ABDUL A. SAID is Professor of International Relations at the School of International Service, The American University. He is author (with Charles O. Lerche, Jr.) of *Concepts of International Politics* and of *The African Phenomenon*, and is editor of *Theory of International Relations: The Crisis of Relevance*. He has contributed to journals such as *World Affairs*, *The American Journal of International Law*, and *The New Republic*.

AMERICA'S WORLD ROLE IN THE 70s

edited by

Abdul A. Said

PRENTICE-HALL, Inc. Englewood Cliffs, N.J.
A SPECTRUM BOOK

For Paul A. Bullock

In appreciation for a job
so necessary, so overlooked,
and so well done.

Current printing (last number):
10 9 8 7 6 5 4 3 2 1

Prentice-Hall International, Inc. (*London*)
Prentice-Hall of Australia, Pty. Ltd. (*Sydney*)
Prentice-Hall of Canada, Ltd. (*Toronto*)
Prentice-Hall of India Private Limited (*New Delhi*)
Prentice-Hall of Japan, Inc. (*Tokyo*)

ACKNOWLEDGMENTS

I gratefully acknowledge Luiz Simmons, President of the Student Association of the American University, 1968–1969, Thomas Block, President of the Kennedy Political Union, and Martin Gold, coordinator of the lecture series, for the generous support which has enabled me to finish this book. They inspired the theme and provided many constructive suggestions.

To the authors of the anthology I owe this volume. Their unsparing cooperation rendered my editorial task a simple one.

As for my student assistants, I will stand always in their debt: Gregory J. Schlesinger dedicated his whole summer and helped in every possible way with all stages of the manuscript preparation; Edward A. Feinberg has been a constant source of inspiration; Richard R. Eurich, Keith R. Rosenberg, and M'Kean Treadway gave their time and enthusiasm to the project. Major Daniel Collier of the United States Military Academy contributed valuable criticism to the editor's commentary.

Mrs. Suzanne McKaugh typed the early drafts with good cheer. Misses Robin Gasperow, Lois Gardner, and Margaret Campbell typed the final manuscript with technical skill and finesse.

Finally, my family tolerated me at every stage of writing and editing.

PREFACE

The invalidation of the premise of the American national mission has been an unusually painful experience for the United States during the past few years. Today, although the world looks on the American standard of living as a desirable goal, it does not sympathize with the American role in world affairs. When the Third World joins many of America's older allies in rejecting the American design for a better world in favor of an active pursuit of their parochial interests, the validity of the American national strategy may legitimately be questioned. It is not the case that the United States is suffering a diminution in stature, but rather that its national security policy is under serious challenge.

The military hegemony of the United States has been under attack from several directions. The United States faces new economic competition and a possibly hostile trading bloc in Europe and the rise of a major economic rival in Japan. American foreign policy no longer derives from a single inspiration on such fundamental issues as approaches to arms control and development. This devolution, furthermore, has already gone so far as to require close examination, careful analysis, and corrective action. This anthology stems from concern for this situation.

During the spring of 1969 the Kennedy Political Union of the American University invited a number of prominent political scientists to explore the issues of changing requirements of American security. Their essays, all originally written for this anthology, demonstrate the serious concern of their authors with our security posture. They explore the changing international environment and recommend new security roles for our nation in the coming decade. The opinions expressed in this book do not reflect the official affiliations of the authors.

The world is anxious for a better life, and much of mankind looks to the United States to provide it. But men stand in need of a set of goals to which they can dedicate themselves unreservedly and an action program they feel to be meaningful to their own purposes. The United States, by its vigorous championing of and identification with the cause of freedom and dignity for all men, has long exercised a powerful fascination on the imagination of struggling peoples everywhere. Here is the real opportunity for a relevant American national strategy and a challenge to present and future policy-makers in the United States.

CONTRIBUTORS

RICHARD BUTWELL is Professor of International Relations at the School of International Service, The American University. He is author of *Southeast Asia Today and Tomorrow, U Nu of Burma, Indonesia, The Changing Face of Southeast Asia* (with Amry Vandenbosch), and *Southeast Asia Among the World Powers* (with Amry Vandenbosch). He has contributed to journals such as *World Politics, American Political Science Review, Journal of Asian Studies,* and *The New Republic.*

WALTER C. CLEMENS, JR., is Professor of International Relations at Boston University. He is author of *The Arms Race and Sino-Soviet Relations, Soviet Disarmament Policy, 1917–1963: An Annotated Bibliography of Soviet and Western Sources,* and editor of *World Perspectives on International Politics* and *Toward a Strategy of Peace.* He has contributed to journals such as *Journal of International Affairs, American Political Science Review, Orbis,* and *The Bulletin of Atomic Scientists.*

THEODORE A. COULOUMBIS is an Associate Professor of International Relations at the School of International Service, The American University. He is author of *Greek Political Reaction to American and NATO Influences,* "Traditional Concepts and the Greek Reality," in Abdul Said, ed., *Theory of International Relations: The Crisis of Relevance,* and is a contributor to *World Affairs.*

WHITTLE JOHNSTON is Professor of International Relations at the School of International Service, The American University. He is a contributor to *World Affairs, Journal of Politics, The Yale Review,* and UNESCO's *History of Mankind.*

JAMES R. JOSE is Assistant Dean and an Assistant Professor of International Relations at the School of International Service, The American University. He is author of *The Political Dynamics of International Organization* (in preparation).

CHARLES BURTON MARSHALL is the Paul H. Nitze Professor of International Politics and Acting Director of the Washington Center of Foreign Policy Research. He is the author of *Limits of Foreign Policy*, *The Exercise of Sovereignty*, *The Cold War: A Concise History*, and *Crisis over Rhodesia: A Skeptical View.*

HANS J. MORGENTHAU is the Alfred A. Michelson Distinguished Service Professor of Political Science and Modern History at the University of Chicago. He is author of *Politics Among Nations, Scientific Man vs. Power Politics, Politics in the Twentieth Century, The Purpose of American Politics, In Defense of National Interest,* and *Dilemmas of Politics.*

JOHN N. PLANK is a Senior Fellow at the Brookings Institution in the program of Foreign Policy Studies. He is editor of the book, *Cuba and the United States: Long Range Perspectives,* and has written articles and essays on inter-American relations.

SAMUEL L. SHARP is University Professor at the School of International Service, The American University. He is author of *Nationalization of Industries in Eastern Europe, New Consitutions in the Soviet Sphere, Poland: White Eagle on a Red Field,* and "National Interest: Key to Soviet Foreign Policy," in Alexander Dallin, ed., *Soviet Conduct in World Affairs.*

LAWRENCE W. WADSWORTH is the Grazier Memorial Professor of International Law at the School of International Service, The American University. He is the author of *A Key to the V. K. Ting Atlas of China,* "Changing Concepts in the Law of the Sea," in the *Free World Forum,* and contributor to *Look* reviews and *The American Journal of International Law.*

URBAN WHITAKER is Professor of International Relations at San Francisco State College. He is author of *Politics and Power: A Text in International Law* (with Bruce Davis), *The World and Ridgeway South Carolina, Nationalism and International Progress, Propaganda and International Relations, Democracies and International Relations: Can They Survive?* and editor of *The Foundations of U.S. China Policy.* He has contributed to journals such as *The Nation, Progressive,* and *War/Peace Report.*

TAKEHIKO YOSHIHASHI is Professor of International Relations at the School of International Service, The American University. He is author of *Conspiracy at Mukden* and (with Elisseeff and Reischaur) *Elementary Japanese for College Students.* He has contributed to *Colliers Encyclopedia.*

CONTENTS

xi

Commentary

CHANGING
REQUIREMENTS
OF U.S. SECURITY

Abdul A. Said

For the past twenty-five years, the United States has been groping for a meaningful framework to guide its foreign policy. It has invoked rhetoric to compensate for objectives and has sought parameters without defining a scope or specifying a magnitude. It has acknowledged its radically altered world role and yet has not departed from its provincial prejudices. The United States has perceived itself as waging a war for the "minds of men" and has done little to instill confidence in the minds of the men for which it is warring.

The 1960s have demonstrated the successive failures of our floundering. Our military and economic prowess has not reduced international turbulence, nor has our surplus of commitments and pledges brought stability and security. We seek alliances to preserve ideals that don't exist. We seek victories against elusive and often unknown enemies. Implicit in our confusion, we seek ordering principles that will provide a foreign policy outlook to give us a clear perspective of ourselves and our role in the world.

Until the recent disenchantment with the Vietnam war, we had convinced ourselves that our world role or "mission" was to act as the defender of democracy, with its assorted synonyms. We took on a contemporary "white man's burden," shielded by the pacifying verbiage of an American foreign policy tradition that we interpreted as benevolent and primarily concerned with the preservation of "free institutions." The basic tenet of this providential policy was a distorted and virulent anticommunism. Every indication of any disequilibrium in the international system somehow became related to communism. As a corollary assumption, we maintained that every nation saw this ideolog-

1

ical struggle with the same intensity that we did. Neutrality thus became a preposterous stance and we rallied to the cause of anticommunism, supporting regimes professing it regardless how sordid they might be.

At the very time we were undertaking new global responsibilities and assessing world conditions, profound transformations were occurring in the international system that were to make anachronistic many of our perceptions. The emergence of non-Westerners as independent participants in the international system, the decline of Britain and France, and the reappearance of a bold China in Southeast Asia disrupted the Europocentric world view to which we were accustomed. We failed to understand the magnitude of these changes and continued to devise policies applicable to the world of the past. "Containment," for example, became extended until we were attempting to "contain" most of the world. A policy devised as a response to aggression in one part of Europe became so universalized and all-inclusive that it demonstrated blatant disregard for worldwide political and cultural peculiarities, assumed that our fears and goals were shared by all nations, and further assumed that nations act with primary concern for ideology.

Ideology has been the tragic element of American foreign policy. By picturing ourselves as the enlightened saviors of all that is noble, we have been able to rationalize our world involvement not in terms of the preservation of a dubious balance of power—but by seeing the United States as the champion of freedom against the nefarious force of communism, with the Soviet Union and China as its tangible manifestations. The world thus becomes a battlefield between God and Satan. Compromise is unthinkable, because collusion with the Devil is ungodly. Only complete elimination of evil is a just goal. As in the two world wars, America sought to transform, not ameliorate, the system.

Unable fully to exercise its righteous wrath without nuclear holocaust, the United States had to accept the notion of limited war with limited goals, limited success, and little transformation of the world. MacArthur's phenomenal reception in the United States after his return from Korea, the McCarthy mania of the early fifties, and the pronouncements of former Secretary of State John Foster Dulles illustrate the frustration and internalized compensations that accompanied our inability to employ total force for total change.

By the early sixties, we had begun to accept reality and hesitantly called for a world made safe for diversity, which presumably meant that we were not about to annihilate the Soviet Union. Yet we persisted in an intransigent refusal to analyze realistically a world not nearly as concerned with ideological professions as we. The United States substituted a fantasy of constitutional parliamentarianism for the alleviation of poverty, disease, and human misery—the real concerns of the non-West.

The seventies will mean a confrontation with radically altered conditions from those that prevailed in the sixties. The legacy of Vietnam will finally convince us that our own security is not endangered by indigenous ideological quarrels thousands of miles away. What endangers us most is the continued irrelevance of our world perspective in an international system that no longer subscribes to our concerns nor symphathizes with our goals.

In analyzing the changing conditions of international relations, the concept of value-free analysis has not served U.S. policy makers well. Security is too much a part of human life to be placed in a vacuum free of human values. When security is considered, emotions, prejudices, and the biases of individuals and groups play a part in every political system. Political considerations, not economic, social, or even physical ones, are most important in determining the objectives and goals of security.

The question of the purpose to which the security is to be put is above all political. In a similar manner, the question of how much one values security is also political. Answer these questions and a political framework for security can be determined. Then, input from other disciplines can enter the picture: likewise, value-free analysis can be of use in determining which systems can be most effective. These two stages may be viewed as *policy determination* and *implementation*.

In past years, an enormous number of books have appeared using other than political forms of analysis. Their authors have used a high degree of academic abstraction in their discussions of various aspects of U.S. security policy. They would have us believe that they can write calmly about such subjects as the number of casualties in a nuclear attack, or the moves of great powers as a game.

Their abstractness has reduced most of these theories to meaninglessness. From hindsight, we can say that their approach misses the heart of the problem of security and some, caring more for method than substance, have constructed theoretical worlds more speculative than those of the medieval scholastic contemplating the angels on a pinhead.

The problems of theorizing about security, however, are intractable to the best efforts of the political scientists; its elusive nature restricts the range of effective conceptualization about it. As a concept, security combines two essential ingredients joined in a complex relationship: an objective ingredient dealing with an actual physical set of conditions, and a subjective one dealing with the feeling of being safe, or the perception of security. The first set of factors is quantifiable, the second defies measurements.

Perception of security, as it relates to foreign-policy making, has historically demonstrated the subjective ingredient of security. The enemy, the x-factor, has always been the paramount fear catalyst in policy formulation. The unknown nature of another nation's capabilities serves to distort security requirements of the perceiving state and create fear. The threat posed by a foreign state is not necessarily congruent with reality.

States often react or overreact for reasons unrelated to the realities of the situation. The idea of reaction to threat is reinforced with the fusion of capabilities and intentions, which leads a government to conclude that everything a foreign state is capable of doing unto it, it intends to do unto that state. This was the rationale behind the NATO land force in Western Europe: that the Russian army stationed in Eastern Europe intended to sweep into the West. Whether valid or not, such a perception is a prime example of the subjectivity of security, whereby capabilities are conclusively interpreted as intentions.

The perception of threat is not restricted solely to fear of one particular national actor within the international system. Fear of a breakdown in the system-process is another source of insecurity. The extensive system of alliances and treaties as described by Kautilya was an outgrowth of sociopsychological drives, rather than a reflection of political necessities.

In addition, rising levels of expectation on the part of a state has historically produced illusions of national missions and hence perceived security roles that are boundless.

Neither our ideas nor our attitudes regarding security have changed much since antiquity. We need to go through the painful exercise of applying, in the words of an old colleague, "massive detergent" to our thinking about security and its problems. The state that defines its security in the old terms and seeks it by the old methods must reconcile itself to living indefinitely with frustration.

This volume of essays returns, often imperfectly, security studies to their rightful place in the political spectrum of things and events. The contributors are not detached scholars separated from real considerations. All of them are well acquainted with the problems of policy making in security. A good number have been consultants, lecturers, and even officials who have undertaken missions on behalf of U.S. departments most concerned with national security.

Before I consider briefly each individual contribution, it should be pointed out that each author wrote his article individually on an assigned topic. The notion of changing requirements of U.S. security indicated that the authors think about change, but no one point of view was demanded or desired. Indeed, as the reader will soon discover, it would have been impossible to do so.

Whittle Johnston invokes the "uniqueness" of American diplomacy to the point where it becomes a political defense. Lauding our aloofness from the world, Johnston brilliantly develops a detailed chronology of our inability to decide between pragmatic deterrence and idealistic consensus orientation, with the latter making an indelible impression on American thought.

He concludes that NATO was one of the most brilliant policies ever conceived in the state system. He also maintains that communism is as strong as ever. We must continue to assert a strong anticommunism, explains Johnston, because its dangers are authentic and omnipresent and may well increase "if the factors which have occasioned moderation are removed." These factors are presumably based on stanch U.S. policy.

Johnston's thesis demonstrates the quandary of the historian in politics. The politician and the student of politics cannot afford to over-analyze the philosophical moods of the past unless he can derive from them some convincing message for the future.

While Johnston explores the roots of the concept of security in the American diplomatic tradition, Samuel L. Sharp examines the milieu of security with the passionate detachment of a Falstaffian cynic.

Sharp recognizes the dangers of overcommitment and overextension. He condemns the volatile and emotional perspective that our foreign policy formulation has taken. Unlike Johnston, he finds the influence of great powers declining and consequently implores the United States to "do less, not more." He analyzes three major factors that have contributed to the depreciation of the role of great powers: thermonuclear war, the nationalistic assertiveness of the medium and lesser states, and the complexities of the Third World. The combination of these factors have led us to conclude that our very existence is in constant danger and that our only rational course, forced on us by our world position, is a militant international posture accompanied by an extravagant defense budget. Chauvinism, rooted in the perplexity of an incomprehensible world, has become our national style. Polarization and military commitments are premised on misguided assumptions and supported by the manipulation of an unwarranted fear.

Sharp explains that security requirements are not based on objective criteria and that perceptions of defense needs are distorted by the clamor of a zealous public and the appetite of a mammoth weapons industry. Sharp condemns the attitude advanced by Johnston. The notion that the United States is a nation of "chosen people" exempt from normal security requirements reinforces the paranoia that has motivated our foreign policy, he argues.

Echoing the theme of a foreign policy orientation constructed on irrationality, Hans J. Morgenthau analyzes the subjective idiosyncrasies that have inspired our relations with Western Europe. He discusses the historical significance of the balance of power as the prime factor in our dealings with Western Europe, thus discounting the importance of the stirring appeals to patriotism emphasized by social historians. Our entry into both world wars and the formation of NATO, maintains Morgenthau, were not responses to nefarious ideologies but exercises in the actual requirements of self-defense.

While Morgenthau recognizes that there have been and will continue to be variations in the policies of the NATO community, he notes that political disagreement will not be obviated by technological pacifiers. We are warned not to subscribe to a naïve overoptimism. Our tendency to vacillate between extremes of exhilaration and despair can only add to the improbability of reaching a rational concord with the Soviet Union and increasingly restless allies of the United States.

Both Sharp and Morgenthau raise the question of the role of a great power in a fragmented world that is gradually renouncing adherence to the two dominant ideologies. Changes in the international system have necessitated a reappraisal of the influence that any wealthy Western nation can exert. Influence cannot be measured in the same terms as in the less complex days when Britannia ruled the seas and divided the globe with the French.

Critics of the traditional style and omnipresence of great powers have recently been labeled "new isolationists." This condemnation fails to recognize that "doing less, not more," may in the long run enhance the great powers' prestige by giving them greater flexibility in their dealings with the rest of the world and also enabling them to establish priorities in order to determine authentic crises and not to misinterpret minor disequilibrium as major catastrophe.

While Western Europe has been at the apex of post-World War II security considerations, the Balkans, with certain exceptions, have remained on the sidelines. Theodore A. Couloumbis inquires whether the security requirements of the United States in the Balkans have really changed since World War II, and to what extent they will be shifting in the future.

The great power loses its selectivity and ability to determine options when it acts as a vigilante, always prepared to intervene and rarely prepared to consider the consequences, he notes. Couloumbis discusses the role of the great powers as stabilizing forces. He maintains that agreement between the United States and the Soviet Union, emanating from the "percentages" negotiations between Churchill and Stalin, have left the Balkans a consistent and peaceful legacy. The improbability of united regional development or supranationalism has permitted the United States and Soviet Union to guard their spheres of influence with assurance that nationalism and factionalism will permit the continuation of political equilibrium. The influence of the United States is dominant in Greece and Turkey, whereas the Soviet Union elicits allegiance from Bulgaria, Rumania, and Albania. Only Yugoslavia maintains an elusive ideological independence.

The highly disorganized nature of the Balkans region makes the presence of the two superpowers act as a shield from the internal quarrels that would occur if the Balkans were left to themselves. The question of response by the superpowers to hypothetical Balkan nationalism is not discussed. Perceptions of balance of power requirements might necessitate an active opposition by one of the great powers to changes in the internal structure of the Balkans.

John N. Plank reemphasizes the need to change our distorted world perspective. He assails the paranoic ideological fears that have inspired foreign policy formation and implores the United States to calmly and realistically look at a world that is suffering not from ideological commitments, but from the disorientating pains of modernization, poverty, and sociopolitical chaos.

Plank traces our paternal attitude to the pronouncements of the Monroe Doctrine and explains that this and subsequent writings have become enshrined in our national thought and action. We invoke the rhetoric of self-determination—and use weapons to maintain unilateral control of political affairs. Yet, for all our military might, we have had little influence in encouraging Latin Americans to take up the banner of anticommunism, though we have not alienated them so much that they have renounced democratic credos and looked to the Soviet Union for comfort and aid. Plank explains that despite our grandiose crusades for progress, veiled for security interests, we have been unable to accustom ourselves to a multipolar political milieu with influence no longer emanating strictly from Washington or Moscow.

Plank thus concurs with the argument advanced by Morgenthau, Sharp, and James R. Jose: we must reorient our thinking from romantic ideological struggle to a recognition that the world is in turmoil owing to the despairing forces of poverty, social disequilibrium, and spiritual detachment. Our role as provider of ideological and crusading epithets is hardly as fruitful as that of contributor of resources to the alleviation of problems that transcend ideology.

Charles Burton Marshall's essay differs from most of the others in developing a rigorous theoretical framework, which transcends his original terms of reference. As a student of the past, Marshall points out that much from bygone times persists in American thinking about security and its requirements. This is quite true; the tendency of American policy makers to take normative positions has been all too evident. On the other hand, this attitude may be changing.

Sub-Saharan Africa and its future, including United States interests, are unpredictable; indeed, if the past is a guide, sooner or later the United States cannot help becoming involved in the problems of Africa directly or indirectly. Ideas as to what constitutes an internal problem in a state are changing rapidly. One is reminded of the dictum that out of Africa always comes something new.

In writing about the Middle East, this editor substantiates the declining influence of the great powers as exemplified in their position in the region. Attacking proposals usually advanced by the great powers that only imposed power can end hostility in the Middle East, the editor asserts that an authentic peace must be concluded by the primary actors involved in the unrest—the Israelis and the Palestinians.

Plans to superimpose a settlement ignore the essence of the conflict. The Middle East crisis is not an East-West confrontation, but a local dispute that is compounded by political and economic interests of outside nations. Although the great powers might wish to establish harmony in the Middle East, their ability to influence the course of events there has declined so radically that their presence is largely irrelevant. Unable to determine the level of priority of the Middle East, the great powers flounder in misapprehensions and misunderstandings.

This editor's description of great-power influence demonstrates the subjective and nonuniversal role the great powers play today. Whereas the discussion on the Middle East underscores the decline of the great powers in that region, Couloumbis regards the unchanging position of the great powers as the chief cause of the Balkans' stability. Yet both imply that to increase the role of the great powers would have little positive effect on the regions in question, whereas Marshall wonders what role any increased activity could assume if it were ever considered appropriate. All three agree with Sharp that the notion of a great power in a polycentric world is archaic and that there is little in our heritage that makes us inspiring as a proselytizing power today.

South and especially Southeast Asia are problematic areas for United States security. With the exception of the denial of communist Chinese influence, there is little consensus among American policy makers regarding our interests in the area. This problem illustrates the fact that the United States has formulated and pursued a policy before it really knew what it wanted to achieve as well as what was possible to achieve in the area.

Discussing security requirements in Southeast Asia, Richard Butwell focuses on the tragedy that deposed a President and disenchanted a nation. He terms the Vietnam war a "colonial" venture, because it was conceived as an extension of the French preservation of empire. Butwell then enlarges this concept and defines colonialism as dependency on any nation to an excessive degree. National independence is unrealistic and unachieved unless defense commitments can be handled by the newly independent nation. If military matters must be handled on a massive scale by an outside nation, then "independence" is meaningless.

Butwell criticizes the United States for its inability to perceive the colonialist connotations of its involvement in Vietnam. SEATO is seen as a remnant of a forgotten era and our fear of imminent Chinese aggression is considered groundless. Butwell implores the American government to reassess its security interests in Southeast Asia, and although he warns against a unilateral withdrawal of forces after the termination of the Vietnam war, he nevertheless counsels us to moderate our interests rationally in Southeast Asia and maintain a less than overbearing armed presence.

The omnipresence of the United States is discussed by Takehiko Yoshihashi in relation to the Far East. Our involvement in the Far East has caused an unjustified and intense fear of China; a precariousness among the border nations surrounding that nation and a breakdown of concord between the United States and Japan. Yoshihashi elaborates upon the remarkable growth achieved by Japan and concludes that only Japan can act as an effective counterweight to the enormous presence of China. Recalling the criticism of Morgenthau—that there are disparities in policies among the NATO members—Yoshihashi explains that we must accept the espousal of independent objectives by an independent Japan. Philosophically, he adheres to Sharp's notion of great powers and summarizes that the nations of the Far East that have recovered from the economic bankruptcy produced by World War II are going to assert an unprecedented degree of independence in accord with their newly found self-sufficiency. Thus, just as this editor refers to the declining influence of the great powers in the Middle East, the Far East is undergoing the same realignment, with the emergence of China and Japan as the two indigenous contenders for leadership.

Prime considerations for the future, writes Yoshihashi, must be the cultivation of closer relations with China and recognition that Japan intends to pursue policies that may differ from the perceived best interests of the United States. Strengthening of the nations surrounding China might lessen the immensity of Chinese impact in the Far East.

Yoshihashi recognizes the necessity of policy reorientation, as do Morgenthau and Butwell. An indication of future prudence as well as sustained greatness by the great powers will be their ability to realize the changing nature of the international milieu and adjust their self-vision in accordance with a world increasingly scornful of greatness and power.

Urban Whitaker extends the discussion of the definitive nature of security mentioned with reference to Marshall. He questions to what extent the maintenance of security is a justifiable end. Clearly empire is one type of security framework that cannot be seen as justifiable today.

In his discussion of world government, Whitaker points out that a world government would be the most efficient form to deal with certain problems. He calls for a neo-Wilsonian multilateralism in the form of an all-encompassing world government. His address is a plea for the elimination of political barriers and a revision of the notion of sovereignty. His implicit premise—that all nations are on the verge or could be persuaded to be on the verge of an unprecedented supranational-ism—reflects an optimistic analysis of the state of the international system.

Lawrence W. Wadsworth approaches the problem of United States security in relation to the community of nations with a realistic perception of the built-in problems of international intercouse. Condemning as self-defeating the search for security by a growing obsession with weapons, Professor Wadsworth interprets our defense posture as having exacerbated world tensions instead of easing world conflict.

Wadsworth differentiates between the desirable and the probable. Although he acknowledges the comforting vision of a universal multilateralism, Wadsworth realizes that discussion of policy formulation must be dealt with on the level of the conceivable. Security maintenance has been the veil that has hidden many unjustified defense moves by the United States. Wadsworth regards the conduct of the United States in the Cuban missile crisis as a dangerous departure from our traditional bias against sea blockades. Our philosophical adherence to freedom of the seas was undermined by support of a policy that violated basic American tenets of world conduct.

Wadsworth's argument falls between the philosophy of nationalism advocated by Johnston and the world community envisioned by Whitaker. He admits that the present framework of international law and organization is an insufficient substitute for national defense and inadequate vehicle for national security. Thus, he feels that nations should act with consideration for the constantly changing nature of the international system.

The theme developed in a regional context by Morgenthau and Yoshihashi is viewed in a theoretical framework by James R. Jose. Regionalism is considered a declining arrangement for security interests, because the defense requirements of great powers are often contrary to the perception of their regional allies. Mutual inhibitions occur when internal pressure disrupts consensus within an alliance and both the great power and its allies are forced to accommodate each other and compromise their own interests.

Regional security pacts further increase the great powers' commitment to the *status quo*, since they are reluctant to alter security alliances—even though their basis may have been drastically altered. Morgenthau invokes this notion in his discussion of our relations with Western Europe, and both Jose and Morgenthau agree that the forces contributing to the founding of NATO have lost their relevance and that a reexamination of United States-Soviet relations must begin with a reevaluation of the premises of NATO and the WTO. Substantiating Morgenthau's thesis, Jose observes that, as in the case of the Nuclear Test Ban Treaty and the nonproliferation agreement, the great powers may find themselves more in agreement with each other than with their allies.

Containment and the fear of a monolithic communism have outlived their utility. The Dulles-devised regional security pacts of the fifties are remnants of a polarization that is giving way to pluralism. Adherence to former premises and alliances not only overestimates our contemporary influence but endangers our relevance as a dominant force.

The recent decision on the deployment of the ABM Safeguard system adds greater relevance to Walter Clemens' discussion. He points to three components as the basic hindrances to control of military technology. The first is technology itself, the ability to produce almost any type of weapons system. The second is the self-escalating nature of the arms race, in which neither nation is willing to assume a position of "second best." The third factor is the self-interest of the military-industrial complex.

Clemens emphasizes the perils of increased military growth and the fallacy that enhanced military preparedness can ensure more adequate security arrangements in the 1970s. He agrees with Sharp that we are in the dangerous midst of a self-escalating arms race and that continued military spending only contributes to the affluence of those now involved in the so-called "military-industrial complex."

Security cannot be achieved by technology, according to Clemens. There is no simple technological substitute for sound political arrangements. Spiraling military costs as the panacea for a world of instability and insecurity is an exercise in self-deception and duplicity. Our inability to recognize that the military must act as a tool and not as the exclusive means of implementing our foreign policy objectives has distorted our world outlook and led us to maintain a costly and lethal arms race.

Security arrangements in the seventies necessitate a sophistication that may well be alien to our diplomatic tradition. We are inadequately prepared to respond to a world asserting itself and in the process of these assertions, condemning their one-time allies and benefactors. Confusion and a policy lacking ends and publicizing dubious means have characterized the past twenty-five years of our security perceptions. A drastic reassessment of a world in the throes of constant change will convince us that a new self-image, stressing moderation and acknowledging the pluralism of the seventies, must be forged. The messages of a bygone era cannot continue to be our clarion.

As we enter the seventies the international system will become less burdened by political constants. The accelerated pace of developments in technology and communications will claim heavier tolls in political stability. The responsibilities of the future will continue to forfeit the debts of the past. Nations will suffer an even greater fragmentation of their world views.

Fragmentation drives states—especially the great powers—into an obsession with isolated parts: national interests narrowly defined and threats vastly exaggerated. Innocuous ideas—battles for the minds of men—are substituted for painful ones—food for their stomachs. The perception of the national purpose becomes increasingly self-centered.

In such a climate, ends are forgotten, as states find themselves compelled to redouble their efforts to devise new and greater security roles. International politics becomes an enormous "caucus race" that forces everyone to run faster and faster just to stay in place. The means become all-absorbing, and national actors become blind to the very concept of ends. The idea grows that ends must wait upon the discovery of means. Hence proceeds a willful and proud commitment to better and bigger guns—a drive that involves escape, substitution, and the undercurrents of anxiety. If the substitution of means for ends is the essence of the self-centered image of national purpose, we can better recognize the perils in which the search for security has and will continue to place states. Sanity is in proportion with placed purpose. There is no standard for sanity or for reasonable perception of security when the whole question of ends is omitted.

The obsession, however, is a great comfort to the obsessed—it is a retreat from the real ordeal. Let us not question the genuineness of the relief when men are allowed to go back to their test tubes and facts, to their bombs and alliance systems.

Ends without means add up to futility; means not related to ends culminate in frustration. Power balancing power, as has been the case traditionally, is nothing more than power challenging power. It is no wonder that the international system has never been more than conditionally stable.

It is the peculiar responsibility—and privilege—of the United States to dare to be different from the imperial powers of the past: to relate our means to the ends of a better world. Only we are reasonably satisfied in the security of our national interest and therefore can perceive the direct relationship between self-interest and international order.

The United States must refashion its outlook toward revolution, supplanting the current notion of synonymity between revolution and an outdated monolithic communism. The United States must adopt a less provincial philosophy that doesn't project its hallowed value of stability *qua* stability as a goal for a world essentially in turmoil. Most of the world is experiencing the heavy pressure of powerful forces and ideas, often accompanied by violence. If the United States persists in classifying all violent change as evil and sanctifies "order" for its own sake, then Americans will have to face the surprising fact that for all its weaponry and technological sophistication, the United States exercises little ideological influence and our indentification as a friend of sometimes ruthless and reactionary regimes has greatly discredited us.

This will be difficult for United States policy makers because stability has had built-in societal value for so long. Because of domestic unrest, the desire to project this value into the international system could become an irresistible temptation in spite of the fact that these policies were ineffective in the past.

It is difficult and perhaps impossible to perceive a world whose problems may resemble those of the United States, but Americans are nevertheless fundamentally committed to a universalization of their peculiar domestic milieu. The gap appears to be widening and will, in all probability, continue to do so. Hopefully, however, a comprehension of the situation will allow a compensation factor to be applied toward the many areas of the world caught in the throes of upheaval.

The primary conditioning element toward revolution will be the domestic rather than the international environment. There are three fundamental reasons for this: (1) The United States is in a stage of development that is substantially different from that of the rest of the world. (2) The problems associated with this stage of development have not been previously experienced in the context of this stage of development. (3) The third reason is an outgrowth of the preceding two and turns on their conditioning the United States' perception of revolution in the international context.

Regardless of what values the United States may or may not hold vis-à-vis revolution, its ability to influence revolutionary trends in the world has been and will be limited. American power in international politics has not been particularly relevant or useful in dealing with revolution because it has focused on its manifestations rather than its nature. If revolution is to be influenced, a great deal of effort and energy is required, which may make the cure unduly prohibitive or even counterproductive. Furthermore, the domestic sources of support for the United States involvement and intervention in revolutionary situations in the world is limited now and probably will be in the foreseeable future.

Thus, the United States' response to revolution should be discriminating. In some cases, short-term instability can lead to long-term stability. At some time in the future, the United States may well support preventive revolution in opposition to weak regimes whose repressive measures often cause violent swings of power. This is not to say that the United States should seek out alternatives for revolution in these countries, but it should always be ready to act in its own interest. Consider, for a moment, the benefits of having had revolutions that supported the aspirations of the people in the hands of other than Castro in Cuba and Mao in China. The regimes that they replaced were no longer relevant, but the United States supported them. In future situations, the United States may choose to aid no side, but it certainly should not support a faction that cannot gain support from its own population.

Unless our policies reflect a realization that the United States is in a stage of development that far exceeds that of most nations of the world and that problems will be handled in a manner that is alien to the idealized American notions of law and "Christian justice," we shall continue to decline as a major power. A rational assessment of the sources of revolution, and a framework of response that lacks the paranoia and ideological obsession that have been our customary reactions, must be sought.

These essays do not represent all the issues of United States security in the seventies. It would be foolhardy to claim that they do. They raise questions to which there are no "right" answers, only judgments of preferability. Even in these judgments, the editor and contributors to this volume differ among themselves. If the seventies have anything in common with the sixties, it will be that the perspective from which we view these issues in the first year of the decade will change vastly by its end.

This is the lesson of our era: change is rapid. Concepts of security that are valid one year are scattered on the refuse heap the next. If it is the task of the state to survive, then those who ponder security problems should not become enamored with their own alternatives.

This must be so because in the final analysis, requirements of security depend on terms of reference as well as a state of mind. Both the perspective and the mentality must be flexible enough to meet the changing demands of the seventh decade of this century. For the world is not about to eat cake.

SECURITY AND AMERICAN DIPLOMACY

Whittle Johnston

In a discussion of the concept of security in the American diplomatic tradition, it is essential to make clear that one is not concerned with security in the "cosmic" sense, which is beyond the ability of any policy to supply. Metaphysical insecurities are a part of the human condition; their resolution is in the lap of the gods. In the issues we explore here our question is a restricted one. Security is taken to mean a situation in which others do not use force against one. How is security in this limited sense to be achieved?

Our most effective model comes from those states within which citizens enjoy a reasonable degree of security. This is achieved by two principal means: the "force from below" (the social consensus) and the "force from above" (the sovereign power). The insecurities states face in world politics derive from the double deficiency in that arena, where both cohesive factors are absent or rudimentary. The basic "cause" of the insecurity of states is a cause in a peculiar sense. It is not operative because something is *present*, as the blow struck by the hammer is the cause of the nail being driven into the wood. It is a cause that makes itself felt in the *absence* of the dual cohesive factors mentioned above, and the *consequence* their absence has for the position and behavior of the units of the system.

States become more secure in world politics as they find surrogates on the world scene for the dual bases of security on the domestic scene. There should thus be two elements in the security policy of any state, which may be called *security through consensus* and *security through deterrence*. The first is designed to maintain, or create, shared purposes among states, so that they will not *want* to threaten each other with force; the focus here is on states' *intentions*. The second is directed to the creation of forces for use against others who might be tempted to use force against you, in the hope that the existence of such forces will

16

deter others from taking such action—or enable one to defend oneself against an attack. The emphasis here is on states' *capabilities.*

What is the proper "mix" between these two elements of security policy? No generalized answer can be given. It depends on two crucial variables, which are themselves undergoing constant change: the state of the actor and the state of the system. With regard to the latter, we must distinguish between stable and unstable systems. When the international system is stable, states often find their security needs adequately met through emphasis on consensus, that is, through reliance on other states' intentions. When the international system is revolutionary the consensus, by definition, is broken; states emphasize deterrence and their rivals' capabilities. Throughout the longest period of its diplomatic history the United States faced a stable, legitimate international system. Its views of security were indelibly influenced by this experience. To understand American views, one must give most careful attention to that long nineteenth century—from Vienna to the "guns of August"— during which the longest span of the national existence was lived. But the United States was not born into a legitimate system, nor has it lived in one since 1914. Hence the mix between consensus and deterrence in the third period has more in common with the mix in the first than either has with the mix in the second.

The state of the actor also influences the mix adopted. Here, too, there have been three periods in American history. In the first, the dominant influence on our policy was Federalist in outlook. Hamilton's view of international politics was inseparable from his view of politics in general: emphasis on the corruption—intrinsic and eternal—of human nature and the consequent need to keep in bounds man's will to power rather than to think of its elimination. In this first period there was a congruence between domestic and international attitude: the Hamiltonian view prevailed, the Jeffersonian view was of secondary importance.

In the second period relations were reversed: the Hamiltonian view declined, internally and externally; the Jeffersonian view grew. The third period domestically corresponds, roughly speaking, with the third period internationally. As one moves into the labyrinth of modern problems in the twentieth century, the hopeful utopia of Jefferson loses relevance domestically and internationally. Wilson is the watershed figure—standing sadly on top of the great divide, that lonely symbol bearing on his own countenance the pain that came with the recognition that America's age of innocence was over. For Wilson was Jeffersonian both in domestic and in international views: In world politics he revived the Enlightenment faith that security could be achieved through global consensus, formalized in the League of Nations. In domestic politics, he revived the faith that the natural harmony of interests of the self-balancing market could be revitalized. But the third era differed from the first, for now the nation had to try to relearn the lessons of a harsher Hamiltonian philosophy. It had to learn them against the backdrop of bittersweet memories of past innocence now lost, and in a world of unparalleled scale and peril.

Thus we get a different mix in components of security policy in these three stages of national history. The proper emphasis on consensus or deterrence changes from the one to the other, as well as undergoing important shifts within each. The indeterminacy of the mix becomes clearer if we make our analysis a bit more refined. Thus far we have used very broad categories; each should be subdivided. If the emphasis be on security through consensus, two paths are open: Is this to be achieved through the power of example or through active efforts? If the former, does one hope for the emergence at some date of a world safe for America, or does one envisage the two worlds existing distinct from one another into the future? If active effort is made, what is to be the content and means of this effort? In the tradition certain elements in the consensus expected are persistent: international law, democracy, national self-determination, free trade, and affluence, along with faith in moral reform, education, development of communications, and so forth. Most of these notions have been rolled into one in the contemporary version of security through consensus, that is, the emphasis on "modernization."

If the emphasis be on security through deterrence, how is this to be accomplished? The early answers placed reliance on geography and on politics. These were to be supplemented by modest (indeed!) military forces. As the nation entered the more hazardous situation of the latter nineteenth century and the geopolitical foundation of its security came to count for less, there was a rise in the emphasis on deterrent forces, particularly of the navy. Finally, as the threats to national security mounted in the twentieth century, there was a willingness to consider some reduction of national freedom of action with regard to deterrent policy in order to increase security.

The mix in American security policy has varied, therefore, depending on the period one is discussing, on the general preference for "consensus" or "deterrence," and on the particular forms seen to be plausible for the implementation of consensus or deterrence.

Let us now turn to a more detailed examination of the different "mixes" in each of the three periods mentioned earlier. In the first, world politics was characterized by almost continuous warfare. Conflict among the great European powers flared up repeatedly throughout the eighteenth century; it reached a thunderous climax in the French Revolution. Thus the "first new nation" was born into a world of peril, in which it faced real threats to its security. As mentioned, the two views that vied for dominance were the Jeffersonian and the Hamiltonian.

Two variants may be distinguished within the Jeffersonian view: a more modest version, which emphasized American withdrawal from the contest, and a more ambitious version, which envisioned the use of American influence to transform the contest. The view that America should withdraw from the contest had been a motive behind the Revolution itself—America should be free so that she would no longer be dragged into "Britain's wars."

Under Jefferson's presidency a sustained effort at actual withdrawal was made, best illustrated in the embargo policy, where the tension between political withdrawal and economic internationalism was to be resolved by *economic* as well as political isolationism. The outcome—the threat of internal disintegration for the nation—was solemn forewarning of America's inability to find security through this means.

Efforts were also made to implement the more ambitious variant of the Jeffersonian approach, best illustrated in the terms of the model treaty drafted in 1776.[1] This was to serve as a guide to American diplomats in their negotiations. Its two major goals were to free international trade from political considerations and to mitigate the impact of war on civilian life. Through the extension of these principles, it was hoped that American influence could bring about a more prosperous and peaceful international order. When, however, the Americans were asked to participate in the League of Armed Neutrality in the 1780s—a rudimentary effort to put collective force behind these principles—another preview of things to come was revealed. The Americans expressed their support for the *principles* of the League, but refused participation.

However, neither of these Jeffersonian variants was the dominant American approach in the first period. The Hamiltonian view dominated, and the enduring testament to its influence is Washington's farewell address, the most significant parts of which were clearly written by Hamilton.

The Hamiltonian and Jeffersonian views differ in ways too numerous to detain us here, but two points may be stressed. The Jeffersonian perspective dreams either of the *avoidance* of the security problem or of its *transcendence*. In the Hamiltonian views there is no way the security problem can be avoided or transcended; at best it can only be contained. The Jeffersonian view stressed the uniqueness and novelty of the American experience, and thus went with the grain of what the Americans most wanted to believe. Hamilton stressed traits Americans shared with men and nations of all times, and went *against* the grain of what Americans wanted to believe. Two factors, in particular, linked the

---

[1] In Chapter 3 of his book, *To the Farewell Address* (Princeton, N.J.: 1961), Felix Gilbert discusses the model treaty at length.

culture with a bent all its own. The Old World valued order, and saw authority as its essential precondition; America prized freedom, and saw permissiveness as the means through which freedom's fruits were to be cherished.

Could one expect a society that altered all other Old World values and institutions to fit its exuberant sense of liberation and possibility to leave untouched the Old World approach to security? We cannot, *and there is as much that is unique in the American approach to the problem of security as there is in the other illustrations of American exceptionalism.* Here the internal and external dynamics rolled together into one to guarantee the triumph of the Jeffersonian vision in the national mind. As Vann Woodward has argued, it may be as important to appreciate the impact of free security on American life as it was to appreciate Turner's emphasis on free land. And right he is; inner and outer experiences each confirmed the other. What the frontier and the absence of a rigid class structure had done domestically, the oceans and our geopolitical setting did internationally: the problem of security was reduced almost to the vanishing point and the vision of an anarchic utopia moved to the center of the stage. There developed in the American mind an attitude of millennial perfectionism—the dream of a world in which it would not be necessary to come to grips with the security problem because the security problem would no longer exist.

It can hardly be said that American diplomacy was much concerned with security problems throughout this long century. To be sure, the Monroe Doctrine professed concern with the possibilities of intervention in the New World; but the concern was known to be unreal when the doctrine was proclaimed, and this shaped the form of its proclamation. John Quincy Adams refused to go along with the British request that the declaration be joint, because he knew the security threat was greatly exaggerated and because he had ambitions for America within the Western Hemisphere, which might be hampered were our hands tied in a joint declaration. In the Mexican war, was security the American concern? Who, after all, threatened whom? In the Spanish-American War, was American security threatened by Spain, a seventeenth century museum piece among bygone great powers?

How are we to describe the American view of security by the end of this second period in her national history? The dominant mood was that of "optimistic possibilism," confirmed by external and internal experiences of that century. America rolled on—this great irresistible force—toward territorial consolidation, toward political consolidation, toward economic consolidation. Nothing seemed to stand long in her way. She was an example to all mankind of what the meaning of its future might be, and felt assurance that universal forces of history were now on her side: that beyond her shores, as well as within them, the world was moving to peace through consensus founded on the universal triumph of democracy, nationalism, and prosperity. America had also learned something about the means by which to play a more active part in furthering security through global consensus. She had confined her activities to a New World theater, but within that theater she had given a record of breathtaking expansionism—but always swiftly and with minimal resistance. The most formidable obstacle that had stood in her path—the crisis of the Civil War—had been overcome through the use of Grant's "terrible swift sword." It was against this century-long backlog of experiences that America entered the third era, with the confident expectation that the Jeffersonian image, dominant now in its own world, was soon to become dominant in the world as a whole. Thus it was that Andrew Carnegie in 1910 could allocate $10 million for "the abolition of international war" and suggest that once this had been accomplished, resources from his fortune be turned to the next most vexatious problem troubling mankind.

With the coming of World War I a new era opened in world politics and in American foreign policy. This third period in American diplomatic history was, like the first, a period of continual conflict and instability. It came into being because the external conditions that had made plausible the attitudes of the second period were all undergoing change. The growth of technology brought about a steady narrowing of the natural bases of our nineteenth-century policy. Of even greater importance, there began to take place in the 1870s a transformation in the distribution of world power, as reflected in the rise of Germany and Japan. Each threatened an aspect of the customary equilibrium, the one in Europe, the other in the Far East. What is more, the advance of these new centers of power signified a relative decline in British power, which meant, other things being equal, a relative decline in American security. At a deeper level, it became increasingly clear that the world itself was caught up in an enormous rolling revolution, whose motive power was the transformation of traditional societies by the relentless pressures of science and technology. At the same time that the world revolution was moving America outward, onto the world, it was moving the world inward upon America: and American interests and the world environment crossed at a thousand and one points. The really difficult questions in American security policy come up as the era of geopolitical separation ended: What is the world system really like? In what way is America to relate herself to it?

The two variants of the Jeffersonian approach still remained, but there were changes in each. The modest variant—security through withdrawal —still persisted, though not without increasing inner doubts. It remains as one approach to the security problem until at least World War II, and we may not have seen the end of it yet. In this view there was a tendency to deny that the changes cited necessitated a deeper involvement of America in "the system," and there was a deep skepticism with regard to the harmful effects that would come from such involvement.

The second, ambitious variant of the Jeffersonian approach was dominant for the first half of this new era, with two powerful proponents: Wilson and Franklin Roosevelt. This view may be described as that of "optimistic internationalism." It saw the involvement of the United States with the system as irreversible, an elemental fact of life. But such involvement was seen more as promise than threat. In a strange irony of history, the third period was to refute the illusion of both Jeffersonian variants: the isolationists dreaded the involvement but thought it to be avoidable; the internationalists welcomed the involvement and saw it as inevitable. As the third period moved on, the involvement did come to be unavoidable, but it also seemed to fulfill the dark forebodings of the isolationists.

The third response has been appropriately labeled "neo-Hamiltonian" (by Samuel Huntington). This view saw the involvement as inevitable, but entertained few illusions about either our ability to transform the system, or our ability to live in it without considerable frustration and effort. It is this view that comes into increasing prominence as the illusions of the two Jeffersonian variants are frustrated.

Wilson was the first great exponent of optimistic internationalism. His "peace strategy" was put together with great care to answer critics from both right and left and harness unified American effort to the cause. Many progressives opposed the war because they opposed force in general, and from the fear that involvement would deflect American resources away from the building of a democratic order at home. The elder La Follette is the most memorable embodiment of this view. Many critics on the right had long pressured Wilson to get into the war earlier to protect American honor. Wilson put together a strategy to answer the demands of both groups, through a demonstration that the war would be the *culmination*, not the *frustration*, of the American dream. He would, indeed, go to war, and thus American honor would be defended. On the other hand, the war would further, not frustrate, the Jeffersonian vision. Think back on those revealing slogans: "a war to end all wars," a war to "make the world safe for democracy." They tell us more about the continuity between the Wilsonian strategy, the Jeffersonian vision, and the mind of America than a thousand details of diplomatic history.

They also put into perspective the provocative but erroneous interpretation Walter Lippmann was to give of the way we saw our security interest in World War I. Writing in World War II, Lippmann argued

that we *really* got into World War I because we *intuitively* sensed that
our security interest, in a geopolitical sense, would have been imperiled
by a German victory.[3] However, if one accepts the Lippmann interpretation he loses sight of the particular uniqueness of the American diplomatic tradition, which is characterized by a relative *absence* of security
concerns as other nations have known them. It is not simply that Wilson did not state as a justification for involvement the concern with our
security in a geopolitical sense. It is that he went to great lengths to
deny that this was our motivation. Time and again, he insisted that our
involvement in this war was unique: we were the only disinterested
power. We did not go to war to protect or further geopolitical interests;
we wanted to end concern by all nations with these interests and to
bring into being a new international system that would transcend them.
Americans have devoted much energy to the criticism of Wilson not
because he represents them inadequately, but because he represents them
all too well. He is a skeleton in the closet that keeps falling out to remind
them of their own illusions and frustrations.

Two implications from this argument have direct relevance for the
remainder of our story. First, the Lippmann-Wilson debate is carried
on in substantially the same terms in World War II and the Vietnam
war. In World War II American policy makers were reluctant to bargain over the specifics of the postwar settlement and were preoccupied
with the formal structure of the United Nations order. Wilson's repudiation of the balance of power and plea for a community of power find
their parallels in Cordell Hull's views. And Lippmann's criticism of Wilson finds its parallel in Churchill's criticism of Roosevelt—most memo-
rably revealed in the title of that last volume of his story, *Triumph and
Tragedy*. The triumph dissolves into tragedy in large part because the
Americans did not understand the nature of the game, and failed to use
their very high cards shrewdly in its playing. Finally, the old debate is
echoed once against in the Vietnam war, in which President Johnson
carried on the Roosevelt-Wilson tradition—justifying our involvement
in terms of a universal concern to transform the nature of the system
rather than geopolitical calculations—and critics like Hans Morgenthau
carried the line of the Churchill-Lippmann critique.

A second implication is that the Wilson synthesis oversold its case
and set into motion an intervention-withdrawal syndrome, in the latest
phase of which we are currently involved. In order to get the United
States to come to terms with the frustrating realities of world politics, it
was necessary to feed her millennial illusions. When the environment

[3] Walter Lippmann's thesis is developed in *U.S. Foreign Policy: Shield of the
Republic* (Boston, 1943). Robert Osgood has subjected this thesis to a careful
critique in *Ideals and Self-Interest in America's Foreign Relations* (Chicago, 1953).

proved recalcitrant to these illusions, there was frustration with internationalism as such and a resurgence either of the older withdrawal impulse or even more exaggerated millennial visions.

In our present time of troubles, by overselling the prospects of what American intervention in Vietnam could, at its best, accomplish, the same sterile dialectic has been refueled. Senator Goldwater has argued that communism is the only threat to our security and has toyed with the temptation to use the "terrible swift sword" once and for all to slay the "red dragon"; and Senator Fulbright has argued that since we have grossly exaggerated the nature of the communist threat, we can afford drastically to reduce our concern and allow the system very largely to take care of itself. Just as Goldwater and Fulbright are mirror images of each other, so each is a reflection of one strand in the "eschatological orientation" so deeply rooted in the American political tradition.

In politics as in medicine, faulty prognosis is the bitter fruit of faulty diagnosis. Roosevelt traced the primary source of Wilson's failure to the deficiency of America, rather than the recalcitrance of the world environment. He devoted his principal energies to the elimination of this deficiency and felt, by 1945, justified in approaching the postwar world with an exuberant optimism. Yet while the failure of the United States to play a responsible role in the interwar world was a contributory factor to the security problem, it cannot be said to have been its principal source. There remained a more formidable source in the nature of the system itself. The Rooseveltian planning for our security problems after World War II was designed to prevent the mistakes that had rendered the League of Nations ineffective. But the proposals for post–World War II security had little more relevance to the dangers the nation would *actually* face than the neutrality legislation had to the dangers of the 1930s.

What, then, went wrong? Roosevelt had been shrewder than Wilson in seeing that a general international security organization could work only if there were the motive power of an effective alliance behind it. Rather than opposing alliances to international organization, he hoped the two would work in tandem: the one giving muscle, the other giving legitimacy. Hence, he went to great effort to maintain the Grand Alliance, but the effort failed. With the collapse of the Grand Alliance the foundations of the United Nations were undermined, and the roof all but fell to the ground; how could one entertain great hopes from an organization the political foundations of which no longer existed? This was the stark fact that became clear by 1946, in two respects of direct concern to the security problem: the inability to implement articles 43 and 45 of the charter, and the inability to establish international control over atomic power.

In some ways, world history paralleled German history a century

earlier; it had come to the turning point—the prospect of peaceful transformation through parliamentary means—and had not turned. And so
with the world: great hopes went into the prospect for world security
through consensus. But the world, too, failed to turn. In both instances,
a darker era was born, a new time of "blood and iron." Arms were to go
up, diplomacy down, and the revival of diplomacy was to await the
establishment of a balance of forces. In short, it was to be negotiation
from positions of strength, and the main energies of American policies
were now turned to the development of those positions of strength.
However, America had to deal with an environment more recalcitrant
than even Hamilton would have dreamed of, for in addition to all the
old burdens of the disorganized states system, three new ones were imposed: communism, nuclear weapons, and the Third World.

Indeed, the world seemed designed with almost diabolical malice to
frustrate the effectiveness of American action. Across that world the
Four Horsemen of the Apocalypse seemed to sweep at will: the red
horse of (cold) war, the pale horse of death, in the balance of terror,
the black horse of famine. And the fourth horse of the Apocalypse rode
within. Under such circumstances how would the nation ever be able
to find an adequate security policy?

The containment doctrine tried to answer this question. It was undertaken in response to a sharp resurgence of the Hamiltonian orientation in American thinking. But there were ambiguities in it at its birth,
which the course of events was to exacerbate. Three may be singled out:
to how much of the world was it to be applied? and for how long? and
by what means? Kennan had in mind mainly the Soviet Union; but
what of China? Or Vietnam? Or the rest of Asia? Or the rest of the
world? How long was this dike to be? And how long was one to be
expected to man it? Finally, by what means was one to "contain"? Here
is the old question of the proper mix between consensus and deterrence.
Some emphasized mainly diplomatic and economic means; others,
tough military power.

Events seemed to determine the outcome. Key events were the brutal
power play of the Berlin blockade, the massive frustrations over the loss
of China, the open aggression in Korea, the swamp of Vietnam, and,
all the while, a Communist challenge to the American identity, which
not only toppled us from our pedestal of innocence but pictured us as
the malignant old man responsible for all the world's ills. These events
led to a hard answer on each of the above questions. Of what use to
build the dam halfway across the waters? Therefore it was to be universalized. Of what use to build the dam half the height needed? Therefore,
it was to be built all the way up so that any pressure could be met:
nuclear, conventional, guerilla. Why build the dam and leave it un-
manned? Therefore it was to be held as long as would be necessary. A

brutal challenge had been given to the American will, and it would be met.

The policy enjoyed brilliant successes, but it cannot be our concern to detail them here. The chief was in Western Europe, where a shrewd blend of security through deterrence (NATO) and security through consensus (the Marshall Plan) was probably the most brilliant security policy pursued by any nation in the history of the states system. The combination also worked elsewhere with varying degrees of success, particularly in Japan. In other parts of the world (for example, Southeast Asia) it was at best a mixed success, and in some (for example, the Middle East) very largely a failure.

But time spares no man—and no policy. The Kennedy era worked on the whole within the context of the containment policy, but there was now a restlessness with it. The phrase that caught the spirit of the Kennedy quest was, "a world safe for diversity." In the Johnson era all security concerns fell into the shadows in comparison with the Vietnam obsession. And it was the Vietnam war that not only brought about the downfall of President Johnson, but signalized to many the final, irreparable bankruptcy of containment itself.

Where do we go from here? A single suggestion, with a few variations, and then we are at our end. After fleeing the swamps of the Old World for three hundred years, we are now back in a swamp more dangerous than that we fled. We shall not get out by struggling aimlessly. Nor shall we do so through the revival of millennial illusions. Quite simply, the nation must gain a firmer control of its expectations through a clearer understanding of the world in which it lives. The lessons of Hamiltonian realism must now be learned, for only if the nation realizes the massive recalcitrance of the vast external realm will it settle down for the "long haul." Only if this is done will the culture have the staying power to devote its great energies to its true security interests. And only if such staying power is demonstrated will our efforts be conservative, pragmatic, and cumulative, rather than moralistic and episodic, with moods of eschatological exhilaration followed by—and often cancelled out by—moods of embittered withdrawal.

If the staying power is achieved, to what policies is it to be directed? We go back to our starting point. It must have the two components, consensus and deterrence, and the proper mix will vary with time and place. With regard to containment, I think it far too soon to celebrate its funeral. Although it is necessary to broaden the doctrine and bring in other considerations to be weighed along with it, I think there is grave danger in its repudiation. Nevertheless there is a grave risk in the continuation of the one-eyed intensity of our preoccupation with communism and containment. In World War II our energies were harnessed against the Axis, and the Communists were thought to share our vision of how the world was to be ordered. We equated the triumph over our most immediate and visible antagonist with the achievement of world order. Little attention was given to the less visible and less immediate foes. Beyond this, it was forgotten that preoccupation with definitive victory over an immediate antagonist may be detrimental to the long-run prospects for world order. And yet in the cold war, though we have learned the substantive lessons of World War II very well, we seem to have missed the larger lessons for an effective security policy. In the cold war our energies have been harnessed against the Communists and we have come to see assorted and sordid anti-Communist regimes as partners in our plans for the future. In both World War II and the cold war our long-run interests have suffered from the narrow intensity of our strategic monism. If our security needs are to be met in the times of trouble ahead, we shall have to try to see the future with both eyes.

SECURITY AND
THREATMANSHIP

Samuel L. Sharp

The theme of this series of papers, "Changing Requirements of U.S. Security," suggests by implication that the participants in the series are more or less agreed on what they are talking about and that their task is merely to apply shared basic notions to specific geographic areas. This assumption is by no means to be taken for granted. This writer, of course, is in no position to impose upon other participants his own views concerning the meaning of terms and concepts, beginning with the meaning of words such as "security" and "requirements." The reader may be expected to be exposed to a stimulating variety of approaches and interpretations. Without claiming exclusive correctness or originality and with the understanding that other presentations need not share them, this author will state here his views and survey some recent critical evaluations of the problem of great-power security from which his interpretation draws inspiration and support.

The title and subject matter of the series convey the following implications:

1. that security is a concept endowed with objective meaning;
2. that nation-states, acting through their authorized decision makers, are actually engaged in a rational pursuit of an objectively definable condition of security;
3. that, specifically, this has been the pattern of behavior of the United States, both in the past and in its current position as a global superpower;
4. that the objectively identifiable requirements of United States security have undergone or are undergoing changes sufficiently significant to call not only for yet another learned symposium but for a rethinking and reformulation of policies designed to meet the changing or changed requirements. A companion implication here is that once a rational course of security-producing or security-enhancing action has been identified and mapped out by scholars, it is likely to be adopted and pursued by the decision makers.

It is hoped that this writer will not be accused of intellectual infanti-
cide (or, in simpler terms, of being a kill-joy) if he suggests at the outset
that none of the implications listed above are to be taken for granted,
certainly not without serious qualifications. The writer is not deterred
from attempting this critical examination by the possibility that he
would merely be storming open doors or reiterating what is obvious to
all serious observers of the game of international politics. In this case,
he would rather err on the side of emphatic redundancy; the obvious
does not appear to be obvious enough to the players of this deadly game
and to those who pay the admission fee, cheer on the players, and ex-
pose themselves to dangers similar to those incurred by people watching
a mad automobile race on an unsafe track.

What is security? The dictionary defines it as the *condition* but also
as the *feeling* of being safe. Incidentally, there is also an archaic meaning of the term, as synonymous with carelessness and a "culpable absence of anxiety," and it is presumably in this sense that Shakespeare
referred to security as "mortals cheefest enemie." The *condition* of being secure is an objective notion, implying the existence of physical circumstances that at the very least guarantee survival; on the other hand,
the *feeling* of not being secure is a subjective notion, which on occasion
may have at best a tangential relation to objective threats to survival
and, in extreme cases, no relation whatsoever to ascertainable reality.
The feeling of insecurity affects actions undertaken in the name of the
nation-state. As Andrew M. Scott put it:

> When an actor perceives itself as being threatened, it will act on the
> basis of that perception, whether or not its fears might be said to be
> justified objectively. . . . Circumstances that would not appear threat-
> ening to an objective observer . . . might seem fraught with peril to
> an actor imagining itself threatened.[1]

Many observers of politics in general and of international behavior in
particular have identified manifestations of exaggerated suspicions or
fears as paranoid. Of course, we must bear in mind that even in paranoid behavior one faces a continuum extending from the "almost
normal" to the hopelessly psychotic. As Ralph K. White has suggested, most of us are at least semi-maladjusted: "In some perverse
way," he states, "the human animal does often actively (though uncon-
sciously) enjoy frightening himself." One likes (or, as psychiatrists
would say, one is compelled) to project the blame for his condition on

[1] *The Functioning of the International Political System* (New York: The Mac-
millan Company, 1967), pp. 184–5. "Actor" here means the state; hence the (puz-
zling) gender.

some external enemy, real or imaginary.[2] Without becoming entangled too much in the psychopathology of politics, we will limit ourselves here to pointing out the presence in international behavior of undeniably paranoid elements in the form of blame projection and, above all, the twin delusions of persecution and of grandeur, both particularly relevant to great power behavior.

Is the nation-state really engaged in a wholly or predominantly rational pursuit of security? Authoritative pronouncements of decision makers, formulations by their intellectual handmaidens, and the very names of various institutional arrangements frequently refer to security as a central preoccupation. Why security is thus advertised or ideologized should be rather obvious: like peace or disarmament, it has the attractive quality of being a reasonable and morally appealing goal. However, as students of international politics know, or ought to know, the rationally cloaked notion of security more often than not transcends the limits of self-preservation. "The quest for security," in the words of Arnold Wolfers, "points beyond mere maintenance and defense. It can become so ambitious as to transform itself into a goal of unlimited self-extension." This is particularly true in the case of great powers, whose spokesmen tend to rationalize the extension of national power either as a quest for "greatness," as a response to a sense of special mission, or by reference to peculiar burdens, challenges, and responsibilities allegedly thrust upon them by history. A major ex-articulator of the American national purpose, W. W. Rostow of the University of Texas, has stated that "we are the trustees of the principles of national independence and human freedom all over the globe; and, given our history, this is a proud and natural responsibility." [3] Whatever one may think of such a definition of this country's mission, it does not suggest a search for security, and certainly not for security first and foremost. It advocates a posture as related to safety as gambling is to a quest for economic security. What we have here is an invitation (by History speaking through Mr. Rostow or other articulators) to risk-taking on an extended scale, as befits the status and self-image of a great power. Similarly, when the spokesmen for the Soviet Union go beyond the very tangible security dilemmas of Russia to present themselves as the global defenders of proletarian internationalism or as the guardians of the integrity of the socialist

---

[2] "Images in the Context of International Conflict," in Herbert C. Kelman, *International Behavior* (New York: Holt, Rinehart and Winston, 1966), p. 268.

[3] *View from the Seventh Floor* (New York: Harper & Row, 1964), p. 53. Mr. Rostow may be personally burdened with the legacy of being named after Walt Whitman, the bard of benevolent American expansionism, who wrote of democracy as "the destined conqueror" and called upon this country to "lead the present with friendly hand toward the future." (Cf. Albert K. Weinberg, *Manifest Destiny* (Baltimore: Johns Hopkins Press, 1935), p. 485.) Recent manifestations of American international behavior have been referred to as "welfare imperialism."

commonwealth (and in the process of carrying out this mandate from history, violate the "abstractly understood sovereignty" of lesser and unappreciative associates), they are reflecting a rather bloated concept of what constitutes the national security of the U.S.S.R. Interestingly enough, this is accompanied by a rejection of the "leftist-adventurist conception" of "exporting revolution or bringing happiness to other peoples." [4] This allows the Soviet leaders to be on record as reasonable —especially by comparison with the allegedly adventurist policies advocated by Mao—yet at the same time pursue a great power policy based on an extended notion of the "red man's burden."

The pursuit of tangible security is obviously not as central a preoccupation of decisionmakers as statements cloaked in reasonable and rational terms would lead one to assume. This poses a serious problem to the scholar: how to analyze rationally a pursuit that is heavily affected by considerations other than rational or—to put it more cautiously— is governed by the specific rationality of the game of international politics. As Raymond Aron points out:

> If security were . . . the preferential objective, it would be possible to determine rational behavior . . .

at least theoretically. However, he goes on, individuals and collectives alike are willing to risk death for certain goals; collectives in particular

> . . . do not seek to be strong only in order to discourage aggression and enjoy peace; they seek to be strong in order to be feared, respected or admired . . . capable of imposing their wills on their neighbors and rivals, in order to influence the fate of humanity, the future of civilization. . . . Security can be a final goal: to be without fear is a fate worthy of envy; but power, too, can be a final goal: what does danger matter once one has known the intoxication of ruling? [5]

Aron also reminds us of the tendency to pursue *glory*, which is a substantial extension of power beyond the limits of security in a desire for "absolute victory."

The peculiar dilemma of great powers has been subjected to a brilliant analysis by Karl W. Deutsch. Such powers, he points out, are "so large that no one could abolish their national independence, even if anyone were mad enough to try." Why is it then that precisely the strongest powers invest so much in money, manpower, and other re-

[4] *Pravda*, Moscow, September 25, 1968 (as reported in *New York Times*, September 27, 1968, p. 3).
[5] *Peace and War* (New York: Praeger, 1967), p. 73.

sources in pursuit of "national security"? Deutsch offers what he calls a simple explanation:

> It is a kind of "Parkinson's Law" of national security: a nation's feeling of insecurity expands directly with its power. The larger and more powerful a nation is, the more its leaders, elites and often its population increase their level of aspiration in international affairs. The more, that is to say, do they see themselves as destined or obliged to put the world's affairs in order, or at least to keep them in some sort of order that seems sound to them. . . . Only the largest and strongest nations can develop some at least plausible image of a world which they by their own national effort might mold, change, or preserve wholly or in large part according to their own desires; and their fears, worries, efforts, and expenditures go up accordingly.[6]

In other words, Deutsch suggests that there is no direct connection between the objective condition of insecurity and the subjective feeling of insecurity experienced by governing elites and transmitted to the people at large. However, there is also a third aspect of the problem, the more or less conscious (though not necessarily deliberately dishonest) manipulation of the feeling of insecurity by what Richard Barnet calls the national-security managers.

Though not really central to the preoccupations of the decision makers, the alleged quest for security is a powerful instrument in the hands of those who preside over the destinies of great powers. Its value is rooted primarily in the cohesion and consensus-producing effects of the invocations of an external threat. In the recent history of this country the manipulation of the "Communist threat," either in a vague and hence totally meaningless form, or concretized as the threat of Soviet expansion and aggression and, more recently, the threat posed by China, provides a fascinating example of the manipulation of the concept. The post-cold war literature abounds in statements indicating that the threat of the invasion of Western Europe by the Russians performed the useful function of "selling" Europeans and Americans alike on the need for NATO and similar "security" arrangements, although such a threat may actually not have existed. Marshal D. Shulman writes: "*With the advantage of hindsight* . . . and with no desire to impugn those who bore the responsibilities for our security, the impression of a planned Soviet military conquest of Western Europe was a misreading of Soviet intentions." Misreading of the intentions of another government is presumably rooted in ignorance; however, Professor Shulman's comments suggest that in addition to what might be called honest misread-

---

[6] *The Analysis of International Relations* (Englewood Cliffs, N.J.: Prentice-Hall, 1968), p. 88.

ing of "signals" or failure of perception, there was also present an element of deliberate exaggeration or misinformation undertaken for "mobilizational" purposes and directed at (or against) the legislative branch of the government or the public at large:

> Perhaps democratic societies cannot be galvanized sufficiently by measured intellectual analysis, and perhaps the strengthening of Western power—which was absolutely essential—could not have been accomplished without the adrenalin of great anxiety.[7]

The result, Shulman finds, was a distortion of the real dimensions of the conflict with the Soviet Union and "disproportionate response to the military challenge." We must conclude that in the ranks of the decision makers and of their advisers there are (a) those who lead from ignorance, lack of foresight, or paranoid tendencies, but also (b) competent individuals who choose, to put it charitably, to operate on conveniently deferred perceptions of reality. This is not the place for a detailed analysis of the habits and rationalizations of those within the bureaucracy who may know better but refrain from advancing dissenting views if only because of the desire "to stay aboard" (sometimes rationalized as desire to preserve "effectiveness").[8] We have the competent testimony of Professor Hans J. Morgenthau about the discrepancy between the public statements and the privately held views of some high government officials on matters not involving "subjective estimates of the political and military situation but hard facts and figures ascertainable by objective calculations." Morgenthau also points out the prevalence of "academic conformism" among scholars who offer their support for policies "regardless of their objective merits" and neglect or betray their proper role, that of "speaking truth to power." Scholarship, he states, has been enlisted as "provider of ideological rationalizations and justification of the government's policies." [9]

It is not easy, in the present state of our knowledge, to sort out with anything approaching definitive clarity the "real" motivations of decision makers, advisers, and articulators. Many sources point out that there was a "real" war scare in official Washington following the seizure of power by the Communists in Czechoslovakia in February, 1948 and that it was triggered by an alarming cable from Berlin under the signature of General Clay. How real, as opposed to useful, was the scare? How factual rather than mobilizational was the image conjured by General Clay or whoever advised him? George F. Kennan, not quite a "revisionist" and

---

[7] *Beyond the Cold War* (New Haven, Conn.: Yale University Press), p. 16.
[8] As suggested by James C. Thomson, Jr., *No More Vietnams?* (New York: Harper & Row, 1968), p. 45.
[9] *A New Foreign Policy for the United States* (New York: Praeger, 1969), p. 153.

not exactly a completely innocent observer, states that what was seized upon as a direct military threat in 1948 was in actuality a series of "defensive reactions of the Soviet side" to the Marshall Plan proposal and moves to establish the Federal Republic of Germany.[10]

The process of administering anxiety-increasing "adrenalin" was repeated in the 1950s, with the invocation of the missile gap, which, of course, existed, but the other way around. The exact proportions of the perception of a threat to American security and the needs of the Kennedy Administration for a prestige victory in the Cuban missile crisis are a matter of lively debate.[11] More recent attempts to "sell" Congress and the public on the need for the installation of an ABM system have also been accompanied by efforts to endow with credibility the image of a vaguely impending if not exactly present security gap which the endeavor is supposed to eliminate. Without going into the merits of the system (which seem to baffle not only laymen but also highly competent scientists), we merely want to point out and stress the manipulational use made of the quest for security, or more precisely, the exploitation of the fear of insufficient security. ("Sufficiency" is a more reasonable sounding term now employed by President Nixon instead of the visceral appeal to "superiority" advocated by candidate Nixon). One may consider too radical the view expressed by I. F. Stone that "the real word for America's nuclear arsenal is not sufficiency but lunacy," but it would be hard to overlook the testimony of Professor Charles L. Schultze, former budget director during the Johnson administration, who pointed out the effects of what might be called "threatmanship":

> The general attitude of the American people is that if you wrap it up in a flag and call it national security, you can't question it.[12]

The effects of manipulation are also eloquently described by Senator George S. McGovern of South Dakota:

> . . . when the [Johnson] Administration yielded to the pressure of the military and agreed to deploy a thin ABM system . . . this could not, in my judgment, be accepted as a security decision based on a broad view of national and international priorities. It was, rather, a

[10] Cf. Nils H. Wessel, "Nato and the Changing Russian Threat," in *The Atlantic Community Reappraised* (New York: Academy of Political Science, Columbia University, 1968), pp. 7–20.

[11] See, for instance, the exchange between Roger Hilsman and Ronald Steel in *The New York Review of Books*, Vol. XII, No. 9 (May 8, 1969).

[12] Statement at a Conference on the Military Budget and National Priorities, Washington, D.C., March 29, 1969. *Washington Post*, March 30, 1969, p. 9. Senator Gaylord Nelson of Wisconsin once described "national defense" as the two biggest "magic words" in the English language. *Time*, April 11, 1969, p. 20.

surrender to mounting political pressure from military-minded senators and congressmen and generals and arms manufacturers and their supporters. And all of this was fed by the tragically mistaken impression that it is possible and reasonable to calculate national security in mathematical terms, related almost exclusively to the capacity of our defensive and offensive armaments.[13]

Needless to say, manipulation of the image of an external threat to national security is not limited to the efforts directed at "galvanizing" public opinion in democracies. It is an ancient device of rulers, and it has been employed for the purpose of legitimizing measures requiring major exertions and sacrifices. A striking example in the history of the Soviet Union is the atmosphere of the war scare promoted by Stalin (and his obedient tool, the Komintern) in the late 1920s in order to justify the sacrifices demanded of the people in connection with the rapid industrialization drive of the First Five-Year Plan, as well as the savage measures against the remnants of domestic opposition. We cannot enter here into efforts to determine the exact proportions of objective reality and distorted or false perception of same in the "mix" on the basis of which Soviet leaders have been diagnosing the existence of threats to the security of their country (and we mean specific threats, from specific sources, not the "basic" and therefore politically meaningless notion of the threat posed by the very existence of "capitalist" countries). On a number of occasions the Soviet leadership resorted to the invocation of threats to the country or to the existing system of government, or both when it knew better.[14] Significantly, though not untypically, the record shows that when actually confronted with an objective threat, the Soviet leadership would react with bluster and a show of alleged unconcern, whereas imaginary threats were met with hysterical outbursts that were at least in part manipulative in origin.

So much for the manipulational aspect of the invocation of threats to security, a crucial factor frequently understated in analytical evaluations of the real situation. However, as suggested earlier, there is at play also what we called the genuine though often objectively indefensible *feeling* of insecurity. We are told, by those commenting on the psychological

---

[13] *Anti-Ballistic Missile: Yes or No* (New York: Hill and Wang, 1969), p. 17.
[14] "A degree of hysteria, a spy and sabotage mania had to be part of the propaganda campaign designed to explain to the Russian people their vast sufferings. Soviet Russia was to appear like a beleaguered camp; every foreign country . . . had to be made part of a concerted plot against the state and its ruler." Adam B. Ulam, *Expansion and Coexistence* (New York: Praeger, 1968), p. 166. Ulam concludes that it is "most unlikely" that Soviet leaders actually considered war to be near. An interesting discussion of the war scare of the late 1920s is in Paul W. Blackstock, *The Secret Road to World War II* (New York: Quadrangle Books, 1969).

aspects of international relations, that decision makers will act on false perceptions of threat, whether or not their fears are justified objectively. A frequent occurrence is the confusion of an adversary's *capabilities* with *intentions*. The assumption that he will do to one all he is capable of doing, though understandable in military thinking and planning (which must include in contingency projections an assumption of "the worst"), often invades political thinking and planning, causing unfortunate enlargement of the scope of worrying. These and other influences create a construct of reality, which in Andrew M. Scott's words, offers "certain overarching ideas about the international scene and the type of behavior that is appropriate to that scene." No decision maker, and consequently no nation-state, is entirely safe from distortions of perception induced by learned response categories, belief systems, and so forth. However, the rational decision maker must be presumed to be able to rise above such conditioning effects and retain the ability to correct errors and come closer to the *objective structure* of perceived stimuli. In fact, one would expect a responsible statesman to show "creative perception," defined as ability to "capture more of the essence of the stimulus than a cursory inspection reveals"; in other and simpler words, he must have insight.[15]

It is not easy to set up an objective scale with clear limits of insightful and rational behavior; tentatively one might classify as "rational" those policy decisions that contain only a nonlethal admixture of the other-than-rational. It is presumably in this sense that John Plamenatz has called the decision makers of the Soviet Union "sane."

We assume that this evaluation, which is some years old and reflects in particular the contrast between Soviet policies as Plamenatz saw them and the aimless and limitless paranoia of Hitler, is still valid, and that Shulman was right when he suggested (albeit with rather irritating condescension) that the record of Soviet foreign policy reveals behavior having "some resemblance to what we know of human behavior elsewhere in the world."

Let us now turn to the *condition* of security, and to changes in the objective components of safety. Among factors contributing to a change in the security condition of great powers the most significant ones are: (1) thermonuclear weapons; (2) the nationalistic assertiveness of medium and lesser states; and (3) the complexity of problems presented by the Third World.

The most important change in the condition of security is, obviously, the advent of thermonuclear weapons of quasi-ultimate destructive capacity. There are, of course, attempts in this country, in the Soviet Union, and elsewhere to overcome the general unwillingness to think the unthinkable. In fact, some suggest that the sheer destructiveness of thermo-

[15] Cf. Joseph H. deRivera, *The Psychological Dimension of Foreign Policy* (Columbus, O.: Charles E. Merrill, 1968), p. 44.

nuclear weapons removes them as a meaningful factor and one can and must therefore continue to play the game and plan for it as if the development had never occurred. As against such attempts there is the obvious fact that the range of rational options available to decision makers has been substantially narrowed down because concepts such as "superiority" and "victory" have become largely meaningless. It has been rather convincingly argued that the possession of excessive power of destruction has rendered the great powers burdened with this awesome gift of technology particularly vulnerable and even impotent.

Faced with the novelty of thermonuclear weapons, some have concluded that the very institution of the nation-state no longer makes sense because it has ceased to perform its historical function of providing security from what John Herz has described as "permeation." There are many voices clamoring for the replacement of the nation-state by a rather dimly perceived higher order or by "the rule of law." Among younger critics of the existing international system, doubts are expressed whether a universal supranational organization is really the answer. A brilliant student of mine, when asked what he would substitute for the nation state, replied with disarming simplicity, "anarchy." In a milder form there are expressions of a populist desire for scrapping the huge national security bureaucracy or for the transfer of some sectors of interaction across frontiers to smaller and informal groups (as if it were self-evident that small groups and spokesmen for particular interests are by definition wiser and more restrained than those acting for what they believe to be the national interest).

Suggestions that we resort to anarchy or to quasi-syndicalism as a cure for chaos are, of course, "way out." However, there can be no doubt that there has developed on the American scene a strong current of doubt concerning the direction and style of the conduct of this nation's international affairs. There are various views about the origin of this critical tendency. Some see in it a cyclical neo-isolationist reaction to a period of overextension of America's international commitments, or—to revive the terminology suggested by Frank L. Klingberg—the advent of a period of introversion following one of extroversion. It has been suggested that we are witnessing a manifestation of the famous generation gap: "People of one generation may well think domestic policy important because their fathers thought foreign policy so." [16] It is obvious that one factor triggering critical reappraisals of this nation's international position and its security requirements is the pointless expenditure of blood and treasure in the Vietnamese enterprise. Nothing succeeds like success, even in dirty business; conversely, signs of failure are guaranteed to feed criticism and introspection.

[16] Samuel P. Huntington in Thomson, *No More Vietnams?*, p. 41.

If we agree that the source of the notion of insecurity is largely in subjective feelings not necessarily related to objective reality, it follows that suggested remedies must take the psychological origin of insecurity for granted. The function of radical criticism is to tell the king or his subjects that His Majesty is naked or else parades around in blood-stained garments. Philip Green has suggested that a radical critique of America's international posture must begin with questioning the assumption that "national decision-makers act always in good faith" and that "the motives they offer publicly for their decisions are in fact their real motives." He singles out for critical reexamination the claim that the United States, as a great power, is somehow trapped in its own greatness and therefore acts within a framework of necessity and compulsion. Decisions presented as an agonizing or tragic choice

> . . . may often be made out of misplaced zeal, bravado, egoism, *hubris*, political malice, or other defects of character and social position that decision-makers possess just as much as natural men.[17]

In essence, Green suggests a therapeutic realization of the fact that

> . . . foreign policy decisions, and the definition of the situation that precedes them, rarely have an immaculate conception in historical necessity.[18]

Denial of semiautomatic and unquestioning acquiescence when national security is invoked will presumably force the manipulators, at the very least, to make a better and more convincing case in specific situations.

Some critical evaluations attack the basic imperial or imperialistic assumptions of great powers about their place in the world, their duties, responsibilities, and capabilities. It is suggested by Arthur Schlesinger, Jr. and others that the end of the age of the superpowers is at hand. Not only are they deterred by the balance of terror from inflicting major damage on each other, but it would no longer be possible for them, even when acting jointly and in harmony, to impose their will on the rest of the world. This is not the place for a detailed discussion of whether the realization that the period of their quasi-omnipotence has ended has by now taken hold of one or another of the superpowers, or both. As Schlesinger points out, "Superpowers are always slow to realize the decline in their capacity to command events." He also suggests that "the drift of the Superpowers toward collaboration . . . has come too late to save their joint hopes of world domination. . . . The events in the rest

---

[17] "Necessity and Choice in Foreign Policy," *A Dissenter's Guide to Foreign Policy* (Garden City, N.Y.: Doubleday, 1968), p. 138.

[18] *Ibid.*, p. 155.

of the world have developed a life of their own . . . and they are passing beyond the reach even of joint American-Russian dictation." [19] This may be a somewhat hasty or sweeping diagnosis, but it would be difficult not to agree with Schlesinger that the failure of the Vietnam venture has triggered "a striking reassessment of the world position of the United States." To the obvious question of whether a similar reassessment is going on in the Kremlin, which appears to be in a mood to reassert its authority rather than trim its commitments, one can only give here the tentative answer that the Soviet Union, once allowance is made for the strictly verbal manifestations of globalism and rare hare-brained probing operations designed to prove the "manliness" of communism, has in fact been but little overextended beyond contiguous areas; consequently, it has less trimming to do. One may also say that the Soviet Union has been deprived of the insights that come with tragic failure and its leaders can therefore engage in attempts to bolster the tottering credibility of the Soviet Union's stance as a superpower by a show of force under relatively safe circumstances. And even here we have not witnessed the end of the story. It is by no means necessary for the United States to delay an intelligent reevaluation of what the requirements of its security are and what the limits are of its rationally redefined interests by using the excuse that the Russians or the Chinese do not seem to feel the same way.

What, in the light of changing requirements of security, should be the general outlines of a new American security policy? Most current suggestions, including many undoubtedly motivated by a deep concern for this country and the values it professes to hold dear, can be reduced to one sentence used by Edmund Stillman and William Pfaff: "America should do less, not more." This is the core finding of recent critical evaluations of America's international position and its security dilemma, often accompanied by a plea for applying the prodigious energies and talents of this nation to neglected internal problems. In the words of Ronald Steel:

> Twice in this half-century we have tried to reform the world and we have failed. We might now contemplate something less exhilarating but more pressing and even more important: the reform of our own society.[20]

Others have called for a channeling of efforts away from the luxuries of nationalism toward what is called *ecological politics*, in order to reduce the threat of a gradual biological disaster likely to result from the pollu-

---

[19] "Vietnam and the End of the Age of Superpowers," *Harper's Magazine* (March, 1969), p. 47.
[20] *Pax Americana* (New York: Viking Press, 1967), p. 353.

tion of the environment and the predatory depletion of resources. None of the serious critics suggest that America should abdicate its greatness; the point here is to define greatness in more relevant and less murderous terms. The adoption of what the Japanese call *tei-shisei* (low posture) is perfectly compatible with dignity and pride.[21]

As we can see, the real nature of the big-power security problems is not too difficult to diagnose; nor is there a shortage of proposed cures, most of them quite sensible. However, we must bear in mind that in severe cases of true paranoia the prospects of *remission* are not very high. We must thus end by returning to the point suggested at the beginning: what is the likelihood of rationally mapped out conduct actually being adopted? Will the actual behavior style of great powers be changed only because it has been convincingly argued by scholars that the one they have used is dysfunctional and even potentially suicidal? Will tired clichés and worn tricks be abandoned by chastened national security managers? Will we really witness an era of creeping rationality? Do most of us as individuals necessarily heed warnings by doctors even if we are threatened with dire consequences? We are told by scientists that in order to survive under changed conditions all the dinosaur had to do was to lose weight (from a hundred tons to, say, a hundred pounds). Did he? Apparently this effort proved too much for the dinosaur's genetic mechanism, we are told by the biologist V. E. Stiers, who concludes:

> The jump from aggressive political self-interest to pure unselfish political rationality . . . is also too much for the genetic mechanism to accomplish in a single mutation. Man, too, like the dinosaur may not have enough time to change his nature by degrees.[22]

In a slightly less conclusive fashion, the philosophically inclined former Secretary of Defense, Robert S. McNamara, in a volume called *The Essence of Security*, reduces the real essence of security to the fundamental question: "Who is man? Is he a rational animal? If he is, then the goals can ultimately be achieved; if he is not, there is little point in making the effort." Mr. McNamara, as befits a born activist, naturally refuses to accept the possibility that man may be incapable of rising above his "animality"; he concludes with a vague hope that the species will somehow continue to "plug away" within the limitations of man's "part-comic, part-tragic, part-cussed, part-glorious nature."

---

[21] A "low-posture foreign policy" has been suggested by James C. Thomson, Jr., along with "de-activism" and "disengagement." *No More Vietnams?*, p. 287. I am grateful to Professor Takehiko Yoshihashi for providing the Japanese term and an explanation of its meaning as the opposite of *kyōko*, or "stiff posture."

[22] *The Center Magazine*, published by the Center for the Study of Democratic Institutions, XI, No. 2 (March, 1969), 27.

WESTERN EUROPE

Hans J. Morgenthau

In order to understand the security interests the United States has maintained in Europe, it is first necessary to dispense with the tendency that has become deeply ingrained in the political folklore of America, that is, the propensity to go from one extreme to the other. Thus, not so long ago, we seriously believed that the Red Army was poised in Central Europe to march west, and that only NATO was standing in the way of this advance. In more recent years, we have come to believe that the Soviet Union's threat to Western Europe was certainly no longer existent, and revisionist historiography has even argued that this threat had, in fact, never existed.

Since foreign affairs—human affairs in general—are not as simple as this, the fear of a physical advance, of a traditional physical conquest of Western Europe by the Red Army, was most certainly a response to the very fact of its existence. The threat that the existence of the Soviet Union has exerted upon the domestic and international *status quo* of Europe and elsewhere was a fact of life twenty or twenty-five years ago, and is still a fact of life today.

The security interests of the United States in Europe exist today, as they have always existed. In order to determine what the present security interests of the United States in Western Europe are, it is first of all necessary to recognize that such security interests exist and have existed since the beginning of the republic. They exist today, however, under different conditions than those that prevailed twenty years ago. And it is the task of theoretical analysis, and of practical statesmanship, to determine in what ways changing circumstances have affected our interests in Western Europe and the policies designed to realize those interests.

From the very beginning of the republic, the United States has had one single interest with regard to Western Europe and with regard to the European continent in general. This was the maintenance or, if need be, the restoration of the balance of power. For the early American

43

statesmen, as their successors in this century, realized almost instinctively that any single European nation that could successfully entrench itself as the master of the continent would automatically present a threat to the security of the United States. As long as there existed in Europe a balance of power, a multiplicity of nations checking each other, none of those competing nations had its hands free to seek conquests or adventures beyond the ocean. It was only when that competition has been terminated, when one nation had made itself the master of Europe, that it could think—could dare to think—of gaining new influence, new power, and new territory on the other side of the Atlantic.

This basic security interest was instinctively present in the minds of the early American statesmen. The example of Thomas Jefferson, who in theory was opposed to the balance of power, is most revealing. It is interesting to note from his diaries and letters during the Napoleonic wars that whenever Great Britain appeared to gain the upper hand over Napoleon, he wished for the victory of the latter; yet, whenever Napoleon was victorious, he wished for an increase in the power of Great Britain. Indeed, the whole diplomacy of the federalist period aimed at safeguarding the security of the United States, surrounded as it was on three sides by the colonies of the European powers, by playing one of those powers off against the others.

Even during the nineteenth century, generally regarded as the classical American century of isolation, the diplomacy of the United States was by no means as isolationist as it has been construed. It was much more neutralist than isolationist, for the United States was always aware that an approximately equal distribution of power was most conducive to its basic security interests. American diplomacy during the Crimean War illustrates this point. The issue of that conflict was of absolutely no interest to the United States; what was of interest to it, however, was the likelihood that not a single European nation would emerge from the struggle as a hegemonious power, and American diplomacy sought to prevent this eventuality.

The intervention of the United States in the two world wars can also be explained in terms of the balance of power. At the beginning of World War I, the United States was by no means certain that it would oppose Germany in that war. As a matter of fact, the United States Army, at the beginning of World War I, had contingency plans for a British invasion of Long Island, an occurrence that never did materialize. The United States finally took the side of the Allied powers only when it became obvious that without the former's massive support, the Allied powers were likely to lose the war and Germany would emerge as the hegemonic power.

The lack of neutrality in the politics of the United States at the beginning of World War II, long before December, 1941, that is, before

Pearl Harbor, is again a vivid commentary upon the instinctive reaction on the part of the United States to the threat of a hegemonial power arising in Europe. And, when at the end of World War II, after a period of hesitation that Churchill called the "deadly hiatus," the United States turned around and opposed the Soviet Union from 1947 onwards, it did so on the same grounds that it had opposed Germany twice before. As Germany had constituted a threat to the balance of power in Europe in World Wars I and II, so did the Soviet Union present the same threat in the years following the second conflict. Both Germany and the Soviet Union, in other words, threatened to transform themselves into hegemonial powers, preventing any possible competitor from opposing them on the European continent. It was for this reason that the United States opposed both countries.

What made the situation in the aftermath of World War II different from the preceding historical occasions that necessitated the intervention of the United States was the fact that there existed at that particular time an extreme imbalance between the would-be hegemonial power and the nations of Western Europe. At the beginning of World Wars I and II, the United States could watch, wait, and see, in order to determine which way the two scales of the balance would move, and then intervene and put its weight in the seemingly lighter scale. After World War II, however, there was no possibility of waiting, because the imbalance was so extreme. Without the immediate intervention of the United States, the balance, in all likelihood, would have turned toward the Soviet Union.

The intention here is not to revive the traditional fear of a westward march of the Red Army; it is merely to point to the enormous political, economic, military, and social weaknesses of the nations of Western Europe in which the Communist parties had become the proponents of national liberation in the underground movements against the Nazis. Even without a direct intervention on the part of the Soviet Union, the very prestige that country had acquired as one of the victors of World War II, coupled with the disarray of the nations of Western Europe and the enormous strength and prestige of these nations' internal Communist parties, would have almost certainly transformed the nations of Western Europe into Communist societies. Because at that time communism was a monolithic force centrally directed and controlled by Moscow, any increase in the power of a Communist movement or any Communist takeover of a government would have meant an extension of and increase in Soviet power.

Since the United States was committed, because of its basic interest in the balance of power, to the containment of the Soviet Union, it was also committed to the containment of communism in Europe and throughout the world. Thus, the intervention of the United States in

Europe, during the refashioning of American foreign policy in the famous fifteen weeks in the spring of 1947, was the direct and admirable response to a threat to the basic security interests the United States has had since the beginning of its association with Europe.

But the soundness of this policy and its success—the policy of containment has been successful, for the Soviet Union has actually been contained—became dubious after 1950. The Korean War marked the watershed of this development. It was misinterpreted by the United States as the beginning of a Communist campaign of military conquest of the entire world. We regarded the aggression of North Korea against South Korea as the opening shot in a worldwide campaign to conquer the world and also identified the Soviet Union as the spearhead of this conquest.

This interpretation was quite erroneous, as later events have shown. It is now quite obvious that the South Koreans wanted to advance north and were restrained by the United States, whereas the North Koreans wanted to march south, and for a time were restrained by the Soviet Union. But when we removed our troops from South Korea, and when the Secretary of State made a speech in which he declared Korea to be outside the security interests of the United States, Stalin obviously yielded to the urgings of the North Korean government. He granted them permission to move and apparently thought the United States would not intervene.

In any event, this complete misinterpretation of the Korean War, aside from leading to the massive rearmament of the United States and to the militarization of American foreign policy, also led to a corresponding militarization of our policy toward the Soviet Union. From then on we were convinced that Western Europe lay exposed to a military attack by the Soviet Union, which would not hesitate to emulate the North Korean's attack on South Korea. We prepared to counter such an attack, and our whole European policy became an attempt to create a military counterweight to the Red Army in Western Europe. NATO was the result.

There have always been two entirely different strategic doctrines concerning the purpose of NATO, and they have not been resolved to this very day. There has been the doctrine that NATO and the troops that NATO has stationed in Western Europe, especially the six American divisions east of the Rhine, were a mere token of the United States resolution to protect Europe in the event of a Russian attack. The divisions the United States had stationed in Western Europe were regarded as a manifestation of the United States decision to use all the military power at its command to deter and, if necessary, to counter the Soviet Union. It was not supposed that NATO could physically protect Europe from a Russian attack. It was only a demonstration to our allies, and particularly to the Soviet Union, that if the latter intended to march west it would automatically instigate a war with the United States, because it could only march west by repulsing the American contingent in West Germany.

The other strategic doctrine assumes that NATO can create a local force sufficient to stop the Red Army if it should attack. At NATO's inception, ninety divisions were regarded as necessary for that purpose. Since ninety divisions were not available, seventy were declared to be sufficient. Today, there are a little more than twenty divisions in Western Europe, and Intelligence—with a capital I—affirms that this is sufficient, but intelligence—with the lower case—insists that this is simply not so.

Here we have an interesting example of a general phenomenon in foreign and military affairs, namely, to what extent professional intelligence is not an instrument to detect the truth—the empirical truth about a certain matter—but rather becomes an ideology by which a certain policy is justified and legitimized in pseudo-elegant terms. The continuous reduction of the number of divisions necessary to stop the Red Army is a classic example of this transformation. Since there are only a little more than twenty divisions available today, intelligence proves that no more than twenty are required to repel the Red Army. But if one considers the size of the Red Army and if one studies the geography of Europe, especially since the defection of France, it is an obvious fact—at least for nonmilitary observers—that Europe is not defensible on the ground. People have talked a great deal about a forward strategy, that is, a refusal to retreat from the Russians, but rather a firm intention to repulse them and counterattack. This writer remembers a discussion he once had with a famous expert in military strategy when the author pointed out to him that the Russians, too, had a forward strategy. This is always true in war; both sides want to go forward, yet the stronger one will succeed in this endeavor while the other is compelled to go backward or else face the possibility of annihilation.

The idea that Europe can be defended on the ground has always been, I think, a pipe dream. It could not have been defended because the members of NATO were not willing, even if they had been able, to put into the field the number of divisions necessary to stop the Red Army. This argument does not even consider the geographical impossibility of deploying large masses of ground troops in that narrow corridor that was left after the defection of France. We should not forget that the Red Army stands a hundred miles east of the Rhine, the boundary between Germany and France.

The only function, indeed a very important function, which in the military sense NATO could have performed and actually has performed, is to inform both the Soviet Union and our allies in Western Europe in unmistakable terms that any violation of the territorial integrity of a member of NATO means automatic war with the United States. It is this simple assertion that on the one hand has kept NATO together, and on the other has deterred the Russians from marching west, provided they ever had the intention of doing so.

In passing, a word must be noted about the revisionist attempt to prove that NATO was unnecessary because the Russians would never have attacked anyway. Nobody, of course, knows that. In any event, in military and political planning, it is always a never-to-be-forgotten rule that one must prepare for the worst. If one is prepared for the worst and it doesn't happen, one can afterwards flatter oneself, or criticize oneself— if one wishes—by saying, "It wasn't necessary at all; they wouldn't have come anyhow." If one wears a winter coat in a snowstorm, he might say he won't get pneumonia. But he could also argue that if he hadn't worn the winter coat, he wouldn't have contracted pneumonia anyway. In matters of coats and pneumonia, an experiment could perhaps be attempted, but not with regard to political matters of such magnitude.

This writer would still defend, without any reservation, the vital importance of NATO, not only in the military sense, but also in the psychological, cultural, or even spiritual sense. It is a visible union, institutionalized, of the nations of Western Europe, which after all have a common civilization, common values, and in the broadest sense a common purpose vis-à-vis the rest of the world. What went wrong with NATO was its mechanical militarization instigated by the misinterpretation of the Korean War.

In the last fifteen years or so, a great change has come over the international environment. The conditions under which NATO arose and was effective are no longer present today. One could say that the basic sickness that has debilitated NATO appeared at the very moment of its conception. It should have been obvious then to our policy makers that one of the foundation stones of NATO was bound to crumble. NATO was in good measure based upon the nuclear monopoly of the United States. This was the counterweight in balance of power to the unchallengeable superiority of the Soviet Union on land. It was the umbrella under which the nations of Western Europe could feel secure. But in September, 1949 it became only a matter of time until the Soviet Union would be able to do to the United States what the United States then was able to do to the Soviet Union, that is, to inflict upon it unacceptable damage. Once this happened—it occurred in the period ranging from 1956 to 1958—NATO's vitality was decisively impaired.

It is to the credit of General DeGaulle—whom this writer had always regarded as the most intelligent statesman on the world scene, though his judgments were sometimes obscured by his love affair with France— that he almost immediately recognized the dilemma that the member nations of NATO, both the United States and the Western European nations, are now facing. On the one hand, it was possible that the United States might want to threaten nuclear war against the Soviet Union for interests of its own, which were not the interests of its European allies. In other words, a nuclear policy of the United States might jeopardize the very existence of the European allies without their vital interests being involved. On the other hand, it was also possible that one of the West European allies of the United States might want to threaten a nuclear war in its own interests, which were not the interests of the United States. And there was the concomitant possibility that the United States would not be willing to jeopardize its existence for interests of its allies that were not its own.

These two theoretically discernible dilemmas were actually experienced in the Suez crisis of 1956 and the Cuban missile crisis of 1962. In the Suez crisis, Great Britain and France pursued military policies to further their own interests, and thus moved Khrushchev to threaten nuclear war. The United States was not willing to risk nuclear war over the Middle Eastern interests of Great Britain and France, so it joined the Soviet Union in preventing those two countries from achieving their objectives. This was a traumatic experience for Britain and France, which the statesmen of these countries have never forgotten.

On the other hand, in 1962 the United States and the Soviet Union came close to nuclear war over Cuba, which was and is an American interest, of a very minor or no importance to our allies in Western Europe. If this war had broken out, the nations of Western Europe would have been destroyed on behalf of the American interest in Cuba. Obviously, the nations of Western Europe were not eager to undergo such a sacrifice, irrational and senseless from the point of view of their respective national interests.

These two basic dilemmas have been a continually devisive force within NATO. The interests and policies of the members of the alliance are divergent, and therefore neither the United States nor the nations of Western Europe want to become the prisoners of the interests of the other side, a contingency which, in the nuclear age, might jeopardize their very national existence. General DeGaulle saw this dilemma, and he also saw, at least in theory, the remedy. He suggested a directorate composed of France, the United States, and Great Britain to coordinate the foreign policies of NATO; for such is indeed the crux of the matter.

Today there are very few issues of foreign policy on which the United States and its European allies see eye to eye. Take any of the current issues—Vietnam, the Middle East, foreign aid, United States relations with China. Wherever one looks, there are basic divergences of interests and policy. But an alliance is the institutional and legal expression of a community, or at least of a parallelism, of interests. There is no point in trying to maintain the institutions of NATO, which have become empty shells performing their routines without much vitality, if the underlying political situation diverges completely from a community or a parallelism of interests. Nor is it possible to remedy the situation by a technological gimmick such as the multilateral seaborne nuclear force, which is now appropriately forgotten, but which a few years ago was offered to us as the great remedy to the problems of NATO. The MLF was, of course, a stillborn child—also a monster of a child with no head and a couple of weak legs. This misbegotten scheme was again characteristic of the mechanistic approach to foreign policy, and also of the approach that refuses to adapt traditional ways of thinking to new circumstances. Yet this technological monstrosity was regarded by intelligent and responsible men as the answer to the problems of NATO!

The problems of NATO are of course political; they are not technological or military. And it is in the realm of the political substance of foreign policy that the remedy must be sought. As long as the United States pursues policies that are at variance with the policies of its allies and vice versa, there is no possibility for the revitalization of NATO.

This is not the only great and drastic change that has occurred in the international environment. It is not only on our side that the ties of the alliance have been weakened; the nature of communism has also drastically changed. The enemy against which we armed ourselves through NATO twenty years ago is no longer the same enemy. Twenty years ago, it was a monolithic enemy; it was a worldwide movement centrally controlled for the purposes of the Soviet Union. Today it is polycentric. National tendencies, national interests of Communist movements and governments have taken the upper hand within the community of Communist ideology and institutions. We are not now faced with one Communist, one monolithic worldwide movement, but with a number of communisms, each of which has a different bearing upon the interests of the United States. They therefore must be met by different policies. One need only look at the profound split between the Soviet Union and China to see the great divergences in interests and policies that have torn apart the members of the Communist alliance, the same disease that has loosened the ties of the Western alliance.

There is today in Europe a movement, in both East and West, which tries to circumvent, as it were, the Iron Curtain; which no longer regards the Iron Curtain as a kind of natural barrier preventing normal relations between the nations of Eastern and Western Europe. This movement has, of course, suffered a setback through the Soviet occupation of Czechoslovakia. But the very fact that the Soviet Union must continually impose its military and police rule upon Czechoslovakia testifies to the enormous strength of the movement toward a normalization of the relations between East and West.

If this movement is visible in the over-all relations between the nations of Eastern and Western Europe, it is more particularly obvious also in the relations between East and West Germany. Here is indeed the crux of the present security interests of the United States and Europe. Today, West German statesmen make statements about their policy concerning East Germany that would have been inconceivable a few years ago, and would then have been regarded as treason. The very idea that one might even recognize the government of East Germany, which, like it or not, has existed for more than twenty years, is a novel idea, almost an original idea. The fact that this idea was propounded by responsible politicians and even members of the cabinet in West Germany is certainly a very significant event.

Germany has, of course, always been the crux of the security problem of Europe. It has been so for the Russians and it has been so for ourselves. The Russians continuously hammer upon the threat they perceive in West Germany to the territorial *status quo* in Europe. In good measure this is, of course, propaganda in order to keep the East European Russian empire together by painting the threat of German revanchism and German neofascism in the most lurid colors. In good measure, however, this is an instinctive reaction to the experiences the Soviet Union and the nations of East Europe underwent during World War II. We have read about Nazism in books, we have seen some pictures, some movies, about Nazism, but the Soviet Union lost twenty million men and the Polish and Czech elites were virtually decimated during the Nazi occupations.

Here is a reaction which is real, which is not put up for political purposes. It is one of the basic facts of political and military life in Europe. NATO has had the unspoken task to limit the freedom of action of West Germany, for the fear that the Russians openly express other nations feel too, even though they are too polite to express it or their interests prevent them from expressing it. This is obvious also from the consideration of the problem of unification. Everybody is in favor of unification, everybody pays lip service to it, but nobody has ever done anything about it, because nobody really wants unification. West Germany today is already one of the strongest nations on earth, and a unified Germany would of course be a rival of the Soviet Union for the mastery of Eastern Europe.

It must be observed that the Russian occupation of Czechoslovakia can be primarily explained in terms of the fear of Germany, of the belief that as Czechoslovakia moves away from Russia it moves closer to Germany. This has always been so, and there is testimony of Czech patriots and historians in the nineteenth century that made exactly this point. No nation of Eastern Europe can stand on its own feet; it must either lean on one of its powerful neighbors or on the other. And if it is not Russia, it is Germany.

This is one of the unspoken basic facts of the security situation in Europe. By embracing West Germany, NATO has also restrained the freedom of movement of West Germany. This author has always regarded this—and many Germans would agree—as one of the major roles of NATO. Regardless of our estimates of the military threat of the Soviet Union, the very fact that Germany is not alone and cannot pursue completely independent foreign and military policies as an integrated member of NATO is in itself worth the price of admission to that organization.

The great unanswered question of the future is the direction in which Germany will go. It is interesting to note that Khrushchev, time and again, in private conversations made the point that ultimately Germany would join the Soviet Union and leave the Western camp. This writer remembers a statement Khrushchev made in which he affirmed that there would be another Rapallo, that is to say, another secret treaty between Russia and Germany after the model of the Rapallo Treaty of 1921. "It will not come under me, it will not come under my successor, but it will come under my successor's successor. It is inevitable and we can wait."

When one considers the relevance of this statement, one should not neglect the key position the Soviet Union occupies with regard to the unification of Germany. The Soviet Union is the only power on earth that can bring about the unification of Germany any time it desires. It can sell the East German government down the river tomorrow and can divide Poland again the day after, if it wants to, if the price is right, if Germany moves out of the Western context and into a closer relationship with Russia. It is not by accident that Poland has been divided four times in the last two centuries, first between Prussia and Russia, then between Germany and Russia, because there is a potential interest for Russia and Germany to find common ground on the prostrate body of Poland.

This is not to suggest that this is going to happen, nor that it is even likely to happen; what is being observed is that within the different possibilities that the European situation contains, this is one potentiality that should not be overlooked, one long-range potentiality that directly affects the security interests of the United States, not only in Europe but in the world. If a united Germany, one of the most powerful nations on earth, should make common cause with the Soviet Union, the other superpower, such a combination would drastically alter the distribution of power in the world.

A similar possibility exists in Asia, that is, Japan and China might enter into a similar arrangement. Again, this author is not predicting anything, but merely indicates that those are possibilities wise statesmanship should take into account in its long-range planning.

In conclusion, the security interests of the United States in Europe exist today, as they have always existed; they are the existential expression of the distribution of power in the world. Though these security interests have before World War II been primarily military in the conventional sense, in the sense of nuclear deterrence and in more recent times they have taken on a distinctly political connotation. It is only on the political level, under present circumstances, that the security interests of the United States in Europe can be met. And one of the political issues that the United States should never lose sight of is the key position Germany occupies in the European scheme of things. The United States ought to be aware of the different potentialities this situation contains, pursue policies that anticipate such potential trends, and turn them in the direction of the security of the United States.

❧

THE BALKANS

Theodore A. Couloumbis

The moment was apt for business, so I said, "Let us settle about our affairs in the Balkans. Your armies are in Rumania and Bulgaria. We have interests, missions, and agents there. Don't let us get at cross-purposes in small ways. So far as Britain and Russia are concerned, how would it do for you to have ninety per cent predominance in Rumania, for us to have ninety per cent of the say in Greece, and go fifty-fifty about Yugoslavia?" While this was being translated I wrote out on a half-sheet of paper:

Rumania	
Russia	90%
The others	10
Greece	
Great Britain (in accord with U.S.A.)	90
Russia	10
Yugoslavia	50–50
Hungary	50–50
Bulgaria	
Russia	75
The others	25

I pushed this across to Stalin, who had by then heard the translation. There was a slight pause. Then he took his blue pencil and made a large tick upon it, and passed it back to us. It was all settled in no more time than it takes to set down.[1]

It was in such a simple and clear-cut fashion that Churchill and Stalin defined the security interests of the great powers on October 9, 1944, at 10 o'clock at night at the Moscow conference at the Kremlin. The notorious "percentages agreement" is one of the best indications of

[1] Winston S. Churchill, *Triumph and Tragedy* (Boston: Houghton Mifflin, 1953), p. 227.

what "balance of power"—that time-tested rule of diplomacy and strategy—is all about. In his memoirs, Churchill recalls with a bit of discomfort the possible cynicism with which decisions involving millions of people were made.[2] But emotion and morality apparently have no place in affairs of state.

The gist of the Moscow agreement was that Britain considered Greece (and by extension, Turkey) nonnegotiable, while the U.S.S.R. deemed Rumania and Bulgaria all-important and wished their exclusive control. Yugoslavia, divided equally, was to be under the influence of him who could best influence it.

The durability of this "off-the-cuff" agreement is unquestionable. The United States has inherited from Britain, via the Truman Doctrine of 1947, the responsibility of guarding the Western world's interests in Greece and Turkey.[3] These interests could best be defined as Western military and ideological presence in Greece and Turkey, or its converse— which is perhaps more accurate—denial of access and utility of this strategic real estate to the Soviet Union. The Soviets, in turn, continue to maintain their presence or heavy influence in Bulgaria and Rumania. Yugoslavia alone has managed, since 1948, to toe an independent line, trading freely with both sides in the cold war, arguing or agreeing selectively with one side or the other, and denying the use of its territory to both.

The story of this paper could end here. Its main premise is that there has been no radical change in U.S. security requirements in the Balkans. The United States still considers its presence (or Soviet absence) in Greece and Turkey fundamental to its strategic interests. Further, it understands the "balance of power" as a situation in which Yugoslavia's

[2] ". . . there was a long silence. The pencilled paper lay in the centre of the table. At length I said, 'Might it not be thought rather cynical if it seemed we had disposed of these issues, so fateful to millions of people in such an offhand manner? Let us burn the paper.' 'No, you keep it,' said Stalin." Churchill, *Triumph and Tragedy*, pp. 227–28.

[3] A. J. P. Taylor seems to contradict the view of the vital strategic importance of the Balkans. Characteristic of his viewpoint is the following quotation: "The policy of forestalling Soviet Russia in the Balkans was an invention of the post-war years, partly encouraged by Churchill himself when he became anti-Russian in 1946. There is no contemporary evidence for it. On the contrary, all the strategies—Soviet, British, and American—were designed with the sole object of defeating Germany however much they differed on the way to do it. The postwar outcry sprang from the belief that the Balkans and east-central Europe were important in the Balance of Power. This is an illusion. They had perhaps some strategic value, though only in the sense that, if Soviet armies were on the Danube, an invasion of Russia by the western powers would have to start from further off. Otherwise the states concerned were liabilities, not sources of strength." Taylor agrees, then, with Bismarck that the Balkans "are not worth the bones of a Pomeranian, or any other sort of grenadier." See Taylor, *English History 1914–1945* (London: Oxford University Press, 1965), pp. 576–77.

neutralist role is insured. Similarly, the U.S.S.R. has made clear that Bulgaria and Rumania rest securely in its own sphere of influence, and has respected Western preeminence in Greece and Turkey; or at least it has not been prepared to risk war in order to gain a foothold in either nation.[4] The United States and the Soviet Union appear, then, to have reached a *modus vivendi* in the form of a stable balance in the Balkans.

But this analysis, so far, presupposes that the Balkan countries[5] have no will or interests of their own, and that they are and will remain obedient or unwitting servants of the interests of their overseers. This has been the case in the past, but will it continue?

The Balkan nations sprang from the deteriorating appendages of the Ottoman empire, as a result of revolution and war, in the nineteenth century. Notwithstanding their common poverty and revolutionary herit-age, they have grown up in an atmosphere of mutual suspicion and hostility, frequent territorial (irredentist) disputes, and strong, at times uncompromising, nationalism—if not chauvinism. They have been so fragmented by hostility that they have systematically invited external powers to control their destinies. There are indeed only three basic characteristics of modern Balkan history. Foreign intervention, extreme nationalism, and politico-economic backwardness.[6] These must be under-stood well by any nation wishing to calculate its security interests in the area.

Great powers have traditionally competed for influence and control within each of the Balkan nations, supporting now one and now another of the local political forces in return for reasonable concessions. Also, these great powers have added their weight to one nation or another in order to maintain the precarious balance that has given the Balkans the image of troublemaker and the "powder keg" of Europe. The post-World War II period is unique in the history of the Balkans in the sense of narrowing the origins of external pressures and influences. This is the result of the division of responsibilities (spheres of influence) between the U.S.S.R. and Britain. (As mentioned earlier, the United States as-sumed Britain's role in 1947.)

Each of the Balkan nations, however, still exhibits a varying degree of susceptibility to foreign control. Yugoslavia probably best represents the

[4] For instance, the U.S.S.R. was cool to the effort of the Greek communists (1946–1949) to turn Greece into a "people's democracy" because it knew that all the Communists were doing was bringing the United States on Balkan territory. See Edgar O'Ballance, *The Greek Civil War* (New York: Praeger, 1966), pp. 53, 78.

[5] Rumania, Bulgaria, Yugoslavia, Albania, and Greece (and by extension, Turkey) will be discussed in this paper.

[6] Charles and Barbara Jelavich, *The Balkans* (Englewood Cliffs, N.J.: Prentice-Hall, 1965), p. 129. See Also L. S. Stavrianos, *Balkan Federation* (Hamden, Conn.: Anchor Books, 1964), also his *The Balkans Since 1943* (New York: Holt, Rinehart and Winston, 1958).

case of successful defection or escape from any great-power control. Rumania has recently become a similar case. But the examples of 1956 Hungary and 1968 Czechoslovakia are somber warnings against any radical severing of the umbilical cord with the Soviet womb.

On the other side of the spectrum, we see, under a climate of detente, polycentrism, and post-Vietnam disorientation, great pressures building in pre-coup 1967 Greece and Turkey toward loosening the American apron strings. Both countries wish to promote low-key, defensive participation in NATO and to increase economic and cultural cooperation with Eastern Europe and the Soviet Union. It has been argued by some analysts that the Greek coup of April 21, 1967, represents the American counterpart of the Czech invasion; that is, that the Greek revolutionary junta acted as an agent of American interests becoming alarmed with the anti-American or neutralist policies that a George Papandreou government (following the scheduled elections of May, 1967) might conceivably have pursued.[7]

Tito's Yugoslavia, by adopting a "diplomacy of balance," [8] has tried to walk the tightrope of non-alignment and play one "cold-warring" power against the other. Tito has been eminently successful, so far, in maintaining his country's independence and sovereignty, although he has frequently vacillated in and out of military and economic dependency, first with the U.S.S.R. and later (1949–1954) with the United States and NATO. In fact, in 1953 and 1954, he reached the point of entering a political and military pact with Greece and Turkey and thus indirectly aligning Yugoslavia with NATO.[9]

The second major characteristic of the Balkan nations is strong, if not uncompromising, nationalism. Suffice it to say that even to the present time, there are basic territorial questions separating all Balkan nations,

[7] Andreas G. Papandreou, "The Greek Dictatorship Not a Domestic Affair," *The Greek Observer*, No. 4, June 1969, p. 5; and "Greece: Warning to the World," *ADA Magazine* (May, 1968), pp. 6-M, also "The Greek Problem is Really an American Problem," *New York Times Magazine* (July 21, 1968), p. 36. For a different point of view favoring the colonels' government, and the necessity of the Greek *coup d'etat*, see Savas Constantopoulos, "In Defense of the Colonels in Athens," *Atlas* (November, 1967), pp. 28–32, and D. George Kousoulas, "The Origins of the Greek Military Coup, April 21, 1967," *Orbis* (Summer, 1969). See also the comments made in a speech by Robert M. Allan (the president of Litton International Development Corporation) delivered at the Statler-Hilton Hotel, Boston, on April 7, 1968, on the occasion of the 147th anniversary of Greek independence. The speech was entitled "Greece: Birthplace of Modern Economic Development."

[8] Stephen S. Anderson, "Yugoslavia, the Diplomacy of Balance," *Current History* (April, 1969), p. 212.

[9] On the Balkan pact, see the excellent study of John O. Iatrides, *The Balkan Triangle* (The Hague: Mouton Press, 1968) discussing the background and causes for the birth and death of this alliance across ideological boundaries.

among them Transylvania, Bessarabia, Macedonia, Kossovo, Northern
Epirus, Voyvodina, Istria, Carinthia, and, of course, Cyprus. These
questions normally lie dormant, but they can appear and escalate quickly
during times of crisis in intra-Balkan relations. All of the Balkan countries are involved with conflicting claims on one another's territories and
populations. There is no doubt, therefore, that nationalism has proven
itself as the most potent and durable force in the Balkans, stronger than
international communism or functional federation, pacifism, or any
other form of regional unity and confederation.

Albania's post-World War II behavior is most illustrative as a case
study of the force of nationalism. Immediately after the removal of the
Axis forces (in 1944–1945) the Albanian Communists, under heavy
sponsorship from Tito's Yugoslavia, gradually established themselves in
power. Yugoslavia poured economic and military technicians into Albania, set up "joint" Yugoslav-Albanian companies (much in the "Sov-
Rom style" of the Soviets in Rumania) and proceded toward the rapid
integration of Albania into an expanded South Slav federation. The outbreak of the Tito-Stalin dispute was all that saved Enver Hoxha, the
Communist leader of Albania, from becoming a regional official in a
Yugoslav federation. He immediately denounced the economic ties with
Yugoslavia, which were allegedly exploiting his country, and joined Stalin
and the Cominform in the shrillest condemnation of Yugoslavia.[10]
"Titoists" in Albania, such as Koci Xoxe, were purged as traitors to the
national integrity of Albania and agents of Yugoslav imperialist designs.[11]

The historic visit to Belgrade of Krushchev and Bulganin in 1955
marked a thaw in Soviet-Yugoslav relations and consequently worried
Albanian leaders as to their fate. Could Albania become a prize for
Yugoslavia's return to the Soviet bloc? Out of despair and isolation in
the late 1950s, Albania frantically sought support from alternative
sources by improving its relations and trading with "capitalist" Italy and
gravitating toward the Chinese once the Sino-Soviet dispute surfaced.
Naturally a lot of ideological sugar coating was spread over the substance of these shifts and maneuvers, primarily designed to accomplish
two things: maintain Albania's sovereignty and independence and insure the continued control of its governmental apparatus by Enver
Hoxha and his deputy Mehmet Shehu.

Yugoslavia's policy, throughout the postwar years, is also highly indica-
tive of strong collective or "federal Nationalism." Yugoslavia has in the
postwar years jealously guarded its territorial integrity. The explosive
question over Trieste, for instance, was solved peacefully primarily be-

---

[10] See Robert Lee Wolff, *The Balkans in Our Time* (Cambridge, Mass.: Harvard
University Press, 1956), pp. 367ff.
[11] Wolff, *The Balkans in Our Time*, pp. 379–80.

cause of Yugoslavia's extreme isolation and desperation resulting from the Soviet-Yugoslav rift.

Greece, in its turn, has come to the brink of war with Turkey three times over the disputed territory of the island of Cyprus. Greek-Albanian relations are still in a technical state of war, and Greek military planners never cease referring to the paper-thin slice of vulnerable territory separating Bulgaria from its coveted "window on the Aegean."

Each Balkan nation, jealous of its neighbor, seeks protection by or augmentation from powerful sponsors; there is no question, therefore, that nationalist issues have kept the Balkans so divided that foreign penetration has been a logical result. This situation has prompted two authors writing on the Balkans to pose the following rhetorical question:

> Since the actions of the non-Balkan powers have always quite obviously and naturally been dictated by their own national interests, a question arises: Why do the Balkan people not cooperate with one another and resist foreign intereference? They are united in many ways. The Albanians, the Bulgarians, the Greeks, the Serbs, and the Rumanians are Orthodox; the Yugoslavs and the Bulgarians have very similar languages. They all suffer from the consequences of foreeign control and economic backwardness.[12]

Notwithstanding all these hard and fast conditions, the Balkan nations have never managed to break through the bounds of narrow nationalism and to attempt functional or political regional arrangements. At best, most attempts for Balkan federation or alliance have been ideological and utopian assertions of rhetoric and at worst, short-lived alliances designed to balance some members of the Balkans against some others.[13] The chief historian of the area, for instance, refers to the Balkan Pact of 1934 as a pact "concerned primarily with the maintenance of the territorial status quo and . . . directed against Bulgaria." [14] The Balkan Pact of 1954 was much in the same spirit, despite the fundamental changes in the social systems of the Balkans after World War II.

The third characteristic condition of the beleaguered Balkan peninsula is economic backwardness coupled with periods of either near chaotic political instability or harsh authoritarian dictatorship imposed from extreme right or extreme left elements. In times of democracy most Balkan nations have gravitated toward multiparty systems, personality-oriented rather than issue-oriented parties, and changing electoral laws.

[12] Jelavich, *The Balkans*, p. 133.
[13] It has been a favorite pastime of *status quo* nations of Greece and Yugoslavia to enter defensive pacts designed to protect them from "revisionist" Bulgaria. See L. S. Stavrianos, *Balkan Federation*, pp. 224ff.
[14] Stavrianos, *Balkan Federation*, p. 258.

As could be expected, these conditions lead to contested elections, coalition governments, frequent party shifts and defections, and a generally fertile ground for intervention, be it external or internal. Internally, such a political melee encourages dictatorial elements to usurp authority. Then, when the dictatorships (whether rightist or leftist) come to power, allegedly to remedy conditions of corruption, nepotism, and instability, they are unpopular enough domestically to need external aid and support to maintain their viability. Once more the invitation to foreign intervention and penetration is ever present.

The economic backwardness of the Balkans has been attributed primarily to factors of climate and geography as well as the debilitating effect of hundreds of years of stifling and inefficient occupation under the Ottoman empire. Whether economic backwardness is responsible for the recurring extremes of political instability (in democracy) on one hand or the oppressive dictatorship (in fascist, Communist, or purely authoritarian regimes), on the other, is a matter of speculation best left to "pantologists," interdisciplinarians, or Marxists.

There is no doubt that in the post-World War II era all Balkan nations have made great efforts and considerable progress in economic development, combatting illiteracy, ill health, and citizen neglect—factors named as the causes of mistakes and misfortunes of the past. Economic growth, it is to be hoped, will continue without destructive and destabilizing social and political effects on the much-harassed Balkan peoples.

The outlook for the future is relatively predictable today. Rumania,[15] with an internally directive regime, is progressively gaining popularity at home and acceptance abroad by employing policies of independence vis-à-vis the U.S.S.R., rapid industrialization (Rumanian style) regardless of COMECON guidelines, and eclectic or pragmatic policies vis-à-vis the rest of the world. The Nixon trip attests to the approval on the part of the United States (perhaps no more than approval and, God forbid, no commitment) of nationalist reassertion in Eastern Europe.

Bulgaria remains the stanchest advocate of Moscow's supremacy in the Balkans and the Communist movement in general.[16] This dependent role is perhaps dictated by the Bulgarian leadership's assessment of what is in the small country's best national interest. As the years go by, the Communist regime in Bulgaria is likely to gain additional acceptance at home and rely less on Soviet external support. In the meantime, however, it is natural for Bulgaria to gravitate toward the U.S.S.R., since her traditional adversaries (Greece, Yugoslavia, and Turkey) currently have cool and correct relations with the Soviets. Undoubtedly—in times of

---

[15] For background see Stephen A. Fischer-Galati, ed., *Romania* (New York: Mid-European Studies Center, 1957).

[16] See L. A. D. Dellin, ed., *Bulgaria* (New York: Mid-European Studies Center, 1957).

detente and thaw—Bulgaria will continue to seek better trade and cultural relations with the West and other Balkan nations, but her close strategic orientation toward the U.S.S.R. is likely to continue for a long time.

Yugoslavia[17] should perhaps receive the highest marks for maintaining relative immunity from external intervention and control and exercizing an independent, self-initiated foreign policy. Tito, in his pursuit of a policy of balanced diplomacy, nonalignment and neutralism, has attained for himself and his country prestige disproportionate to his nation's size and power. Yugoslavia will most likely continue to play the role of the "honest broker" between blocs in times of East-West friction. In times of detente, however, Tito (or his successors) could spearhead federative or confederative schemes in the Balkans and eastern Mediterranean (strongly assisted by Rumania) designed to create neutral, denuclearized safety zones. Such a zone would result should the Soviet and U.S. Sixth fleet leave the Mediterranean—a recent Tito wish—to avert a future accidental clash that might have catastrophic nuclear consequences.[18] All these schemes, of course, are likely to remain unfulfilled suggestions as long as the present balance of power situation perpetuates itself.

Albania[19] maintains and will continue to maintain strong, nepotist, authoritarian rule in a backward and poor country that exists in utter isolation from its Balkan and European environment. The leaders of Albania will continue advocating the appropriate "doctrinal mix" designed to secure external support—be it from the U.S.S.R. or China—against two relatively powerful neighbors (Greece and Yugoslavia) that would allegedly divide and devour her given a free hand. These fears may be somewhat exaggerated in view of the fact that few nations (including Greece and Yugoslavia) would welcome the burden of inheriting territories that would become economic liabilities for their relatively more advanced populations.

Greece[20] (and under very similar conditions, Turkey) finds itself a

[17] For background, see Robert F. Byrnes, ed., *Yugoslavia* (New York: Mid-European Studies Center, 1957).

[18] Tito answering a question in a news conference said recently: "We had thought the presence of the Soviet fleet would contribute to a solution [of the Middle East crisis] and we felt it was positive. But we are now afraid that one day it might come to a conflict between them [U.S.S.R., United States], because one never knows when a situation may explode. It would be better if neither fleet were there, that they did not concentrate there, but we must accept the facts as they stand." Anderson, *Current History* (April, 1969), p. 217.

[19] For background see Stavro Skendi (ed.), *Albania* (New York: Mid-European Studies Center, 1956). See also Nicholas C. Pano, *The People's Republic of Albania* (Baltimore: The Johns Hopkins University Press, 1969).

[20] C. M. Woodhouse, *The Story of Modern Greece* (London: Faber & Faber, 1968), D. George Kousoulas, *Revolution and Defeat* (London: Oxford University Press, 1965), T. A. Couloumbis, *Greek Political Reaction to American and* NATO

stanch ally of the United States, bound to it through NATO and direct bilateral agreements. Postwar Greek progress and redevelopment had a late start owing to the costly and traumatic (in terms of political aftermath) civil war in 1946–1949. The 1950s, however, were years of relative governmental stability and considerable economic progress. But throughout the 1950s the Greek military establishment enjoyed large-scale independence from political control. When, in the mid-1960s, Greece was visited by a series of political crises, a small team of army mid-career officers assumed governmental control by *coup d'etat* and established an interim dictatorship whose long-range aim was to reestablish a "modern and safe democracy." [21] Following over two years of military rule, the George Papadopoulos regime shows few, if any, signs of repeating the Turkish pattern of the 1960s, which returned the control of power to politicians, proclaimed elections, and maintained the armed forces only as an auxiliary guarantor of the stability (that is, Western orientation) of the country. Instead George Papadopoulos appears to be digging in for a long term in power. He has purged large numbers of military officers, restaffed the governmental apparatus with reliable men, and put "plaster over an allegedly broken-boned Greece." [22] Pressures from NATO countries and the United States are likely to intensify in the direction of reestablishing democracy in its birthplace; however, if Papadopoulos survives, it is not unlikely that he, too, will make a dramatic *volte-face* to gain external support from the "best bidder." And so it is possible, in the personalized vocabulary of political science, a new term will appear timidly next to terms such as "Stalinism," "Titoism," and "Nasserism"— "Papadopoulism."

What has the post-World War II policy of the United States been toward the Balkans? The application of the balance of power system vis-à-vis Soviet (and more recently, Chinese) presence in the area is perhaps the best summary description. Toward Greece and Turkey the United States has followed an alignment policy of close association, heavy military and economic aid, the construction of American bases on

---

Influences (New Haven, Conn.: Yale University Press, 1966), and for perhaps the most valuable survey on modern Greek politics, see Jean Meynaud, *Les Forces Politiques en Grèce* (Montreal: Etudes de Science Politique, 1965). See also Keith A. Legg, *Politics in Modern Greece* (Stanford, California: Stanford University Press, 1969).

[21] The suspension of constitutional freedoms in Greece was the source of considerable embarrassment to the United States, under whose protective umbrella this retrogressive development occurred.

[22] For elucidation see Marcus Wheeler, "Greek Political Perspectives," *Lo Spettatore Internazionale* (English edition), III, No. i (January–March, 1968), 339. See also Theodore A. Couloumbis, "Greece: Ballots or Bayonets," *World Affairs*, Vol. CXXX, No. 4 (March, 1968).

their territories, coordination of armed forces through NATO, and good cultural and economic relations.

Toward Yugoslavia, since the split with the U.S.S.R. in 1948, the United States has followed a most benevolent policy indeed. It has spent well over $2 billion in helping Tito with economic and military aid. By encouraging the Balkan Pact (between Yugoslavia, Greece, and Turkey in 1954),[23] the United States has almost found itself in the paradoxical position of having to rush to the defense of one Communist regime against the possible encroachments of another.

The U.S. policy toward Bulgaria and Rumania, as with the rest of Eastern Europe, has been one of economic isolation and political condemnation (at least verbally). More recently the United States has adopted a "new look" toward Eastern Europe by abandoning policies of "liberation," or "rollback," for "building bridges" or employing "peaceful engagement." These tactics are designed to increase trade, ameliorate cultural relationships, and more or less consolidate the East-West detente, thus relaxing the cold war somewhat but not enough to disturb the institutional trappings of the East-West adversary relationship.[24] Even more recently, the policy of peaceful engagement seems to have run into some great snags. First there is the psychological reaction to the Czech invasion, which sobered up many prophets of "gradual autonomy-building" in East Central Europe. Also, the lack of any substantive response from the United States has once more—as with Hungary and Poland—reminded the world of the imperatives of "balance of power," of "spheres of influence," and of the necessary gap between the ideal or desirable and the real or prudent policies. Further, the continuing Vietnam stalemate has antagonized large segments of the U.S. Congress to the point of opposing policies of freer trade with Eastern European countries, which are simultaneously supplying Hanoi with war materials.[25]

So the prospects for the next ten years are for a continuation of the geopolitical and geostrategic balance of power policy of the United States toward the Balkans based on the triptych calling for alliance

[23] See Iatrides, *The Balkan Triangle*, pp. 133ff., for an excellent discussion of the ramifications of the pact.
[24] See Andrej Korbinski, "East Europe and the United States," *Current History* (April, 1969), pp. 201ff. For the most clear-cut statement of this "new look," see Lyndon B. Johnson's address before the National Conference of Editorial Writers, New York, October 7, 1966, *Department of State Bulletin* (Oct. 24, 1966). For a scholarly substructure to this "new look" see Zbigniew Brzezinski, *Alternative to Partition* (New York: McGraw-Hill, 1965). And for a brilliant criticism of the Brzezinski position see Stanley Hoffman, *Gulliver's Troubles: Or The Setting of U.S. Foreign Policy* (New York: McGraw-Hill, 1968), pp. 485–92.
[25] See Korbinski, *op. cit.*, pp. 203ff.

with Greece and Turkey, support for an independent, non-hostile Yugoslavia, and maximum feasible economic and cultural cooperation with Bulgaria and Rumania, designed to encourage the liberalization of their regimes and (but within prudent limits) increase their autonomy vis-à-vis the U.S.S.R.

In the short run, therefore, it pays the United States as well as the U.S.S.R. to support in deeds, if not in words, policies of national exclusivism (within safe limits) rather than federalism in the Balkans. As long as the Balkans are divided, suspicious of one another, and warring, they will be fertile ground for external intervention. Of course this attitude may change as the U.S. government's estimate regarding the "objective" requirements of security (which are usually subjective) changes.[26] For instance, the day may come when we cease relying on overseas fixed bases for logistic support, or military capability for definition of influence and strategic presence. The nuclear equation may very well push the superpowers toward a policy of mutual disengagement and the development of mutually guaranteed "pacification" zones. Our very understanding of terms such as power, influence, and security may take altogether new forms. Instead of units of military or institutionalized presence, influence and power may be gauged in economic and cultural and, in any case, interpersonal rather than intergovernmental terms. This is a vision, indeed, of the far future, when the present alliance systems have been dissolved, the cold war lines blurred, and the division of Europe ended.

What will the Balkans do then? What can they do today? The road for the Balkan people is two-branched and they are at the crossroads today; it seems they will continue to be at the same crossroads for many decades to come. If they stay on their present path, extreme nationalism and protracted conflict will remain their lot. Even if the United States and U.S.S.R. should decide to disengage from Balkan politics, middle-range powers such as Britain, France, Germany, Czechoslovakia, and China would rush to fill the vacuum. Penetration would continue as in the past, only from different sources.

What, then, are the lessons of history for Balkan planners? If they wish to minimize external intervention, they must create a regional

---

[26] President Richard Nixon addressing the North Atlantic Council in Washington, D.C., said: "We in America continue to consider Europe's security to be our own." And then he added, "It is not enough to talk of European security in the abstract. We must know the elements of insecurity and how to remove them." In Robert Ellsworth, "The Future of the Atlantic Alliance," *Department of State Bulletin,* Vol. LX, No. 154 (June 16, 1969). Of course Mr. Nixon is approaching impatience or extreme optimism in hoping that elements of insecurity can be removed. Professor Samuel Sharp in his lecture entitled "Changing Security Requirements by Great Powers" (appearing elsewhere in this volume) wittily referred to "perfect security" as "death."

union, which would naturally limit narrow national ideals, interests, and prerogatives. Before countries like Rumania, Yugoslavia, Greece, and Turkey can seriously advocate schemes for federal or confederal union in the Balkans, some hard, empirical studies must be conducted to determine the "integratability index" of the Balkan peninsula. Is it economically advantageous, for example, for each of the Balkan nations to enter into a regional customs union or common market? How far is integration to go? Should one begin with economic and social cooperation as the "functionalists" would argue, or should one admit that unless there is a fundamental political understanding all partial efforts toward cooperation will meet with failure? To borrow Karl Deutsch's term,[27] is the Balkan peninsula a "security community"? If not, if the chances for integration are miniscule because of economic or geographic or ethnic or religious or even myth-made incompatability, then all talk urging a Federal Balkans is either irrelevantly utopian, an exercise in frustration, or a ritualistic weaving of a phrase merely because its texture is good.

Whither, then, the Balkans? Todor Zhivkov, the Premier of Bulgaria, made the following impassioned pleas on the twenty-fifth anniversary of Kemal Ataturk's death. He said:

> May the Balkan peninsula never again become a battlefield, nor a beachhead for military operations, but may it become a region of peaceful coexistence, of mutual economic and cultural cooperation between the states for the welfare of our peoples.[28]

But the hard question still remains: Cooperation and welfare and peaceful coexistence on *whose* terms and how implemented? And so we pessimistically return to "Balkanization" as usual.

[27] Karl W. Deutsch et al., "Political Community and the North Atlantic Area," *International Political Communities* (Garden City, N.Y.: Doubleday, 1966), pp. 1–91. See especially p. 37 where he outlines essential conditions for community amalgamation. It would be an extremely useful contribution indeed if a study were completed measuring the "security-community" indices of the Balkans, using the methodological guidelines of the Deutsch school.

[28] See Todor Zhivkov, *For Peace, Friendship and Socialism* (Sofia: Foreign Languages Press, 1966), p. 468.

LATIN AMERICA

John N. Plank

Security planning is seldom fully appropriate to the situation for which it is devised. Events move at an extremely rapid pace and are affected by the equally rapid onslaught of technology. Change is anticipated, of course; probable outcomes are isolated, analyzed, and planned for, yet in many instances "security" can be no more readily guaranteed at the end of planning sessions than at the beginning.

In one respect, this uncertainty derives from the fact that security— for societies as for persons—is a vague and indeterminate thing. So many components comprise security, so few are examined, so many are influenced by other—supposedly extraneous—factors, that the ultimate attainment of security exists only as a chimera. Security assessments can never be accurate. No country, no matter how powerful or inspired, can prepare appropriately for every contingency.

Lack of prescience and the "insecure" condition that resulted from it have historically not bothered Americans. They have not been overly disposed to thinking in "domino theory" or fear-ridden terms. Rather, confidence has been their distinguishing characteristic, a confidence generated largely from their geographic situation. In the first century of its existence, and for sometime there after—until around 1900—the United States enjoyed the blessing of isolation from stronger European nations. This isolation bred security and its offspring, confidence. During this period, the United States was in effect an insular continent, a position that enabled it to move into a situation rapidly and with assurance, to "take care of things," and then get out and return to safety.

This has not been the position of the United States in the post-World War II period. Revolutionized technology and rapid communications have effectively terminated America's former isolation. As a result of the cold war, Americans have felt threatened, and their reaction has been one of fright and sometimes terror. Generalizations carry within them the seeds of their own contradiction, yet the general approach of the

United States to the world has been defensive, even in the Western Hemisphere, which it has long considered its special domain.

The cold war alone is not responsible for this defensive orientation, although it has proved much easier for Americans to detect communist conspiracies, particularly in their own back yard than it has been for them to live comfortably with ambiguity, uncertainty, and creative challenge.

One can, of course, exaggerate the intrinsic importance of Latin America as well as its importance to the United States. But for every excess on the side of exaggeration, there is a larger one on the other side, the side that views Latin America as some kind of poor country cousin toward whom the United States feels a vague kinship relation—not quite a member of the family but still a member of the household. We acknowledge a degree of responsibility for the creature—we strive to ensure that the area not starve, that it not be ravaged by seducers from other parts of our global environment. We prefer that Latin America not venture abroad, not take up with strangers. We have arranged what we think is a reasonably comfortable place for it, down in the kitchen next to the hearth. We protect Latin America as any rich and decent relative would, expecting in return only that Latin America stay in its place, do some routine work for us. We are not prepared, of course, to accept that Latin America is yet ready fully to make its own decisions, take responsibility for its own destiny. We certainly are not prepared handsomely to endow it and set it off on its own. That day will come, we insist, but it is still far distant. Latin America still needs our solicitous care, Latin Americans being too immature, too irresponsible, too weak really to understand and advance their own best interests. As good relatives we are obliged to define and further those interests for them.

This is a caricature, of course, but it is not an outlandish one. Persons in high positions in the State Department refer to Latin America's "adolescent rebellion" against the United States; language attributed to former Presidents of the United States—including one very recent President—is literally shocking in its condescending, patronizing tone toward Latin America and Latin Americans.

Because we have largely defined our relationship toward Latin America in this way, we have identified our security interests in ways compatible with that definition and have arranged our security capabilities in accordance with it. It is time, however, that we reassess our whole security posture. It would be disruptive of the symmetry of many of the titles of papers in this series to suggest alterations, but as far as Latin America is concerned a more appropriate title is the *changed*, not the changing, requirements of U.S. security in Latin America.

What underlies our security posture vis-à-vis Latin America is qualitatively different from that which underlies it in other parts of the world, particularly the Third World. A specious geographic propinquity is part of it, of course—if Mercator had employed a North Polar projection instead of the one he did, the Western Hemisphere idea might not have got such a grip on us, for geographically nothing unites North and South America except an impassable land bridge, conveniently cut by the Panama Canal. Our cultural affinities are with Europe, not with Latin America; our trade relations are with the North, not with the Western Hemisphere.

What makes our security posture different is history and ideology. The Monroe Doctrine is now part of our national store of operative ideas, ranking not far below the Constitution, the Bill of Rights, the Declaration of Independence, and the Gettysburg Address. As a people we *believe* that the Western Hemisphere is a special place, a special community, ideologically and strategically off limits to extrahemispheric powers. The Monroe Doctrine dates from 1823, although it did not really acquire force and power until sometime later. It remains at the root of our security concern as reflected in the Rio Treaty of 1947, as reflected in the writings not only of the Admiral Mahans of his and subsequent generations, but also in those of such men as Hans Morgenthau and Walter Lippmann. Complementary to it, but still very much a part of our store of hemispheric security concepts, is the Roosevelt Corollary of 1904. In that year President Theodore Roosevelt said: "All that this country desires is to see the neighboring countries stable, orderly, and prosperous. Any country whose people conduct themselves well can count upon our hearty friendship." It was, in Theodore Roosevelt's interpretation, left to the United States to determine whether the countries of the region were conducting themselves well or ill. In 1965 it was again left to the United States to determine whether the Dominicans were conducting themselves well or ill. Should the Chileans in 1970 elect a Socialist president who has the overt support of the Communists, will it again be up to the United States to determine whether the Chileans are acting well or ill?

The point here is that *security* for the United States, as it has been defined for the Western Hemisphere, is a much more embracing concept than it is for the rest of the world. In this hemisphere we feel our security to be threatened not only when an effort is made to install missiles in Cuba—something that happened once and is extremely unlikely to happen again—but also when the Latin Americans veer away from us in matters ideological, economic, social, or political. Why do we equivocate about this? We think of this hemisphere as being *our* hemisphere, and our psychological and political security depends to an unhealthy degree upon our paramountcy in this area along *all* dimensions, not just military or strategic. We have no confidence in the Latin Americans, and there is something unwholesome in the whole relationship. In a perverse kind of way, we are as psychologically, almost pathologically, dependent upon the Latin Americans' remaining in a subordinate position to us—or, to put it the other way, our remaining in a dominant position vis-à-vis them, as the Latin Americans are psychologically, politically, economically dependent upon us. We stand to Latin America as a neurotic parent stands to a child, a relationship that is as deleterious to one member as it is to the other.

Here precisely is where security interests, as conventionally defined, enter in. But in a perhaps too categorical statement, there is no longer a meaningful security threat in this hemisphere, neither one directed against the United States from Latin America nor one directed against the states of Latin America from external sources. We all recognize that the prospect of an across-the-water invasion of Latin America—the kind of thing that marginally preoccupied us during World War II as emanating from the Nazis and Japanese—is now altogether remote. The nuclear standoff between the United States and the U.S.S.R. defines the terms of the great power confrontation in military aspects—and Moscow has no interest in directing its missiles toward Latin America. The insurgency threat, at least any insurgency that can be reliably traced to either Moscow, Peking, or Havana, has diminished to the point of disappearance. The Venezuelan defense minister recently announced that there has been no such activity in his country in half a year. And as we know, Venezuela was a prime target. By extension, our own officials tell us that they know of no major activity of this kind *anywhere* in Latin America since the death of Che Guevara in 1967. Wherein, then, lies the security threat to us? or to the Latin Americans?

And with the disappearance of these threats, wherein lies the justification for our security posture toward Latin America? Our security policy there has been almost *too* successful. If the Latin Americans can handle their own insurgency problems, what justification is there for our continued involvement there, particularly when the costs—political and other—we pay for that continued involvement are considered? If there is no longer a strategic threat from outside the continent, what justification is there for our expressed desire to maintain a supply and training monopoly for Latin America's armed forces—again, when the costs of that monopoly are so heavy?

One of course cannot assert that a meaningful security threat will not reemerge; but what is important is that we define our security interests in the region much more carefully than we have in the past, that we do what we can to restrict them to considerations of vital relevance to our national interest rather narrowly conceived. The notion that an indigenous insurgency in Guatemala, for instance, represents a threat to the Panama Canal and that therefore it represents a threat to us is appalling; those who advance it are either silly or disingenuous. One does not have to go to Guatemala if his objective is the blowing up of the canal. Or the notion that the demise of Duvalier—which must occur one day in accordance with one of nature's more inexorable laws—obliges us to intervene in order to prevent chaos, which in turn might lead to a communist takeover, which in turn would represent a threat to our national security interests—that notion needs very careful examination. There are good reasons why we and the other states of the hemisphere should strive to devise mechanisms and programs for the resuscitation of Haiti, but preoccupations with United States or hemispheric security ought not to be predominant among them. Should turbulence emerge in Bolivia, the sequel to Barrientos' death and Siles' accession, we should not assume that either the security interests of the United States nor the security interests of neighboring Latin American countries require major intervention there. It is interesting that we detect no security threat in the hostilities between Salvador and Honduras; and yet their full implications are ominous.

The Russians are following a different route toward establishing a presence in Latin America, the route of diplomacy and trade; all the evidence—and it is persuasive—indicates that they frown upon adventurism in Latin America. The Cubans and Chinese are in no position to exploit opportunities, if indeed opportunities can be found—and Che's melancholy Bolivian experience indicates that they are not plentiful.

Let us be a bit more precise about this. The free election of an anti-American, overtly pro-Soviet regime would not, *ipso facto*, constitute a threat to our security. It would be a shock to our pride and it would be interpreted presumably as reflecting a potentially dangerous shift in world power dispensations. But that interpretation would reflect both a too-rigid conception of the kind of world we live in—which, as Henry Kissinger has pointed out, may be militarily bipolar but is increasingly politically multipolar—and a misreading of the Latin American reality, which is a manifestation, still largely latent, of a yearning to escape from dependence upon the United States, not to switch sides in the great-power confrontation.

The outbreak of major civil strife in a Latin American country, which eventuated in the assumption of power by a group that announced itself as being communist, would not in itself represent either a threat to our security interests or those of its neighbors. This has happened already, of course, in the case of Cuba. Two points: First, all of our elaborate security machinery—and remember that Fidel was building his base during the heyday of John Foster Dulles, when cold war security considerations were predominant as they never were before, and have not been since—did not prevent Batista's downfall and Fidel's triumph. Second, Fidel failed miserably to export his revolution; and it is hard to believe that the United States was responsible for that failure. Fidel's principal target, Venezuela, handled the challenge overwhelmingly by itself under the leadership of strong but enlightened leadership. We should recognize that we cannot, at acceptable cost, maintain incompetent, corrupt, unrepresentative regimes against strong insurgency movements that have significant popular support—and the interesting feature of those insurgency movements we can identify in Latin America is that those movements are weakest which have the most pure, most overt lines to international communism. It is the nationalist insurgencies that are most powerful; of these, it has to be said that they are not highly successful, largely because revolution is not at all an easy thing to get underway, as hundreds of frustrated if idealistic Latin American young people will attest.

Do we have to be reminded of the price we paid and continue to pay for our Dominican intervention? By that precipitous action we forfeited for an indefinite future any prospects for a viable regional multilateral alternative to unilateral intervention—the idea of the Inter-American Peace Force is moribund if not totally dead. Do we have to be reminded that the intervention revived or aroused suspicions and fears among broad sectors of important Latin American opinion that we thought had been successfully quieted? Our policy makers should be more aware than they sometimes seem to be that the memories and expectations young people today bring to inter-American relations are not those of the policy makers. Forty percent of Latin America's population today is fourteen or younger. What are their memories? The Bay of Pigs, the Dominican intervention, the Brazilian coup of 1964, and the subsequent coups in Argentina, Peru, and Panama. The identification of the United States with the military establishments in all these countries is asserted, if not demonstrated.

No, it is not only that U.S. emphasis upon security—which leads it to adopt a far too negative, defensive posture in its Latin American policy— is likely to prove unavailing in the future; it is also that the indirect costs are likely to be far too great. The United States is already too strongly identified as a *status quo* power; it would be tragic if it were to continue to lend its military force to what are regarded as *status quo* or reactionary elements and trends. This is not fair to us and what we stand for—or, at least when we are true to ourselves, what we should stand for—nor is it fair to the Latin Americans.

Security questions must bulk large in a country with an $80 billion defense budget, in a country in which it is assumed that the only way an AID bill can be presented with any hope of passage is through trotting out the bogey that if we don't give aid our security interests will be threatened, in a country in which we seem incapable of mobilizing ourselves except in adversary relationships, relationships of confrontation. But this security focus is not only misleading, it is downright dangerous.

Our challenge in Latin America has precious little to do with security as conventionally defined. One of the things that gutted the Alliance for Progress was precisely its ambiguous nature as conceived in the United States. The Latin Americans quite legitimately ask, Was the Alliance mounted to help us or to frustrate Fidel Castro and the communists? We can say, it was not either/or, it was both. We can say that, and we can believe it; behind the sword and shield there is the plow. But as seen from Latin America the reality looked different. Latin America seemed to be viewed as a theater in the cold war, a territory in contention between us and the communists.

Now, it is one thing, if you are a pretty girl, to be vied for by two men: it is quite another if you conceive yourself as a chattel to be allocated to one of the two men. And the record is too clear, at least as it appears to the Latin Americans, that—all rhetoric aside—the United States is really not interested in them except in derivative terms, derivative from its own rather narrowly defined national interest concerns. There is no question that we take the place for granted, that it is at the bottom or next to the bottom of our priority areas. This is always vociferously denied, yet the record is clear. Only for a very brief period during the very last Eisenhower and the very early Kennedy years was it different. Almost anything can distract us from Latin America: Europe is more important, the Middle East is more important, Asia is more important, clearly the Soviet Union is more important. As long as Latin America is relatively tranquil, or as long as something more exciting exists elsewhere to attract our attention, we ignore Latin America. We recognize that in the last analysis Latin America can't go anywhere; and the Latin Americans recognize this too.

The danger now existent is that, because of the marked diminution of the security threat in this hemisphere, we shall once again relegate Latin America to oblivion or close to it. President Nixon has told us that Governor Rockefeller embarked on his Latin American journeys with an open heart, an open mind, and open eyes. As a Latin American diplomat said, however, he did not go down with an open pocketbook. Indeed, it is hard to escape the uncomfortable and disconcerting thought that in this context "open" may translate to "empty." We have been told that the formulation of this administration's Latin American policy awaited Governor Rockefeller's return and the submission of his recommendations. Our expectation, all things considered, can hardly be an optimistic one.

Actually, the diminution of the security threat presents us with a real opportunity if we will seize upon it and put it into the broader global context. Let it be said, in the first place, that the dying out of the security threat is fully recognized by the Latin Americans themselves and that, in an odd way, it gives them flexibility that they perhaps would not otherwise have. Particularly does it give them an opportunity openly and aggressively to taunt the United States. Nationalism in its various forms —whether in Peru, Argentina, or Brazil—is flourishing in Latin America today, not only because of the workings of the forces of what we call modernization in the region, but also because Latin Americans recognize that the cold war is no longer what it was in the region a decade or even five years ago. They no longer feel themselves to be between the eagle and the bear, to use Salvador de Madariaga's formulation. It will be a test for us to permit them to have their rein as they seek their national identities, seek to define themselves, often enough by distinguishing themselves, asserting their independence, from the United States.

What we must understand is that Latin America is awash in emanations from our culture—scientific and technological, cultural, economic —in all dimensions. As seen from Latin America, we are the great expansionist force, particularly today, when the identifiable Communist threat is so rapidly diminishing. Unfortunately much of what we *consciously* project toward the region is negative and defensive—and this is particularly true in respect of our security preoccupations. Can we not project what even in this troubled period in our own domestic development, is more truly, more legitimately us? Namely, an attitude of confidence, of willingness to take risks, to experiment, an attitude of boldness and assurance? Can we not try to get the spirit of the Alliance for Progress to match its rhetoric? Can't we let Latin America go, following, supporting, encouraging, but stopping this anxious mother-henning, this far-too-prevalent view that the Latin Americans are not capable of determining their own course and destiny? What today do we have to fear? Anti-Americanism? We shall not eliminate that by following the policies of the past. Communism? Can't we credit them with the right to determine their own courses—and can't we accept that in the Latin American context today, in almost all cases a man who calls himself a Communist is a nationalist first and a Communist second, and is very seldom the kind of person Moscow—which is the only real security threat in today's world—would want to welcome into the fold?

Yet something transcends all this, something vastly important. What is most distressing about the security concerns that have underlain our hemispheric policies for so long, and particularly since World War II, is that they distort our whole perception of the world and its challenges. The real challenge that confronts us in the United States is not the East-West one, in accordance with which Latin America becomes an element in the East-West struggle for power, prestige, and perquisites. The real challenge is the North-South one. It is grotesque and obscene that the thriving North, of which both the United States and the U.S.S.R. are parts, should be pulling away toward ever-increasing material affluence if not opulence, leaving the South farther and farther behind. We define poverty levels in this country as beginning at about $3,200 a year, for a family of four. That is five to ten times the income of families in most of the world, including Latin America. *That* is the problem that should preoccupy us, not the confrontation—with its ideological overtones—between the United States and the U.S.S.R. But we cannot even begin to get to work systematically and with adequate resources upon that problem so long as we are devoting such a disproportionate amount of money, time, and energy to the United States-U.S.S.R. contest, characterized by reciprocal suspicion, hostility, and fear. The only way the scaling down can be begun, and certainly the only way it can be accomplished, is for us to reassess the nature of the world in which we live. Our concern with and for Latin America ought not to be security, it ought to be development; and we should begin to believe and to act as if development were indeed our concern, devoting to its requirements the kinds of resources we are now devoting to defense.

One thinks often these days of the astronauts, and most specifically of what Archibald MacLeish wrote for publication on Christmas morning: "To see the earth as it truly is, small and blue and beautiful in that eternal silence where it floats, is to see ourselves as riders on the earth together, brothers on that bright loveliness in the eternal cold—brothers who know now they are truly brothers."

Can we transfer that intellectual awareness to which Mr. MacLeish so poignantly alerts us to a living awareness? Can we persuade ourselves that what he says is really true, that we are all here together, infinitely precious, each of us on an infinitely precious and infinitesimally small island in space? Can we get our priorities straight? In Latin America the changed security situation permits us to do that, and the requirements of simple humanity demand that we do so.

SUB-SAHARAN AFRICA

Charles Burton Marshall

Two of the words in the topic need a preliminary expounding. One of them is "requirements." The term denotes actions, objects of actions, or a quality pertinent to either. That quality is intensity of desire, demand, or constraint, approaching or amounting to necessity. The nuances range over want, need, indispensability, requisition, obligation, and compulsion.

The other problematic word is "security." What first comes to mind is Edward Gibbon's reference, in *The Decline and Fall of the Roman Empire*, to how the Emperor Honorius' court "enjoyed the security of the marshes and fortifications of Ravenna" against the Goths. In that context the term means something tangible. It is equivalent to material conditions of safety: absence of threat, abatement of risk, or shelter from physical harm. The word has, however, meanings more impalpable. In Harold Laswell and Abraham Kaplan's *Power and Society*, for example, security is defined as "high value expectancy, position, and potential; realistic expectancy of maintaining influence" and is linked to "demands and expectations of the future value of the self." [1] The anxieties assuaged, the troubles warded off, and the benefits assured pertain to the subjective realm of existence. Security means confidence of enduringly amounting to something worthwhile.

Fallacies may result from analogizing too readily between general affairs and personal circumstances—a point ably argued by Robert A. Nisbet in his *Social Change and History*. We should be on guard against applying that latter meaning of security to a society, a state, or a nation precisely as it applies in individual life. Nevertheless, in general affairs security is not merely material safety but pertains to civil morale as well. The broad pertinent questions of security in relation to external policy are: What is needed in order to forestall hostile penetration of the

[1] Harold D. Laswell and Abraham Kaplan, *Power and Society: A Framework for Political Inquiry* (New Haven, Conn.: Yale University Press, 1950), p. 61.

national domain or intimidation through threat of such penetration? What is called for in order to sustain external conditions favorable to confidence in the validity of national purposes among a determining proportion of the populace?

The aspects are linked. The linkage is portrayable, up to a point, by a diagram of a sort sometimes found in textbooks in international relations, representing diverse states in world affairs by an array of congruent rectangles, each with a top portion marked off to indicate the governing establishment. Arrows pointing up and down within each rectangle depict interaction between regime and populace. Horizontal arrows, both projecting and impinging, connect each top portion with their counterparts to indicate interaction among governments. Each interactive circuit feeds into the other. That is to say, government operates at a crux.

Trouble comes in getting overdrawn either way, as when resources cannot be raised at home to match external exigencies, or when pressures generated domestically push a government to seek more than its power can avail abroad. This applies to security aspects particularly. General confidence in national capacity to cope with dangers from abroad is a necessary element in civil morale. In turn, civil demoralization—disintegration of accepted and affirmed public values, or incapacity to agree on what has intrinsic worth in general affairs—is likely more than anything else to render a nation vulnerable at the periphery.

The apotheosis of security would be to combine a location beyond reach of material threat and an external situation so marked by unity of precept and harmony of interest in world affairs that no external entity would even be disposed to raise a challenge. That first element was assumed to be a reality for the United States in a now long departed past. The second element was a durable anticipation and goal, reflected, as Felix Gilbert's *To the Farewell Address* reminds us, in the early American motto of *Novus Ordo Seclorum*, "a new order of the ages."

That anticipation, drawing on rationalistic modes of thought prevalent among French intellectuals of the latter eighteenth century, looked to a time when all peoples would share in the blessedness that Americans ascribed in their own case to the factor of remoteness from foreign embroilments. A free people could wish no harm to another, it was postulated. International enmities were the aberrant works of rulerships. The general blessedness—for which the United States would set a model —would be achieved by rendering all peoples free of foreign impingement and making all governments popularly accountable.

As a shelter for the United States in earlier phases, distance in retrospect seems to have been less important than luck—luck represented in prevailing conditions of world affairs, of which the Americans were beneficiaries but over which they had small influence. The decision makers were concentrated in Europe. None was in position or of magnitude to dominate the others. Their brief and infrequent wars were fought over modest issues, with relatively light havoc resulting. Their rivalries were focused on stakes of empire overseas but, thanks in large part to dissuasion exercised by British policy buttressed by dominance in sea power, generally spared the American continent. With the dissolution of these conditions, mostly within a lifetime, the safehold once relied on has vanished.

The preceding discussion has a bearing on the proper compass of security policy and on its requirements. Will to cope with palpable threats and to avoid the circumstances of intimidation in external affairs is wholly salutory and necessary. The corollaries present difficulties. The matter of maintaining safety for the national position may involve assuring access to resources essential to an adequate military basis. Depending on circumstances, it may require initiatives to forestall an adversary from gaining positions likely to give irreversible advantage. The possibilities are problematic. Conditions for a nation's safety may be conceived in exorbitant terms. Initiatives to forestall danger may be taken with too ready a zeal, with a result of precipitating a nation into more trouble than it can handle. So a wary, rather than an absolute, approach is called for even with respect to security in its most tangible aspect. Emphatically, we should be watchful about the implications of conceiving national security in terms not simply of safety but of assurance about values. Assurance about values entails determining what values to assure. That question has to do with identifying friends and adversaries. It is possible for a nation to become divided, tentative, and abashed about values to the extent of forfeiting capacity to perceive enemies or to recognize friends. Oppositely, a nation's values may come to be perceived and evoked in terms compulsively universal and bellicosely imperative, so that hostilities are exacerbated far and wide and the nation concerned is impelled into struggles beyond its capabilities, impairing the security it sought to insure.

Specifically, we should be on guard in respect of the traditional precept linking security with the vindication of self-determination. It is so easy to bend the principle back upon itself, so that it militates against the principle of independence that it purports to uphold. This consequence—implicit in the Wilsonian version relating security with the universalizing of democracy—was made explicit in President Lyndon Johnson's State of the Union message of 1966. The "most important principle of our foreign policy," he said, "is support of national independence—the right of each people to govern themselves—and shape their own institutions. " He went on: "For a peaceful world order will be possible only when each country walks the way it has chosen for itself." So far, the line of reasoning seemed clear enough and plausible too, as universal respect for national autonomy would be essential to peaceful world order. Then the President reversed: "We follow this principle, abroad as well as at home, by continued hostility to the rule of the many by the few." Thus a security requirement was adduced in terms of imposing requirements within another jurisdiction. True, it was only in a speech, but one wonders whether "only" is appropriate to faulty doctrine in a stately utterance.

On the globe, one readily discerns the expanse called Asia, Europe, and Africa as sectors partitioned into autonomy by fingers of sea but constituting together, nevertheless, one great land mass of the Eastern Hemisphere. Asia, the largest by far, appears as a rough spheric isosceles triangle. Its base is a jagged arc from Singapore to Aden, 4,500 miles apart. Its equal sides of 6,000 miles each form an apex on the Bering Sea. Europe, put in modest proportion, is seen as an adjunct to Asia consisting of two compound peninsulas (plus the nearby British Isles) marked out by complex extensions of the Atlantic. The more southern of these extensions, in a section called the Mediterranean, almost reaches an opposed finger thrust northwest from the Indian Ocean. The territory set off by these nearly intersecting inlets is Africa. A strip of it delimited at 20° north, more or less, is excepted from the scope. The lands comprising it are deeply affected by their nearness to the Mediterranean. The manner of their intersection, in strategic and other respects, with Southern Europe and the nearby corner of Asia differentiates them from the rest of Africa. Their populations have largely Arab identity. That northern portion merges into a conceptual area called the Middle East. The balance of Africa focused on here is the more autonomously African four-fifths, with offshore Malagasy included.

This broad characterization of the topical area is in a non-geographer's and non-demographer's approximations derived from data no more refined than what an almanac affords. In gross measure the area embraces somewhat under ten million square miles—thrice enough to enclose the United States without Alaska, and roughly a sixth of the earth's total land. Forty-three distinguishable politico-geographic entities make up this area. Four of these entities are in an undisputed status of dependency. Another, although unquestionably a dependency, is a focus of dispute as to precisely how it is so and whose it is. Two others are territories with independence asserted but controverted. The remaining thirty-six are independent with clear title, amounting to slightly less than three-tenths of the world's total. Thirty-three of these have reached independence in the last dozen years. These constitute about half the profusion of states which have popped off the production line in a quarter century. The most numerous cluster of states deposited since World War II by the sudden ebb of imperial authority based in Europe is found in this portion of Africa. Measured in numbers of governments, as distinguished from people, they constitute a major constituency of what, in a phrase first applied by Alfred Sauvy in 1956, is called the Third World—signifying the aggregate of necessitous states, mostly new and nonwhite, which together assertedly determine their alignments in international politics on the basis of their ambitions for internal development. The concerned area's populations—here statistics are far from firm—add to something under a quarter billion, amounting to perhaps a fifteenth of the world's total. The independencies average about six million each, but the average is misleading, because five of the countries share half the aggregate and one in particular, Nigeria, is greatly disproportionate (though perhaps by less than claimed, since figure-passing for prestige is suspected in this instance). As a more illustrative figure, the median population is about three and a half million.

The existence of a so-called white redoubt at the southern end of Africa is a circumstance of considerable significance. The territory embraced in the topic must be differentiated into two disparate zones divided by a zigzag averaging at about 20° south.

The more northern of the two zones is larger than the other by about four to one in territory and five to one in people. It embraces regions customarily known as West, Central, and East Africa. Thirty-five politico-geographic entities are included. Only one is anomalous—namely Biafra, which is a rebellious minor region of Nigeria according to the Nigerian version accepted generally, an independency by the Biafran contention supported by a handful of outside governments, and in any event a source of internecine war over the issue. Thirty-two of the lands are unequivocal independencies, giving the zone a distinguishing feature in the almost complete elimination of rulership from abroad. Two of these, namely Liberia and Ethiopia, are long established in that status, although the latter experienced a decade of Italian occupation that ended in World War II. The other thirty are new to independence. Half of them emerged from subordination to France. Ten were formerly British-ruled. One was in part British-ruled and in part Italian-ruled. Three were formerly under Belgium. One was under Spain. With two or three exceptions, the independencies are black-ruled. The more northern zone is black Africa most unequivocally.

The other zone is Southern Africa, extending to about 35° south. Of its eight politico-geographic entities, four are undisputed independencies. Three minor ones new to the status, varying in numbers from less than a third of a million to almost a million, are black-ruled. The fourth, independent in its present configuration for six decades, is the Republic of South Africa, with a population well on the way to twenty million, a fifth of it categorized as white, or, in local usage, European—the pre-eminent factor accounting for Southern Africa's being called the white redoubt. Here, as in the remaining five territorial components, political authority rests with the white minority. In adjoining and subordinated South West Africa—with a population around six hundred thousand, black over white in a ratio of perhaps five to one—South Africa's authority, dating from 1915, continues as an energetic reality, notwithstanding its having expired in 1966 according to a fancy entertained by the United Nations General Assembly. Rhodesia, with numbers approaching five million, preponderantly black in population and dominantly white in polity, is a third component, also of controverted status. In the British government's version seconded by both the General Assembly and the Security Council of the United Nations, that country was reduced to crown colony status and subsumed to London's direct control in 1965. A Rhodesian claim to juridic independence—made after more than four decades of self-government—dates from that same time. What, if anything, may rise to vindicate the British and United Nations version is not now discernible. Finally there are two long-established extensions of dominion from Portugal, which, despite much pressure, betrays as yet no intention of following the time's fashion by relinquishing overseas empire—namely Angola and Mozambique, together numbering over twelve million.

Africa as a whole and the portion concerned here in particular rank far down in the scale of security interest measured in explicit United States policy undertakings. Collective defense arrangements contracted through treaties and otherwise engross the American continents, traverse the Atlantic to the western segment of Europe, extend along the northern littoral of the Mediterranean and through a tier of states to the Asian subcontinent and embrace mainland and insular portions of Southeast Asia, Taiwan, the Japanese islands, South Korea, continental Australia, and insular New Zealand. For distance, numbers, and heterogeneity, the potpourri of United States commitments exceeds anything ever before undertaken in any nation's security policy. Africa, however, is completely omitted. As outposts of its strategic interests, the United States operates a far-flung system of bases for transit, supply, and communications. The number has been tending downward. Of a remaining total of 343 major and 1,927 minor bases (minor being those staffed by fewer than two hundred persons and costing less than $2 million each) only one, a major communications and electronic observation center in Ethiopia, is within the geographic scope of this topic.

Security requirements are not necessarily correlated to documented commitments and actual installations. Being a preeminent maritime power with wide-ranging strategic obligations, the United States clearly must have a concern about Africa's southern cape as a key to the security of one of three accesses to the Indian Ocean. With one of these accesses, the Suez Canal, blocked since 1967, and perhaps destined to remain so for a long time to come in view of the problematic chances of a settlement between Israel and its Arab neighbors, the importance of the Cape of Good Hope is made drastically greater. Reopening of the Suez Canal, if it ever comes, will not greatly diminish the cape route's importance. Sea commerce has adjusted to the new circumstances. The trend is toward larger vessels, bulking too deep for the canal. Restoring reliance on a thin artery vulnerable to the vicissitudes of those environs is not likely to be attractive, anyway. Reopening of the Suez, if ever, would probably sharpen the strategic significance of the northeast reaches of black Africa flanking the Bab el Mandeb and the Gulf of Aden. Whether the Suez Canal should be reopened or remain shut, a circumstance of great potential significance is the revision, now developing, of strategic relations in the Indian Ocean. For reasons of retrenchment, the British are now in a course of retracting the naval power whose dominance made that ocean the single most stable of strategic waterways for a century and a half after Waterloo. The Soviet Union, embarked on what the Georgetown University Center for Strategic and International Studies has described as "a maritime strategy designed to help it break out of its long history of continental confinement," is manifesting intentions of becoming a naval power there in the British wake.

It is only reasonable to note a high probability of continuing and increasing commercial and strategic importance for the cape. What circumstances may alter the American mood is hard to say, but for the present that mood is mostly negative about commitments and involvements. Present questions turn on whether and how to hold on to ones existing rather than whether and how to pick up more.

Noteworthily, the first instance in recent decades of immediate and preponderant opposition at the Capitol to incipient involvement abroad was related to black Africa, specifically the Democratic Republic of the Congo. In the summer of 1967 the Congolese regime, professing to believe itself to be in great danger, sought help in bolstering its forces fighting rebels and some infiltrators from Angola at a remote scene. The United States government, which had done the same sort of thing several times before as well as having spent some $500 million on helping the Congo, provided three jet transports and sent along, though explicitly not for combat purposes, a small military complement including a paratrooper platoon. "There was a political purpose to the move," as the *Los Angeles Times* observed, in that aid to a black regime against white-led troublemakers might garner credits and counteract Soviet propaganda. The State Department adduced an additional purpose—succor to imperiled missionaries. The gesture—made at a time when the Vietnam war was dragging on, the seven-day war in the Middle East was still reverberating, and Cyprus was tensing up again—precipitated a congressional uproar against courting more trouble. The State Department's reassurance of riskless prudence for the gesture failed to convince the objectors. The awkward venture was soon phased out.

A contrast to events involving the same country only a few years before is worth emphasis. In 1960, the Congo had become a scene of domestic turbulence, with native forces rising against Belgian forces in the immediate sequel to receiving independence. Alleging great international danger, the new Congolese regime sought aid from the United States, which prompted a referral to the United Nations Security Council. The concerted powers responded as if disorder in the Congo were a phenomenon of highest danger and exigency. Without waiting for detailed comprehension, they made up their minds what to do. A heterogeneity of military components from a diversity of nations was rushed in, purportedly to save world peace under United Nations aegis. As argued in Ernest Lefever's *Uncertain Mandate*, the original instant response was prompted rather by competitive zeal among the powers to display anti-imperial credentials than by genuine perception of great general peril. Whatever the line of reasoning, the underlying premise was that an issue of widest importance turned on the Congolese domestic situation. It is difficult now to understand the alarm. The Congo crisis was a crisis not for intrinsic reasons but because the major powers concurred in treating it so. Details as to how different from the Congo crisis the response has been to Nigeria's war since the summer of 1966 against breakaway Biafra will be spared. The recession of concern in external affairs, noted as a development of the American outlook in recent years, applies with emphasis concerning Africa. That is the point, and it is demonstrable without need of much research.

The African movement into independence surged in 1960. A spate of singularly unprophetic scholarly books about the continent began appearing. The press abounded with novelties about exotic places. The high expectancy, the sudden burst of public interest, and the signs of busy concern in Washington and Moscow are recalled in an article by Dr. Lefever in *Orbis*.[2] That same year, "for the first time in American history," as recalled in Arthur Schlesinger Jr.'s A *Thousand Days*, "Africa figured prominently in a presidential election." An index to Kennedy campaign speeches contained 479 references to Africa. A chapter devoted to policy about Africa in Schlesinger's history of the Kennedy presidency is replete with phrases such as "endless lengths," "new adventure," "an unending stream," "special effort," and "greatest success." Designation of a new Assistant Secretary of State for African Affairs preceded even that of the Secretary of State. The event was big news. In the President-

---

[2] Ernest W. Lefever, "State-Building in Tropical Africa," *Orbis* (Winter, 1969), p. 984.

elect's appraisal, the post carried "responsibility second to none in the new Administration." [3] In the 1968 campaign—according to Lefever's account—the aspirants, candidates, and platforms discussed Latin America, the Middle East, Eastern Europe, the Soviet Union, Western Europe, Communist China, and (voluminously, of course) Southeast Asia, but said nothing whatever about Africa beyond a reference to Rhodesia by the third-party candidate, George Wallace. Designation of a new Assistant Secretary of State for African Affairs waited until late spring and was only routinely reported.

A State Department hierarch's appraisal of emerging Africa's significance in early 1961 emphasized the prevalence of Western constitutional modes: elections, parliaments, accountable executive power, judicial restraints, bills of rights. The new states constituted history's greatest single accretion of free governments. There, in essence, he said, America's early self-projection was being realized and vindicated. Just as the United States in its time had emerged youthful, vigorous, unencumbered by old grudges, to be an exemplar to nations, so the progressive new Africa could become mentor for the world. In retrospect, it is now safe to assume that he overdid it a bit. In words from Robert A. K. Gardiner of Ghana, it has been "a decade of discouragement."

The phrase brings Nigeria to mind. My wife used to receive letters of gloomy analysis and dark prediction from a former Foreign Service colleague then serving at a lower echelon in our embassy at Lagos. How could the higher-ups there and in Washington remain so oblivious of what was going on and where the country was heading? She put that question at the close of a particularly foreboding account. The succession of events—coups, counter-coups, massacres, secession, and internecine warfare—vindicating our friend's private assessments began two years or so later, at the start of 1966. The first casualty, *Le Monde* of Paris observed after the opening coup, was Nigeria's reputation in the West as a model African country. "In Washington," *Le Monde* added, "the State Department is all the more concerned precisely because it occurred in Nigeria, considered as a land with a future." [4] Nigeria is the most dramatic example because of being the largest in population and the most overvaunted, but it is far from being a sole one. Order has been difficult to maintain in many places, with a resulting tendency to resort to the military, which has recurringly played politics by coup, often by lethal coup. The more northern of the two belts of Africa—the coup zone, as Frederic Hunter calls it in a *Christian Science Monitor* article —has produced twenty-three violent overthrows of governments since 1960, about one-third of the world's total for the interval.

[3] Arthur M. Schlesinger, Jr., *A Thousand Days: John F. Kennedy in the White House* (Boston: Houghton Mifflin, 1965), pp. 551–84.

[4] *Le Monde* (Paris), January 18, 1966.

As for causes, Stanislav Andreski's *The African Predicament: A Study in the Pathology of Modernisation* supplies some answers. Independence, it reminds us, was mainly the work of leaders in urban enclaves touched by western ideas received through contact with European rulerships and cultures. Their ideas were not much shared over the countryside. Independence substituted these leaders for the departed colonial apparatus. Their foundations among the populace were weak. Traditional identities—tribal bonds—have remained strong. Leaders striving as competitive politicians have found in them something to appeal to, so that what there is of democratic process has not proved a counter to tribal identities. As distinguished from that problem, there is the problem of loss of identity, disorientation, anxiety, and anomie in individual lives in connection with the great influx to cities, leaving nothing between the isolated person and the mass, and regrettably often resulting in the politics of bloodshed.

Policy making—meaning resolution, articulation, and effectuation of public purposes—has proved unexpectedly difficult. Before accession to authority, it had seemed to be only a matter of getting office and issuing edicts—the gist of Kwame Nkrumah's aphorism about seeking first the political kingdom, whereupon all else would be added. Reality, however, is obdurate, and for many reasons. The cash nexus is usually so limited: a problem of itself and a circumstance that constricts solutions. It is hard to get the word around so as to match obedience to decision. "Authority varies inversely to the square of the distance from the capital," is how I once heard the idea expressed. More basic is what Russell Warren Howe, writing in *Foreign Affairs*, has called "secular inertia," a condition tied in with meagerness of sense of history, or lack of an agreed-on past that provides a guide for coping with the future and serves as a foundation for what Rousseau called the General Will.

Pronouncement is tempting where policy is out of reach. Faced with shortcomings in the domestic scenes, some of black Africa's leaders—not singular in this respect—have been wont to turn compensatorily to external activities to fulfill the idea of nationhood. Several years ago an African diplomat at the seat of the United Nations explained the tendency to me. Great principles and hopes of political life should not be deferred merely because one could not perform on them. What was good about international politics, he went on, was that it gave opportunity to preach what one could not practice. His own country did not have free elections, but it did demonstrate fidelity to the idea of them by being for them in far places. Black Africa does fully its portion of the busy work of international affairs. "The search for identity, the need for self-affirmation, the desire to confirm an independent existence the reality of which is perhaps subconsciously questioned . . . all directly underlie the moves and countermoves, the aspirations and pretentions of African leaders in continental and global politics," [5] Professor Victor Ferkiss has observed in *Africa's Search for Identity*. Nationhood does not fulfill itself vicariously, however. What the new African states ever make of themselves will be realized essentially through what they do within, not by stands they take on affairs within other peoples' jurisdictions.

The black African governments lean to neutralism and in utterance eschew warlikeness. That is to say, like governments of many other regions, they are against all war except the kind they are for. The point is related to their shared repugnance for having culturally and ethnically differentiated authority ensconced in the region—an understandable attitude, especially in view of the contrast presented by the principal entity of the white redoubt, South Africa, in respect of effectiveness as a policy-making entity and an economic going concern. Again to quote Professor Ferkiss, "they would exempt from their general antipathy war actions aimed at reducing what they regard as colonial oppression. African nations—though retaining a theoretical preference for nonviolence —increasingly regard the overthrow of white power in Rhodesia, South Africa and Portuguese Africa as desirable even if force is necessary." South West Africa should be added to the list. In a sense all black Africans are brothers, according to Professor Ferkiss. If so, the sense is reflected in policy most clearly in purposes affirmed regarding Southern Africa—a circumstance implicative of a parallel to Arab unity and the outlook regarding Israel. The goal of ousting the white rulerships is what lends most of what unity obtains in the Organization for African Unity, formed in 1963 as an instrument for articulating and coordinating common policies among the governments.

The goal is tied in with endeavors of black dissident groups, which seek patronage abroad for militant activities within the respective Southern African countries. The character of the forces disposed is that of freedom fighters or terrorists—depending, of course, on who is characterizing them. Their numbers and formidability are similarly matters for variant estimates from different sources. On balance, however, their supporters among black African states and elsewhere seem to have heeded too little the wisdom of Niccolo Machiavelli, who in *The Discourses* titled a chapter, "How Dangerous It Is to Trust to the Representations of Exiles." The likelihood of fulfillment through such agency seems much less than was being widely alleged, with presumptive authority, only a few years ago. The wars that the black African regimes' aspirations would entail are likewise beyond their own doing. Distances are great. Means are meager. The military strength to be contended

[5] Victor Ferkiss, *Africa's Search for Identity* (New York: George Braziller, 1966), p. 103.

against, South Africa's in particular, is much too much. "If the African nations could mobilize military force the situation would be different," as the former United States Under Secretary of State, George W. Ball, has written in *The Discipline of Power,* "but they have no effective armies or aircraft or submarines to match those of the one modern military power on the continent, and their impotence only adds to their outrage." [6] The cause looks vain unless powerful outsiders can be mustered to make a go of it.

The quest, perennially pushed at the United Nations, draws affirmations regularly from all the Third World, Communist bloc states, and a heterogeneity of others not in position to do anything for the cause besides voting for it. Support from major Western governments—and above all from the United States—is what proponents covet. The United States has shown some disposition to honor the purpose by gesturing sympathy. The reasons and rationalizations are various. Former President Lyndon Johnson has stated a case in terms of national self-projection. "The foreign policy of the United States is rooted in its life at home," he has said. So precepts subscribed to within our jurisdiction should be pressed for beyond our jurisdiction—a matter of refusing to live by a double standard, in his explanation. In his book, *The Insecurity of Nations,* Charles H. Yost, the United States Ambassador at the seat of the United Nations, has invoked a conceptual debt owed by the great powers to the Third World.[7] Arthur Goldberg, a predecessor in that post, has discerned opportunity to "strengthen the defense of American interests in the rest of Africa and the non-white world" by bearing down on Southern Africa. Professor Ferkiss' book, already cited, finds justifications and impulsions in hypotheses concerning ruinous race wars by which Africa might be "politically and to some extent physically destroyed" in part as a result of "America's failure to take appropriate action." In some ultimate exigency the United States might find itself forced, too late, to intervene. The disapproval generated by its defaults among the black African states might bring on "a major political defeat for the United States," in his view. "Time grows shorter day by day," [8] he has written in urging drastic initiatives to head off catastrophe. Similar alarms over a course headlong to disaster have been rung in dozens of articles and books.

Since 1961 this Government has concurred repeatedly in General Assembly resolutions calling for relinquishment of Portuguese authority in Angola and Mozambique but has avoided endorsing steps to compel

---

[6] George W. Ball, *The Discipline of Power: Essentials of a Modern World Structure* (Boston: Little, Brown and Co., 1968), p. 253.

[7] Charles Yost, *The Insecurity of Nations: International Relations in the Twentieth Century* (New York: Praeger, 1968), p. 250.

[8] Ferkiss, *Africa's Search for Identity*, p. 336.

that result. Over the same time span the United States has voted for successive General Assembly resolutions calling for redesign of internal policies and governing patterns within South Africa, and from 1963 on has gone along with a Security Council action calling for curtailment of sales of arms and munitions to that country. From 1965 on, the United States has supported a series of General Assembly resolutions and Security Council actions invoking progressively severe commercial restrictions against Rhodesia in attempts to compel displacement of the regime and restructuring of the polity, while opposing alternate measures for unequivocal hostilities. In 1966 this Government voted for a General Assembly resolution purportedly dissolving South Africa's authority in South West Africa, and subsequently has participated with ten other governments in a council supposedly authorized by the Assembly to administer the territory as South Africa's surrogate pending fulfillment of independence. On the literal record, Southern Africa bulks large and dire as a concern to United States security. There this Government has been drawn into laying down precepts for governing in five countries beyond the span of American jurisdiction. In two instances, the United States has taken positions denying the rightful existence of actual regimes. With respect to one of these the United States is party to declaring the regime's very existence to constitute a threat to the peace within the meaning of Chapter VII of the United Nations Charter and its prescriptions for commercial discriminations, ostracism, and hostilities.

In international affairs one has to learn to measure by results rather than by precepts and expectations—a point applicable to Southern Africa, where what happens seems signally disproportionate to declaratory portents. The Rhodesian instance is illustrative. The British government cried alarm to the world on Rhodesia in hope of coercing the regime there to submit to basic revision of the polity as a precondition for Britain's formal acquiescence in independence, which the country already largely exercised in practice. Early in 1966, in a notable but not singular example of unprophetic anticipation of events in Africa, Britain's Prime Minister gave official assurance of determinative success within a span of weeks, not months, for economic sanctions that the British prompted the Security Council to invoke. Two and a half years after that utterance he was repining the dilatoriness of Appomattox in Rhodesia. Under sanctions the Rhodesian regime has experienced limbo but not extinction. As observed by C. Gordon Tether in *The London Financial Times*, sanctions have "failed to make things more than mildly uncomfortable for Rhodesia"—for Rhodesian whites, anyway. They have adjusted production patterns, become adept at patent infringement, learned to produce more than five hundred kinds of articles previously imported, found out how to dissimulate in commercial documentation, and shown up the fallacy of a British belief, concurred in by the Security Council including the United States, that closing down a volume of international trade amounting to only .25 per cent of the world's total would be easy—bringing to mind a metaphor about a needle in a haystack.

It is not that sanctions have been ineffective. Rather, they have not had the effects intended. As Dean Acheson has said, they "have served only to encourage the British government to frustrate a settlement by insisting on untenable conditions, to push the isolated Rhodesians sharply rightward, to retard the Rhodesian blacks' economic progress, and to make the United States improvidently dependent on the Soviet Union for chrome." Under the momentum of success, and perhaps with a touch of hubris, the Rhodesian electorate has voted to sever all connection with the Crown, to declare a republic, and to revise the constitution with a view of ensuring their ascendancy in perpetuity.

Now that sanctions have unequivocally failed of their purpose, the rationale for persisting in them is, as put forth by Colin Legum, writing in *The London Observer* of June 29, 1969, a hope of generating "internal pressures" which, he says, "might produce a more purposeful African role." "The absence, so far, of a significant black factor," he adds, "is the basic weakness of the struggle to alter the balance of power in Rhodesia; and this should be squarely faced." The meaning is plain enough. Sanctions, prolonged, might eventually help induce the sort of warfare they purportedly were designed to avoid. The point tells something of the dangers of perceiving security in terms of how someone else's realm is to be governed.

In the instance of South West Africa—focus of most enduring of issues at the United Nations and of the most voluminous and intricate international litigation ever conducted, as well as one of the most futile —the General Assembly's presumption of prerogative to terminate and to take over South Africa's governing role seems likely to go down in annals as a paper event. By the same resolution the General Assembly undertook to rename the place Namibia and to designate the heterogeneous inhabitants as the Namibian people—an appellation by which no existing aggregate of people knows itself. The source of the General Assembly's power in the matter remains a mystery. The Charter assigns it no relevant dispositive authority. A question of means is pertinent. How independence for South West Africa could be realized without South Africa's acquiescence, and how that acquiescence could be achieved under conditions short of specific military defeat of South Africa, are questions left unanswered in the Assembly's action. As a concrete circumstance, distinguished from abstract precept, South Africa's command of accesses to South West Africa inheres in geographical conditions irrespective of any authorization from outsiders. South Africa's authority in South West Africa, moreover, stems from conquest by military operations against German forces in 1915. The League of Nations mandate confirmed rather than established that authority. The General Assembly's declaratory termination of South Africa's rule in the territory was a gesture. South Africa's government of it as if it were an integral part of its own domain—a concept authenticated, though not established, by the League of Nations mandate—is a continuing reality.

I, for one, am loth to venture predictions, because Africa in general has proved hard on prophets. In 1961, exiled dissident leaders from Portuguese Africa were being received in Washington virtually as prime ministers-designate. The United States government was hurriedly and surreptitiously arranging university training in administration for some dozens of their followers in anticipation of an imminent accession to offical responsibilities, an eventuality that seems remoter now. The earliest of many books in which one reads about impending cataclysm for South Africa was dated 1922. The theme had wide acceptance a few years ago, and lingers still in many minds. Yet, as C. W. De Kiewiet observed in a distinguished article in *The Virginia Quarterly Review*, now "The South African government is at a peak of confidence and self-assurance. It faces its critics and opponents with a level eye. It has income to back bold decisions. It feels that the movement of events throughout the world has been predominantly in its favor, and continues to be so. Its supporters, who grow in each election, breathe easily. . . . The country is visibly relaxed." [9] The embargo on munitions and armaments has occasioned some expense and inconvenience, but the principal effect has been to spur that country notably closer to a self-sustaining defense.

Growing in material resources and in self-assurance, South Africa in recent times has been articulating a policy of initiative toward expanding economic relations and establishing diplomatic ties in black Africa —a development which, in Jerome Caminada's appraisal in *The Times* of London, "has a significance that will not be sponged out by hostility from afar." Concomitantly, pressures for action at the United Nations have been focusing on South Africa as strategic epicenter of the white redoubt. Having been drawn into subscription to goals requiring fundamental redesigns of governing patterns and transfers of political authority through Southern Africa, the United States has been, is, and will continue to be, pressed to follow relevant implications through to logical conclusions by permitting itself to get involved in unequivocal war or, at least, in some systematic program of economic hostilities against South Africa. Hearings in 1966 by a subcommittee of the House of Represent-

[9] C. W. De Kiewiet, "The World and Pretoria," *The Virginia Quarterly Review* (Winter, 1969), pp. 7–8.

atives, canvassing possibilities for riskless further lines of action against South Africa, elicited little besides suggestions for various pinprick gestures. The notion of economic and commercial discriminations as a way of levying hostilities without the risks inherent in belligerency persists in some quarters. A formula for economic and commercial confrontation put forward by former Ambassador Goldberg as a design to bring the South African regime to capitulation (paradoxically called a "program for disengagement") would be conditional on concurrence in the Security Council—a contingency subject to several doubts, including one as to how the necessitous British could possibly afford to slough off a signally favorable trading relationship. Professor Ferkiss would have the United States venture the course alone. Imaginatively, he depicts the United States obtaining and exercising sovereign purchase, through manipulation of trade discriminations, on the pattern of rulership in South Africa. Nothing in experience, however, warrants such an assumption of efficacy for economic warfare or of plasticity on the part of others.

To premise security requirements on how other domains are to be required to be run is to invite danger. To view the concept of self-determination in a way that assumes for outsiders a prerogative to interpose in how any polity manages its internal affairs is to get involved in contradiction. While avoiding prophecy in such a matter, this author would rate it a receding probability that the United States will permit itself to be drawn further toward hostilities in Southern Africa. How to ease away gracefully from consequences of having humored expectations beyond our intentions of fulfillment, how to vacate policy positions entered into on a basis of faulty perception of trends of events, is more likely to be the next stage of the problem.

THE MIDDLE EAST

Abdul A. Said

American scholarship and statesmanship have spent a quarter of a century in a massive attempt to understand the Middle East. Students and diplomats alike have busied themselves in mastering Turkish and Arabic, Hebrew and Persian, the ins and outs of Islam and the multi-faceted history of the region.

Yet, strangely enough, this deepened appreciation of the Middle East has not brought about any great elevation in the level of performance of the United States in the region. The scholars, assuming that all that can be dissected theoretically must operationally be an entity, dissected the Middle Eastern subsystem. It was declared that there does exist an "Arab World," a "Maghreb Personality," a "Northern Tier," when in fact the units of the region are viable only because they are fragmented. The age of independence has legitimized social superiority and inferiority in the region with its corollary of conflicting interests. This is not to suggest that there have not been valuable scholarly works on the Middle East. We are deeply indebted to the normative as well as empirical studies of historians and political scientists. Without their illustrious labors we would have a still cruder understanding of the region, but policy oriented studies remain few and far between.

The diplomats consciously attempting to apply rules distilled from sizable volumes of reporting to the problems of the region are divided into maximalists and minimalists, a division that characterizes the thinking of the American foreign policy establishment in other parts of the world.

The maximalists contend that the Soviet Union has substantially improved its position in the area since the mid-1950s. Although Moscow may not now be capable of an outright takeover anywhere, it can influence policy decisions by certain governments and is in a position to capitalize on unexpected developments. Apart from official ties, a generation of Middle Easterners is growing up that accepts the political values and friendship offered by the Soviet Union. By comparison, the United States is less and less in touch with this generation. Not only does Washington fail to provide a standard around which it can rally, but it all too often appears to be actively opposed to its goals and aspirations. As a result, an anti-United States feeling is developing in the region that redounds to the advantage of the Soviet Union. In brief, argue the maximalists, if the American objective is to encourage the evolution of compatible nations and deny the area to Communist control, the United States has lost much ground and has only dim hope of avoiding further setbacks. What is required is a more aggressive, purposeful program—one intended to blunt the Russian thrust wherever it is most pointed. This means a massive program of economic and military assistance to American allies, a willingness to compete with the Soviet Union, and an effort to elicit additional efforts from Western European countries.

At the other end of the spectrum, the minimalists contend that the Middle East is not vital to United States interests, that the Soviet effort in the area is a natural by-product of geographic propinquity and receptivity of local forces, and that a reasonable basis of East-West coexistence in the region does exist. The minimalists argue further that no power will ever again have the degree of influence and control over the destiny of the region that was recently enjoyed by Britain and France. The Middle East of the foreseeable future will be an arena where all the great powers will exercise some influence but where none will dominate. Finally this group contends that indigenous nationalism will ultimately prevail over communism—that it will reject Moscow's domination and become a force with which we can find a reasonable accommodation. The United States can gamble, in brief, that local nationalism will thwart the Soviet Union. Hence, the United States should not seek to involve itself in every problem or crisis in the area. Rather, it should seek to strengthen its attachments to friends and allies and permit nature to follow its inevitable course.

Thus suspended between these two attitudes, American diplomacy stands firm on indecision in the Middle East, with our diplomats adopting a hands-off posture toward the region. American scholars and diplomats have in recent years seen their best efforts reap a harvest of frustration and failure in the Middle East. Crisis has succeeded crisis in the region, United States responses have been less and less effective as the foreign policy establishment is gripped by inhibitions. Washington finds itself tortured by the glaring disproportion between effort and result in its foreign policy toward the region.

The distempers of American foreign policy in the Middle East are aggravated by developments in recent years, which have created a set of entirely new conditions in the region. American diplomatic, cultural and commercial relations with the Middle East can be traced to the early days of the republic, but it was not until the United States entry into World War II that Washington began to develop a national strategy regarding the region. A national strategy may be most simply defined as a general plan for the accomplishment of national purpose by the employment of national resources. This definition indicates the three essential ingredients of any strategy: purpose (ends), resources (means), and plans (the relating of ends and means).[1]

A national strategy thus requires first, a formulation of national purpose to serve as a constant criterion of choice; second, an over-all estimate of the operational environment in which the state must act in the future (from the generalized purpose as applied to the predictable situation is derived a set of goals and objectives); and third, collecting and committing adequate capability to the accomplishment of each objective. A key element in strategic planning is what is often called a strategic concept: a composite formulation of national purpose, situational estimate, and practical principles, which becomes the working doctrine of government in carrying out its foreign policy. It is in terms of the accepted strategic concept of a state that most objectives are selected and most courses of action carried out.

The United States has chosen to emphasize the element of protection and thus has committed itself to a strategy of defense in the Middle East: striving primarily to turning back the threats to the position of power it enjoyed in the region. It is a strategy that seeks stability. Whatever means it chose to implement its policy in the area—the Truman and Eisenhower Doctrines of 1947 and 1958 respectively; the admission of Turkey to NATO in 1952; the Bagdad-CENTO alliance in 1955; or bilateral defense agreements with selected states (in 1958 with Turkey, Iran, and Pakistan)—the United States has consistently pursued a dual objective of containing the region from hostile powers, and guaranteeing the territorial integrity of the states of the region.

The United States embarked upon its Middle Eastern strategy with overwhelming advantages vis-à-vis its rival, the Soviet Union. Although neither competitor was without political liabilities, the Soviet Union, whose threats and efforts at intimidation were of a fairly recent vintage, labored under greater disadvantages than the United States. United States success in thwarting Communist subversive efforts in Greece in 1947, its firm support to Turkey against Russian territorial demands in 1946, and its endeavors in rescuing Iran's rich northern provinces from the Red Army occupation in the same year enhanced further the position of Washington in the Middle East.

[1] The author is utilizing the concept of strategy as developed by Charles O. Lerche, Jr., *The Cold War and After* (Englewood Cliffs, N.J.: Prentice-Hall, Inc. 1965), pp. 21–25.

Granted that America's containment policy proved to be a deterrent to Russian expansionism in Turkey and Iran, this success however was no guarantee for continued Arab friendship in the face of Washington's support to Israel, beginning in 1948. So far as they were concerned, the Arabs knew little and cared still less about Russia's threat to Iran and Turkey and about the cost in human life that the Soviet Union paid in achieving a rapid industrialization of the country. The primary concern of the Arabs was not with communism or democracy, capitalism or socialism, but with Zionism. It was this transnational religious ideology that posed a serious threat to the Arabs.

That United States relations with the Arabs have slipped badly is evident in the fact that the American government has no formal diplomatic ties with nearly half of their governments. Americans are the object of severe reproach because of their seeming lack of impartiality on the Arab-Israeli question, their provision of arms to Tel Aviv, and their declining aid for all but the most favored few.

By contrast the Soviet Union has made dramatic inroads in the Middle East since 1955 and today maintains close ties with such states as the U.A.R., Syria, Algeria, Iraq, and Yemen. Moscow has successfully cultivated friendly relations with Turkey, Iran, and Pakistan, three Middle Eastern members of the Central Treaty Organization. It has become an arms purveyor for such peripheral areas as Morocco, Sudan, and South Yemen. The Soviet entry into the arms market was in itself symptomatic but the significance of this move is enhanced by Moscow's decision to maintain a permanent naval fleet in the Mediterranean. Not since the Franco-Russian alliance of the 1890s had the Russians given serious consideration to becoming a Mediterranean power, but within a period of less than fifteen years the Soviet Union has assembled a formidable force and virtually checkmated the power of the American Sixth Fleet.

From the mid-fifties through the mid-sixties the Soviet Union emphasized the element of promotion and committed itself to a strategy of attack: seeking opportunities while capitalizing on a dynamic environment. In the process the Soviet Union elevated its security role in the region from a low to an intermediate level of intensity. The U.S.S.R. acts at three distinct levels of intensity, which we may simply identify as high, intermediate, and low. Each of these can be matched with an equally revealing priority judgment and a controlling idea of interest.[2] The high-priority policies judgments have all concentrated on a single concern and a related set of problems: the physical security of the state, particularly as it is threatened from just across its border. Moscow's adventures in areas outside its own security orbit are all low priority and

[2] It was Charles O. Lerche, Jr., who alerted the author to this notion; see Ibid., p. 43.

low risk, involving a conspicuous willingness to retreat in the face of strong opposition or possible escalation. In the intermediate zone between high risk and low risk, the prosecution of security role is much less critical to the Soviet Union than is the defense of its boundaries but of greater importance and higher priority than any possible project to be won outside its recognized sphere of influence.

Both the United States and the Soviet Union were pulled into the power vacuum created by the withdrawal of the colonial powers from the Middle East; both feel compelled to define and pursue exclusive, if not conflicting, interests in the region. But especially since the declining importance of the Suez Canal, neither set of interests in the region is supported by vital and historically permanent principles of foreign policy. The United States has chosen to pursue vaguely defined interests from Vietnam to Suez in much the same style as that of the colonial powers of the nineteenth century. The Suez is America's lifeline to nowhere. Such behavior raises the question: should today's great powers legitimately claim interest identical with the great-power interests of the colonial era?

As in Southeast Asia and the Far East, Soviet Middle Eastern interests are manifested in a pattern of increasing response to the pressures of an expanding American influence in the area. Russian interests in the defense of her own real estate in the region and, to a lesser extent, the strategic values of the Persian Gulf oil reserves, are intense. Furthermore, the positive gains resulting from a spirited Soviet response to American initiatives are often of some value, however temporary. Nonetheless, the goals of Soviet policy in the Middle East are essentially limited.

In the classical balance-of-power system, strategic interests could be achieved only by the maintenance of local forces; similar results are possible in today's world, dominated as it is by the superpowers, without the permanent presence of power. This concept takes on added significance in the Middle Eastern context. The issue is not whether we must consolidate United States perimeters of defense in an increasingly undelineated arena but whether the overlapping of spheres of influence by its very nature will not create such a delineation. In the classical system, Napoleon's Egyptian campaign was intended to secure protection against other European powers, rather than expanding the perimeter of French influence. Conversely, in the present international system, United States strategic interests must be determined not by the presence of power, but by the power of influence.

In today's world, where it is possible for the superpowers to confront one another from within their own territories, it is increasingly difficult for them to justify their continued presence in such areas as the Middle East, where the presence of a great power is immediately taken to imply ambition rather than charity.

Traditionally, influence took the form of actual physical presence. At a time when defense technology was less advanced, it coincided with Soviet-American confrontations more directly than it does today; hence the Middle East was of immense strategic importance to the United States. Strategic bases were built in the region to allow for a variety of American attack routes on the Soviet Union and to protect the United States from medium-range Soviet bombers. Wherever we could, we attempted to establish strategically important bases; our presence was designed to counter rather than exert local influence.

Despite the fact that the United States and the Soviet Union are able to conduct their strategic roles from within their own territories, both powers have chosen to focus their confrontation in the Middle East. In so doing, they are vulnerable to the violent forces of the regional historical experience, including conflicting nationalisms and revolution.

By June, 1967, Washington and Moscow inherited a cargo of woe in the Middle East. Both powers lost much of their ability to control events in the Middle East and much of their eagerness to formulate all regional questions in cold war terms as well. Although the momentum imported by earlier decisions still carries both of them forward along familiar paths, their present talks about the Arab-Israeli dispute suggest that both are decreasingly optimistic about the prospects of salvaging much out of the region.

In the Middle East are found an infinity of human, social, economic and political variations. With all the conditions of conflict so dramatically evident, it should come as no surprise that the conceptual integrity of the strategies of both major powers has been seriously compromised as they have sought to prosecute the struggle in this region. The struggle has been neither ideological nor military-political. Instead, it has been an only partly successful attempt by both sides to capitalize on circumstances of local vacuum of power.

Early Soviet successes in the Middle East have come from its skill at capitalizing upon local conditions of unrest and potential revolution. Eventually the Soviet Union has also been baffled by the cross-currents of the policies of the region. Obviously counting on local Communist parties to spearhead subversion while at the same time working for improved diplomatic relations with native regimes, Moscow appeared to be developing a double-pronged offensive in such states as Egypt and Iraq. But these regimes refused to play the game the Soviet way: they suppressed their indigenous Communist parties. The Soviets discovered that one cannot buy an Arab, one can only rent him at a very high cost. Of course, the Sino-Soviet split compounded Soviet difficulties in the region.

No matter what form the Soviet-American conflict took, and no matter what level of threats and indirect action was reached by either or both sides, it seemed almost impossible to secure an unequivocal victory or defeat for either party. The dazzling complexity of Middle Eastern politics produces ambiguous results. The United States, preferring a single dichotomy of Communists to fight against and anti-Communists with whom to be allied, found itself caught several times in artificially polarized situations. Washington often acted forcefully to destroy all alternatives except those of the extreme right and extreme left. Iraq in 1958 is only one such illustration.

In assessing the changing requirements of United States security in the Middle East we must recognize that there are few positions as difficult as that of the United States in the decolonized areas, particularly in this part of the world. The fact that in 1778 the United States courted the regencies of Rabat and Tunis and the Court of Fez and that it even went to the point of asking Louis XVI for his *bon offices* in bringing the United States closer to North Africa, or the fact that Morocco was one of the first units to recognize the independence of the United States, has little significance in the contemporary international system. There are hardly any cultural or psychological ties linking the United States with the region. Differing internal organizations, economic structures, customs, language, aspirations, beliefs, philosophy, and religion constitute major obstacles.

Wilson's idealism, Roosevelt's stanch stand to see these states become independent, and American benevolence and humanitarianism do not often meet with expectations and conflicts yielding unpredicted reactions. Without entering into complex social analysis, perhaps it would be wise to recall a few fundamental notions before labelling instability in the Middle East as an extension of ingratitude or incomprehension.

The superior quality of the resource materials and technicians provided by the United States may in the long run bring about a closer relationship with the recipient states assisted. Now, however, anti-Americanism is rampant. Resentment of the United States is aggravated by Communist propaganda perfectly adapted to entertaining logically simple minds. Imperialism and colonialism are favorite topics for discussion in a region where traditionally there have always been appreciative audiences and garrulous orators.

In the Middle East the conditions of life, dictated by the scarcity of natural resources (or a lack of skill), have developed a passion for "easy money," considered a blessing one should not have the naïveté to reject. This process, in the mind of the people of the region, can be traced to the naïveté of the donor, which is formulated in the following way: He who gives money has much more, inevitably. His gift can be but a modest one in relationship to that which he really possesses; the giver's only intention has been to buy at a low price a commodity whose value he feels the recipient does not know (hence he is ignorant). This is charity—a charity that is insufficient but pretends it will yield much more. In the Middle East, a subcontinent ravaged by wars, invasions, schisms, the locusts, the south wind, and tribal hatred, the Pax Romana or the Pax Gallacia, the disinterested gesture, does not exist. A gift is but a trap, an insult, or both.

The United States as well as the Soviet Union, being "equal partners in the game," have chosen to continue the competition using traditional, if not classical, methods of political gaming. In such a system, the rules of providing military assistance, the presence of military advisers, and the like, including at times rather sophisticated weaponry, replace the traditional military base, and in so doing create a political base equal to a center of military power in the traditional system.

In the Middle Eastern context, democracy represents an attempt to organize progress, whereas communism attempts to disorganize tradition. Both ideologies operate in an environment where change is viewed as detrimental because it challenges tradition. Economic and social advancement in the region is a slow process in which democracy, in its attempt to organize change and understand tradition, has merely permeated them. Communism has been appealing only when Soviet or Chinese seduction can be invoked to gain and consolidate one's position momentarily. Western democracy is not synonymous with modernization nor is communism synonymous with exploitation. The Middle Easterner finds his identity by comparing himself to East and West: concluding that he is different, he rejects both.

Similarly, democracy has had little lasting effect in the Middle East except to the extent that it has moved a United States driven by military imperatives to bestow economic favors on countries that demonstrate accommodating attitudes. Tunisia and Morocco, for example, continue to receive American aid primarily because of their approval of the United States role in Vietnam and their moderate stand in the Arab-Israeli conflict. Algerian and Syrian radicalism and Tunisian and Moroccan moderation characterize the only clear-cut successes of revolutionary communism and Western democracy, respectively, in the entire area.

Today the American approach of containment and the guarantee of Israeli and Arab territorial integrity is clearly counterproductive; it both perpetuates interregional tensions and accelerates regional hostilities. As a foreign policy style, anticommunism is particularly inappropriate to the Middle East because (beyond clan loyalties) no ideology, including Islam and more recently developed pan-Arabism and Arab socialism, has stimulated an enthusiastic, sustained popular response. Middle Eastern Communist parties are notoriously lacking in real political power.

The American anti-Communist approach has resulted in a divided region, with reactionary, often monarchist, United States-supported client states in complex confrontation with revolutionary, populist, essentially nonaligned states, which tend to gravitate toward the Soviet Union. Similarly, the American objective of guaranteed Israeli and Arab frontiers merely reinforces Israel's overwhelmingly centripetal isolation. It has allowed the Israelis the luxury of ignoring the several compelling reasons for them to adjust to the realities of their regional environment. The stubborn American commitment to Israel has, at the same time, provided Arab leadership with a scapegoat—Zionist-American Imperialism—on which to blame all the ills of the Arabs.

As the United States charts its strategic plans for the coming decade, certain forces and indigenous elements will insure the success or, perhaps equally plausibly, distort its purpose. These are the so-called constants and variables of Middle Eastern politics.

1. Group tension and rivalries are endemic. Some are religious in nature and character, ranging from the religious animosities of Maronite Christians and Sunni Muslims to the ethnic conflicts of Arabs and Kurds. Others reflect more contemporary collisions, such as between doctrinaire socialists and conservative monarchists, labor chieftains and labor ministry bureaucrats, civilian leaders and military commanders, youth groups and government technocrats.

2. Most societies are predemocratic and largely guided by authoritarian principles. Within the Middle East, the aggregation and preservation of power is the principal goal of ruling elites. Their style and techniques vary, but the elitist view of power is based on a zero-sum perspective. Any diminution of their power is regarded as a threat to the whole of the political system. (With the passage of time, however, fewer and fewer Middle Easterners have a stake in the preservation of existing political orders.)

3. Regional political constellations and alliances are of relatively short duration. The moribund state of the Baghdad Pact, together with the failure of Egypt, Syria, and Yemen to form a cohesive unit, are but the most obvious examples of political security arrangements that have "gone wrong." Alignments among ruling monarchs and petty sheiks have proved as impermanent as those negotiated by the area's "progressives" and revolutionaries.

4. Arab unity shall have proven to be an illusion and a justification for conflict rather than a means for consolidation of the Arab peoples. Pan-Africanism will find common interests and a Black Destiny, but in the process it will reveal or uncover more African *differences* than similarities. The horizontal line separating Arab Africa from the rest of the continent will be firmly delineated. North African vertical boundaries will be subjected, on the other hand, to numerous pressures brought about because or in spite of Algeria's ambition in leading the Arabs. Leadership of the Arabs, however, necessitates often spectacular and

unpredictable political maneuvers; and there is good reason to believe that Algeria and Egypt will compete very heavily in the years to come. Arab ideological justification will continue to be invoked; however, considerations of exclusive national interests will inspire to a greater degree the foreign policies of the states involved.

5. An end to Arab-Israeli hostilities is not imminent and could only come about by means of an indigenous settlement. Ultimately, the conflict must be settled by the Palestinians and Israelis. A solution imposed by outside powers will be an inauthentic attempt at resolving a situation that few outside powers appreciate or understand. Invocations by Westerners that the Arabs and Israelis seek amelioration in a "Christian spirit" only illustrate their incomprehension of the magnitude of the dispute and an ignorance of their own history.

Those who argue in favor of a superpower agreement to stop the armament race in the Middle East must recognize that even if such an agreement could be reached, the disputants would not be starved of the arms they need. With just such an eventuality in mind the Syrians are already exploring other avenues for acquiring sophisticated arms, including, perhaps, missiles from Communist China. Neither the United States nor the Soviet Union could restrain other arms producers from selling arms to the Middle Eastern countries. Furthermore, by the early 1970s it would not be difficult for Middle Easterners to purchase from private dealers large quantities of sophisticated arms such as M-47 and M-48 tanks and F-104 jets, which will be phased out by European members of NATO.

6. The United States will continue to be confronted with a situation that can no longer be labeled as direct. In recent years, France has made a comeback in the region, and its ability to perpetuate a mediator's policy within the present context is recognized by both the U.S.S.R. and the Arab states. Though France's military capabilities are limited, her influence in the Middle East has increased. The potential of France's cultural and psychological role in the region effectively challenges American and Soviet influence.

Communist China has established diplomatic relations with the United Arab Republic, Syria, Iraq, Yemen, the Sudan, and Algeria. Chinese moves in the region have not been too effective, but China will continue to intervene in the politics of most Middle Eastern states in opposition to American and Soviet interests.

The Chinese accuse the Russians of "ideological softness" and "bourgeois" compassion with the West (in view of strict Communist orthodoxy, this accusation is not false). The result is that the Middle East will be subjected to Chinese reward and punishment. China might even equip some of the radical states of the region with thermonuclear weapons.

7. The greatest challenge facing Arab revolutionary states is the creation of a viable ideology to attract the Arab masses. The Palestine liberation movement is currently groping for a philosophy that will break the impasse that the Baath and other recent revolutionary ideologies have met. Their appeal is not just limited to the liberation of Palestine but extends also to the liberation of Jordan, Syria and Egypt. This may explain the infatuation of the Arab masses with *al-Fateh* and the Popular Front for the liberation of Palestine, an indication that mass participation is the most effective means of achieving results.

Although the unity of the Palestinian liberation groups is not yet a reality, they appear to be moving in that direction, and are beginning to look to the next stage—that of linking up with the Arab masses. Both *al-Fateh* and the Popular Front realize that their success will depend on their ability to spread the revolution to the Arab masses. It is in this stage that they will encounter their greatest challenge. Linking up with the Arab masses will require an ideology and the creation of what may be called "parallel organization."

Although ideologically uncommitted, *al-Fateh* has so far rejected the Marxist-Leninist approach of the Popular Front on the grounds that it is part of the traditional revolutionary approach and thus fails to free the Baath and other Arab socialist ideologies from their impasse. It has so far relied on a nationalist and anti-imperialist (Israel) approach. This approach has been more successful than that of the Popular Front, and its simplicity is made more attractive by the activities of *al-Fateh* inside Israeli-occupied territory. Greater emphasis must be accorded, at this stage, to structures and organization. If *al-Fateh* or the Popular Front fail to develop these structures, they will lose control over the non-Palestinian Arabs, and the whole movement may suffer from "warlordism." On the other hand, the Arab governments will be alarmed at the development of an organized mass movement that can only threaten their continued existence, and they will thus not countenance the development of these "parallel organizations."

The prospect of a peaceful settlement may hasten these developments and may bring about with it a major confrontation. There may be an attempt by the Palestinian liberation movement to take a shortcut: a direct bid to the masses without the benefit of parallel organizations. In such a situation, it may find itself stalemated, emotionally supported by the masses, who, lacking organization, will not be a match for the organized, repressive force at the disposal of their governments. Such a stalemate can only hurt the Palestinian liberation movement.

This over-all preoccupation with the Palestinian cause may serve as the vehicle for a Pan-Arab movement of liberation. The cause of Palestine, many involved Arabs feel, can be served correctly only through a Pan-Arab union. This has resulted in a state of affairs in which liberation from without is pushing fast the agenda for liberation from within—from rulers reluctant to gamble over sectional, particularistic interests. When a molding of the Popular Front and *al-Fateh* takes place, the direction for liberation from ruling elites will inevitably be intensified, and liberation from demoralization and regressive regimes becomes as much of a priority item as is liberation from Zionism. Events can develop so fast that this may not take long to occur.

Whether the Palestine liberation movement continues its upward rise in effectiveness and non-traditionalism will depend upon its leadership ability to capture the Arab youth. If the past two years are any indication of the direction of the movement, the Arabs may have a revolutionary experience coming, one that will rank among and parallel those of the United States in 1861–1864, Russia in 1917, or Italy in 1871. The question now seems not whether this will happen, but what will be the price. To many Arabs, no price ceiling is worth the alternative.

Thus, a prominent element in Middle Eastern politics is inconstancy. The result is a profusion of bewildering paradoxes, such as current financial transfusions by oil-rich rulers to regimes that until recently were considered their implacable foes; or the provision of material support to liberation movements by governments that preside over rigidly conservative policies at home. Almost by way of reciprocity, the United States has itself responded to such paradoxes with apparent contradictions of its own. None was so evident as the case of Yemen during the early 1960s, when the United States provided food to the U.A.R. and an aid program to the U.A.R.-supported republican regime in Sana—while also offering military assistance to the Saudi Arabian government together with food for the Saudi-backed royalists operating outside the Yemini capital.

Before discussing proposals for a new American security role in the Middle East, it is necessary to recall that United States policy in the region is inherently limited by at least two basic considerations. Military intervention provides, at best, only a temporary and precarious base for the extension of national power. Nonmilitary policy options, including economic aid, technical assistance, and diplomatic pressure provide no certain guarantees of American success in influencing local politics.

Recognizing these limitations upon American foreign policy, what are the changing security requirements of the United States in the Middle East? Politically the United States should attempt to encourage the inherent fluidity of the region. It should, however, also attempt to structure the shifts of political alignments by inducing Turkey and Iran to assume a more active role in regional politics. Third parties such as France, Yugoslavia, and other European states should be encouraged to participate in the exercise of this policy. The existence of such powers could offer the other states of the region alternative outlets for the external expression of sovereignty.

This political dimension of a positive American policy can be implemented only by considering the possibility that democracy can be counter to United States interests and communism counter to Soviet interests. This would allow us to support or oppose governments without regard for their domestic or external ideological commitments. If we deemphasized our identification with our client states, they would no longer be able to play with us and would become more inward-looking and viable. In short, the United States should support governments with the purpose of fracturing the transitional alignments that now exist in the region.

The United States should admit the inherently counterproductive effects of the Truman and Eisenhower Doctrines and CENTO, which have merely introduced cold war tensions and polarized the Middle East into pro- or anti-Western camps. It should realize that the cost of American "military presence" or bases in Saudi Arabia, Libya, and Morocco has outweighed strategic American gains. Instead, the United States should concentrate on its ability to influence from the Mediterranean. Naval power can replace land bases, a phenomenon the Soviets are capably demonstrating. Because the Middle Eastern brand of revolutionary communism threatens totally to disorganize regional traditions, the United States should exploit the resulting social disruptions and political chaos with the assurance that the people and governments of the areas will eventually incline toward the lesser of the two evils.

The second dimension of a positive United States policy consists of Middle Eastern-American social and economic cooperation to affect revolution in the area. The United States should concentrate on what is satisfactory to it and not on what the region can expect from it. This concerted effort must rest on the elaboration of those areas of interest that are common to the states of the area and the United States. Generally speaking, these may be limited to questions of development of regional cooperation, trade agreement, and narrowing the widening gap between human needs and resources.

This common effort should take a decidedly regional cast; it must not remain a part of cold war calculations. Rather, it must rest firmly on the identity of specifically Middle Eastern and American interests. Extraregional cooperation should proceed on an *ad hoc* basis, and divergent interest and resultant policies should be tolerated.

What would this fluid regional system with several poles of power imply for the states of the Middle East? The polarized camps of reactionary, monarchist, anti-Communist states and of revolutionary, populist, socialist states would dissolve into nonideological alignments. The security of all states in the region would be increased by diminishing the possibility of hostile and rigid coalitions being formed against them; all would find increased safety in multiple centers of power competing with one another, perhaps, along constructive channels.

Middle Eastern-American cooperation implies a mutually beneficial relationship among the states of the Middle East and between them and the United States. It does not describe objective realities as much as it indicates worthwhile possibilities. It does not assume the existence of an indivisible Middle Eastern-American community of interests; rather, it points the way to realistic achievements, which can be gained through coordination. It requires little but inspires much.

This concurrent effort should not be conceived as a means of perpetuating Washington's leadership of the free world but rather as a way to increase jointly the ability of the Middle East and America to deal effectively with identifiable common problems, including aggression from outside or inside the region. Admittedly, these concerns will be qualitatively different from those originally assumed by the United States since World War II in the Middle East; Washington must decide between realistic achievements and improbable possibilities.

SOUTH AND
SOUTHEAST ASIA

Richard Butwell

American relations with South and Southeast Asia, political and economic no less than military, have changed dramatically in the years since World War II. Vietnam, above all else, testifies to this modified relationship. The change is in part the result of a more important American presence in general in the world, but it is also partly the almost inevitable outgrowth of the process of decolonization of the countries of this region. The stability that so recently characterized this widespread area became a thing of history with the termination of the old Western colonial presence.

By 1940—indeed, probably well before that date—the Western colonial presence had outlived both its relevance and its usefulness in South and Southeast Asia. When the Japanese attack occurred, the colonial powers could not protect their possessions against this assault from the north. The Americans fought heroically to defend the Philippines, but the historical fact is that they failed to do so successfully. The British and Dutch defense of their colonies was also unsuccessful, and France actually acquiesced in the Japanese presence in old Indochina (today's troubled Vietnam, Laos, and Cambodia). It was from their base in what is today South Vietnam, in fact, that the Japanese embarked upon their starfish-shaped pattern of aggression against the Americans in the Philippines, the British in Burma and Malaya, and the Dutch in Indonesia.

Decolonization—which received a major boost from the Japanese conquest and occupation, which toppled the old colonial empires—did not begin in 1946. What did happen between 1946 and 1963—was that an outdated state of *formal* dependency came to an end. In 1946, the Philippines, ruled by Spain for more than 350 years before the Americans succeeded to colonial control of the islands in 1898, regained its independence. Indonesia had announced its independence a year earlier. Vietnam's independence was also declared in 1945, the day the Americans officially received the Japanese surrender. Laos and Cambodia gained their independence as by-products of the Vietnamese freedom struggle. India and Pakistan were the first newly independent lands to emerge from Britain's once-proud South and Southeast Asian empire in 1947, being followed by Burma and Ceylon in 1948, Malaya in 1957, and Singapore and the two former northern Borneo colonies of Sarawak and Sabah in 1963.

The new countries soon found that they were by no means wholly independent in fact, as contrasted with form, as a result of the departure of their former colonial rulers. Domestic capital was far from sufficient for the proclaimed goals of development and had to be obtained from wealthier countries—some of which were their old colonial rulers. Technical help also had to be obtained abroad, and students in the tens of thousands were dispatched overseas for specialized education. The ex-colonies, moreover, were by no means effectively integrated internally, most of them possessing pressing minority problems.

The process of decolonization in its many internal manifestations—the search for the appropriate in political institutions, insurrections by ethnic minorities as well as by ideological movements, and economic reorganization and development—continues today. The weak face shown the outside world by most of the South and Southeast Asian countries, big India and Pakistan no less than smaller and less developed Laos and Cambodia, is largely the consequence of this circumstance.

Decolonization in terms of external relations has been even slower in fully manifesting itself. Least of all were the new states of South and Southeast Asia fully free (though nominally politically and economically independent) in terms of their security. Curiously perhaps, some of these countries (India, Burma, and Ceylon, among others) seemed to pursue otherwise seemingly independent foreign policies, which the world came to call "neutralism," but which failed to provide the protection needed against various real and potential external enemies.

Decolonization internally, in the sense of the departure of the once ruling foreigner from the country (at least as the controlling agent), has by now largely if not completely taken place. But decolonization of this vast area's defense dependence upon nations beyond its shores is only just beginning. And it could be more than a generation before this process completes itself.

The Philippines provides a particular case in point. It was the first former Western colony in Asia or Africa to have its demand for independence recognized by its imperial ruler after World War II. But Philippine independence was far from complete when the Stars and Stripes were lowered for the last time on July 4, 1946. The departing Americans, fearful in part of a revival of Japanese militarism, retained possession of twenty-three bases in the islands under ninety-nine-year leases. The Philippine leadership, rather than initially seeking the complete withdrawal of the Americans from the country, sought actually to involve the United States more intimately in their nation's defense, even though the Americans had failed as colonial ruler to protect the islands from the Japanese. The 1951 Philippine-American mutual defense pact, part of Secretary of State John Foster Dulles' network of bilateral and multilateral agreements, was as much of Filipino as of American asking. In 1954, in the wake of the Geneva Accords (terminating the eight-year Franco-Viet Minh war and legitimatizing a Communist regime in Vietnam north of the Seventeenth Parallel), the eight-nation Southeast Asian Collective Defense Treaty, which became SEATO, was signed in the Filipinos' de facto capital of Manila. The Philippines was one of only three South and Southeast Asian nations to put its name to the treaty, the others being increasingly anti-Communist Thailand and Pakistan (which figured, wrongly, that this action would line up the Americans on its side against India).

In the eight-year period 1946–1954, the first eight years of resumed Filipino independence, dependence of the Philippines on the United States for security purposes actually grew rather than declined. The Philippines was more closely tied militarily to its former colonial ruler by the end of 1954 than it had been on July 4, 1946. The number of American bases in the islands was subsequently reduced and the leases cut back to twenty-five years, but the United States still uses these facilities more or less as it wishes and in imperfect consultation with the Philippine government. Since the dramatic escalation of the Vietnam war in the middle 1960s, and especially since the first signs in 1968 of the likely American withdrawal without victory from Vietnam, there has been much questioning in the Philippines of the value of the present heavy military reliance on the United States. But the fact remains that, nearly twenty-five years after independence, the Philippines plays only a very modest role in its own defense. The process of decolonization, which has manifested itself internally both politically and economically, is only beginning with respect to the defense policies of the independent Philippine nation.

The circumstances of the other countries were different only in degree. Even fiercely independent Burma retained a British training mission for a few years. India had to obtain its military equipment from other countries, as it nervously viewed first Pakistan, and then China, as threats to its security. Pakistan joined both SEATO and CENTO—and gladly accepted American military assistance. Post-colonial Indonesia did not depend on the Netherlands in any way militarily, but Sukarno excessively mortgaged his country's economic future for Soviet arms and other military equipment. Even never-colonial Thailand solicited American defense protection—more actively perhaps than did any of the former colonies.

In the years 1946–1963, independence was in fact obtained from the former colonial rulers and economic life within the new nations increasingly reorganized, but the defense of both South and Southeast Asia was never really "decolonized." SEATO, which was to establish its headquarters in the Thai capital of Bangkok, was symbolic of the continuing "colonial" defense of the area against external enemies. Thailand, the Philippines, and Pakistan were members, but so, too, were the United States, Britain, France, Australia, and New Zealand. Though the Americans and the two South Pacific states might be said to have a legitimate security interest in the area, Britain and, even more so, France were very much declining colonial powers. And all five countries were not "of" Southeast Asia (as most of the NATO nations were "of" Europe and all of them "of" the North Atlantic region).

SEATO was largely anachronistic on the day of its birth. Secretary Dulles seemed to miss the point of the defeat suffered by France in Vietnam. The Geneva Accords may not have adequately provided for who should rule Vietnam, but they left no doubt as to who would not do so: France. Yet French membership was almost pathetically solicited by Dulles, although it was to be the successor Kennedy administration that would have to discover, during the dangerous Lao crisis of 1961, how little stake France still had in the region. Britain's interest and involvement were much greater, but it was still only fourteen years after SEATO's creation, in 1968, that Britain announced its intention to withdraw altogether militarily from Southeast Asia within three years. During its first fifteen years, from 1954 to 1969, SEATO for all practical purposes was the United States (plus Australia and Thailand). The Philippines, so vocal in its regional aspirations through the years, played a much less active role than these three countries, and Pakistan and France ultimately came to espouse policies directly opposed to those of the organization or a majority of its membership.

SEATO's justification and contribution, however, appear more formidable in retrospect when the alternatives are considered. Although only Thailand, the Philippines, and Pakistan joined the alliance, other states of the area expressed interest in defense cooperation (if not this particular pattern of cooperation). Burma's Premier U Nu suggested an alternate arrangement among the powers of the region itself, and Ceylon's Prime Minister Sir John Kotelawala offered to host such a meeting. These two states—plus Pakistan, India, and Indonesia—had been periodically meeting together as the so-called "Colombo Powers" (indicating, among other things, that Indians and Pakistanis might patronize the same institutional arrangements if it were in their interest to do so). But both India and Indonesia opposed security alliances of any kind, even among themselves. India's Nehru in particular carried great weight with the Burmese and Ceylonese leadership.

In a very real sense, SEATO represented a half-way house—a step in the direction of greater decolonization of the defense of South and Southeast Asia. A former colonial power in Southeast Asia, the United States, largely organized the alliance; Britain, France, and even Australia formerly governed, or still possessed, colonial holdings in the area. But Thailand, the Philippines, and Pakistan, whatever their respective motivations and however small their number, represented a step towards indigenous responsibility for the region's defense. The step could be compared perhaps to the beginnings of internal self-government in various of the colonies at an earlier date: something less than self-rule (as SEATO was something less than self-defense) but still a significant change and part of the process of decolonization.

SEATO was always more of a symbol of the American commitment to Southeast Asia than it was any kind of real regional security community. That commitment was made after one defeat by Communists—that of colonial France by Ho Chi Minh's Viet Minh—and in advance of a subsequent intervention of literally enormous proportions by the United States in support of the anti-Communist successor regime to the French in South Vietnam. The United States had been tempted to intervene in the spring of 1954—in the form of air support of the besieged French fortress of Dienbienphu—but Army Chief of Staff General Matthew B. Ridgeway, among others, prevailed over Vice-President Richard M. Nixon and Secretary of State Dulles in counselling President Eisenhower. As a result, the Americans did not intervene in Vietnam in 1954 in compensation for demonstrated French weaknesses. The United States did intervene, however, in the post-Geneva period, and especially from 1965 onward, because of the absence of internal military and political strength on the part of South Vietnam.

The point to be made about Vietnam here is not that foreign (meaning American) military might was unwisely used to try to substitute for largely lacking indigenous political power and prowess—though this was the case—but that if intervention could in any way be justified, it was probably effected in the wrong manner and by less than an ideal combination of partners. The United States intervened unilaterally and subsequently sought to develop a coalition of concerned nations, which ultimately included significant contributions from Thailand, Australia, and especially South Korea and token contingents from the Philippines and small but concerned New Zealand. Nor did the intervention take place within the framework of SEATO, the protestations of Secretary of State Dean Rusk that the United States acted in response to its SEATO obligation notwithstanding. When the American military buildup began in the early Kennedy years, moreover, South Vietnam lacked concerned allies altogether in East and Southeast, not to mention South, Asia.

The point of the mistake made by the United States in intervening in Vietnam in the manner it did was not missed by later President Richard M. Nixon. As early as October, 1967, writing in the journal *Foreign Affairs*, Nixon said, "One of the legacies of Vietnam almost certainly will be a deep reluctance on the part of the United States to become involved once again in a similar intervention on a similar basis." Nixon also urged "other nations" to "recognize that the role of the United States as world policeman is likely to be limited in the future." The President-to-be did not seem to be saying that South and Southeast Asia were not important to the United States, but he was reflecting a realization that the nature of the problem was such that it was impossible for America to try to continue to shoulder the responsibility by itself. In the *Foreign Affairs* article, Nixon stated quite positively: "To ensure that a U.S. response will be forthcoming if needed, machinery must be created that is capable of meeting two conditions: (a) a collective effort by the nations of the region to contain the threat by themselves; and, if that effort fails, (b) a collective request to the United States for assistance." Nixon suggested the development, to deal with future "Vietnams," of a military dimension to the ten-nation Asian and Pacific Council, created in 1966. This may not be the most desirable approach to the problem—and is probably also impossible—but Nixon did demonstrate an awareness of the need for Asians (and not just those of South and Southeast Asia) to shoulder more of the responsibility for the defense of their own part of the world.

The problem that confronts the United States and other interested powers (such as Australia and the Soviet Union) is the fact that the process of decolonization as it relates to security, and possibly even to foreign policy more broadly defined, is only really just beginning. The cast of characters has undergone considerable change since SEATO's formation in 1954, but not the play itself. It is still basically the story of the defense of Southeast Asia by non-Southeast Asians.

"Colonialism" refers to the fact of an outside power doing for a country what it ought to be doing for itself. In this sense, and in this sense only, Vietnam has been a "colonial" war. But it has been a "colonial" war largely because of the weakness of South Vietnam. If the countries of South and Southeast Asia remain weak in the future, it is difficult to see how the process of decolonization of the defense of the region can advance very rapidly. The countries of the area must possess strength of their own to meet their security needs.

The fact of the continuing process of decolonization of South and

Southeast Asia is important in yet another respect. In his October, 1967 *Foreign Affairs* article, Nixon seemed to be suggesting a NATO-type solution to the security problems of South and Southeast (as well as East) Asia. But it might well be asked if a NATO-type solution is relevant to the contemporary and seemingly future security problems of this area. The answer is partly "yes," if such a region-wide security alliance could be brought into being (which is open to question)—partly "no" (because South and Southeast Asia's problems today are not what the NATO countries' problems were two decades ago). There has been overt aggression by North Vietnam against Laos (and there were at least 50,000 North Vietnamese soldiers in Laos in mid-1969). Cambodia has also been the victim of both North Vietnamese and Viet Cong aggression. But it is doubtful that there has been Chinese or other Communist aggression against any other South or Southeast Asian state—India excepted—since independence. India and Pakistan have both aggressed against the other, but a regional approach to the chronic friction between these two opposed states has nowhere been suggested. Conspicuously, neither the United States nor the Soviet Union has wanted to involve itself in a partisan way in such Indian-Pakistani differences. The Indian-Chinese conflict is another matter, however, both countries being willing to expand their military assistance programs to the New Delhi government to checkmate their common foe, the Chinese—much to the annoyance of the Pakistanis, who moved closer to China.

When the Vietnam war ends, as it will one way or another, the fierce political struggle in that country will by no means terminate. Nor will it probably have any appreciable effect on civil wars in most other parts of South and Southeast Asia, except for Laos and Cambodia, where already deteriorating security situations could worsen as a result of any Vietnam settlement that recognizes the real strength of the Communists in South Vietnam. Burma's twenty-year-old war against its Communists, however, backed more openly and strongly today by China than ever before, will continue unabated. Thailand's three Communist fronts—the troubled northeast, the Malay-inhabited peninsular south, and the northern region of roving Meo tribesmen—will probably not see less action because of an end to the fighting in Vietnam. Indonesia's Communists, seemingly literally decimated in 1966 in the wake of the earlier abortive Communist attack against the country's ranking military leaders, still managed to mount mini-revolts in 1968 and again in 1969 (and presumably will not be deterred from doing so in the future by anything that is likely to happen in Vietnam). Malaysia's continuing Communist war in the southern jungle reaches of the Borneo state of Sarawak, sparked in part by Indonesia under Sukarno, today enjoys Indonesian cooperation across the frontier between the two countries (but will probably persist anyway). Nor will an end to the Vietnam war in any probable way lessen the resort to violence of India's Communists, least of all in troubled West Bengal.

Moreover, Communist insurrections or other uses of violence may not be the primary source of the most immediate threat to the survival of various of the governments of South and Southeast Asia. Differences between majority and minority groups underlie many of the problems of Burma and, to a lesser extent, Thailand—and could cause Malaysia, among other countries, more trouble in the 1970s than previously.

In light of these varied and complex factors, what are the United States security requirements in South and Southeast Asia today? The United States cannot change its role as protector of much of the region, especially Southeast Asia, overnight without inviting new trouble for itself and its friends. Unilateral disengagement from Vietnam, as urged by many critics of the American military presence in the United States and abroad, could be disastrous. A rapid American reversal of role in Vietnam could unduly stimulate both known and unknown adversaries of the United States and various of its allies. Such states might be tempted to probe anew the limits of tolerance of American security policies—with the possible result of new problems for other peoples (not necessarily even in the same part of the world). This would not be responsible conduct on the part of the United States, and it could result in the loss of even more lives of Americans and others.

The same can be said of the American military presence in the broader area of Southeast (if not South) Asia, especially in the short run. The United States did agree to an interpretation of its SEATO obligation vis-à-vis Thailand in 1962 that in effect established a bilateral defense relationship between the two states. The Thais were visibly and understandably worried in 1969, in an environment of seemingly inspired press reports of the beginning of American troop withdrawals from Vietnam, that the United States might not honor its commitment to Thailand. The Philippines displayed similar fears, President Ferdinand E. Marcos declaring that "there is the possibility that, once Vietnam is over, the United States may not want to commit any of its soldiers to putting out grass fires in this part of the world." These two countries have been the United States' closest allies in South and Southeast Asia, and they should not be brushed aside as if past American commitments could be voided wholly because the United States failed to attain its objectives in Vietnam.

The question is not whether the United States should honor existing commitments (or, at the very least, free itself slowly, cautiously, and responsibly from them) but whether it should assume new responsibilities in the future, and under what circumstances. There are at least two important considerations to keep in mind in this respect: one is the nature of the security problem as it presents itself in South and South-east Asia, and the other is the need for multinational and significant internal contributions to meeting this problem. It should not ever again fall to the lot of the United States to fight another nation's civil war on its soil largely without considerable outside help or support. There is no area in South and Southeast Asia so vital to the United States that it should run the risk of another defeat such as it has experienced in Vietnam, whatever it may call its lack of success in that country.

There is no little evidence of the American realization that the nature of the security problem in South and Southeast Asia is largely internal and that a foreign power, such as the United States, is limited in what it can do by itself to meet this problem. There is the danger, however, of also reading too much into Vietnam's experience. It is always possible, if not probable, that we will soon forget the lessons of Vietnam that foreign military might can never substitute for internal political weakness and that multilateral external help is almost always preferable to single-power aid; but it is even more likely that we may miss one of the main meanings of Vietnam altogether (which may well be that Vietnam was the wrong place for the policy in question). Thailand, for example, is in no real way a "second Vietnam" today nor will it probably be in the future, the fears of the Honorable J. William Fulbright, Chairman of the Senate Foreign Relations Committee, to the contrary notwithstanding. Thailand was never a colony, it has no Ho Chi Minh, it is not divided (and has not been historically), and it is one of the most rapidly developing countries in all Asia economically.

The probable future security problems facing Thailand (and Cambodia and India and other states) raise the very important question of whether South and Southeast Asia are in fact "vital" to the United States (a question which, if it were ever asked in the Johnson years, was never effectively answered in public). The answer is that this part of the world is no more vital—probably not as much so—to the United States today than it was to Britain in the era when Britannia ruled the waves.

Cooperation with the Soviet Union in the defense of South and Southeast Asia, at least until such states as India and Indonesia are more able to provide effective regional military leadership, raises the question of the American attitude toward communism in South and Southeast Asia. Can the United States cooperate with the U.S.S.R. and still oppose indigenous Communist regimes (even if they come into being as a result of revolution)? And should it do so? It is open to serious question whether the United States ever considered a Communist Vietnam as such as a major security threat to itself. The fact is that the United States, because of its own fears and blindness, mistakenly perceived North Vietnam to be China's agent in the war that was renewed in the divided Vietnamese peninsula in the late 1950s. It cannot afford to make this mistake again—so high has been the cost in lives, dollars, and domestic disruption. At the height of the American escalation of the Vietnam war, Senator J. William Fulbright argued unsuccessfully that the United States should primarily concern itself with the behavior (not the ideological basis) of Communist states. Communism, he said, should not be opposed in somebody else's country just because it is communism.

The United States has long regarded China as the chief threat to both South and Southeast Asia; this at different times was not the view of India, Indonesia, the Soviet Union, or even Japan. These times have changed, however, at least as far as these four states are concerned. China has clearly intervened in both South and Southeast Asia, along the Burmese border and in support of Thailand's civil insurrections as well as along India's northern frontier. It has also supported Communist North Vietnam in its military activity against South Vietnam—although to nowhere near the same degree as the Americans have aided the Saigon regime. Its intervention, however, has almost nowhere taken the form of direct aggression, and, if the truth is to be recognized, the chief threat tomorrow, as today and yesterday, comes from within the several countries of the area.

SEATO's chief shortcoming was the fact that it did not bring together those states most concerned with Southeast Asia even at the time of its inception. France and Britain, whatever their past contributions, were, or were becoming, historical "has-beens." Southeast Asia, moreover, would not as a whole benefit appreciably from the Thai, let alone the Filipino, contributions to its collective defense. The U.S.S.R., Japan, and Australia (as well as the United States) have growing interests in the region—unlike the now departed French and British—as does India (considered outside Southeast, if not South, Asia). Indonesia's serio-comic renaming of the Indian Ocean as the Indonesian Ocean under Sukarno was at least suggestive of its realization that it is a two-ocean country like the United States, fronting both the Pacific and, from the Indonesian point of view, the long-neglected Indian Ocean. India, Indonesia, and Pakistan have a much greater present as well as potential contribution to make to the collective defense of South and Southeast Asia than Thailand and the Philippines will ever have.

The new shape of the strategic situation in South and Southeast Asia —deriving from the British pull-out, *de facto* American-Soviet agreement on the need to contain China, and India's seeming re-emergent interest in its important neighbors to the east and southeast—might well be the occasion for a new and imaginative attempt to structure the security of turbulent Southeast Asia. The Indian concept of a multi-nation guaranteed "peace zone," may be the best approach. But as Vietnam and Laos have both tragically shown, an agreement without effective enforcement machinery may turn out to be less satisfactory than no agreement at all.

The United States, the Soviet Union, India, Indonesia, Australia, and even Japan—if it can see the need to play a political role in Southeast Asia commensurate with the economic contribution it already makes to that part of the world—should take the lead in bringing into being a "Southern Asia Security Council" as the instrument for overseeing such a peace zone. The other regional states—Thailand, the Philippines, Malaysia, Singapore, Ceylon, and ideally, Pakistan and Cambodia—would also be participants. It will be argued by some that such an instrument smacks of great power dominance and runs counter to present trends, especially within Southeast Asia, of more indigenously oriented regional institutions. Such an approach should no more supersede such regional institution-building, however, than NATO prevented the emergence of the European Economic Community.

The process of decolonization as it effects the defense of both South and Southeast Asia has by no means spent itself. It is in fact only starting, and it would be very foolish to ignore this fact. The result, indeed, could be another American or Soviet or Indian or Indonesian unilateral intervention with no less disastrous consequences than Vietnam. The Americans were drawn into their Vietnam involvement in part because they did not perceive the possibility of its happening. Unless tomorrow's "Vietnams"—which will surely occur—are foreseen and planned for, there will be more such tragedies in the future (the wishful thinking of present-day American public opinion notwithstanding).

At the same time, the non-area powers such as the United States must help the countries of South and Southeast Asia to evolve an increasingly indigenous regional security system that most efficiently provides the kind of protection that is necessary in this less than perfect world. This will not come about overnight, any more than the several South and Southeast Asian lands are solving their internal political and economic problems overnight. Colonialism brought many benefits, but it also deprived peoples of their natural right to try to solve their own problems. Nations that were protected by other nations, sometimes for centuries, do not spring full-blown into adequate regional security communities. They may, of course, never be able to stand on their own militarily; neither can Denmark, Greece, and various other states. Hopefully, at some future date truly effective international peace-keeping machinery will have evolved.

But for the present there is a vacuum in once colonially controlled South and Southeast Asia. The process of decolonization still has a long way to go as far as the defense and security functions of the states of the area are concerned. Even if the United States were to attempt dramatic disengagement from its far from largely self-assumed responsibilities in the region, it might not find this all that easy to do. Nor should all of the American military personnel in the area be withdrawn when the Vietnam conflict finally ends. An American military presence continues in Europe today, long after the threat of direct Soviet military intervention has passed. The presence is symbolic of a persisting commitment. There is need—and justification—for the same kind of commitment in South and Southeast Asia.

THE FAR EAST

Takehiko Yoshihashi

Immense and increasing populations, frightful contrasts in the living standards of different nations, along with the converging interests of three powerful nations make the Far East the most varied, confusing, and uncertain area of the world. Whatever we do, it is essential that our future approach to Asia on matters of security be guided by a feasible set of concepts which are meaningful in terms of what we as a nation are and are capable of doing and which are at the same time applicable to the realities as they will evolve in the Far East.

There is a danger that in the post-Vietnam era this country may beat a hasty retreat from the Asian scene as we did in Europe after World War II. On the other hand, we cannot continue in the same role we have played for the past three decades. Irrespective of our wealth and strength, there is little that this nation can do to alter changes that are taking place on the mainland of Asia, a bitter lesson we are just now learning.

Our leaders in the past were often perplexed and uncertain as to how to deal with Asian matters because the situations existing there were alien to them. The problems we faced in Asia were quite different from those in Western Europe.

Until the late 1930s, it was this country's policy to steer clear of European affairs. Our entry into the first European war became necessary when Germany's meteoric rise to power upset the balance of power in that part of the world. But when peace was restored, we again lapsed into isolationism, which prevailed until 1939. Since World War II, we have departed from our traditional policy and have returned to Western Europe to help guard against Soviet encroachment.

In the Far East, from the outset of our involvement in the early nineteenth century, there existed a set of conditions that bade us to assume a much more positive stance, notwithstanding our preoccupation with domestic issues. Having annexed Hawaii (1893) and the Philippines

(1899), by the turn of the century we had planted ourselves squarely in the Pacific and the Far East.

This happened to coincide with the declining period of the Ching Dynasty in China. Western powers vied for concessions and extensions of their spheres of influence in China, thereby further weakening a country already ridden with internal malaise. For a brief period, there was even serious talk about cutting up the Chinese "melon."

Initially, in line with a suggestion from the British together with prodding from a domestic interest group, this country circulated a note in the latter part of 1899 enjoining other powers from seeking unfair commercial advantages in China. The wording of the so-called Open Door note, which nevertheless made allowances for spheres of influence, was decidedly commercial. However, when this note is considered together with one that Secretary Hay circulated shortly thereafter on the occasion of the Boxer Rebellion calling for the preservation of Chinese territorial and administrative entity, it is clear that our interest in China was political as well.

During the four decades following the Russo-Japanese War (1904–1905), our principal concern in the Far East was to contain, restrain, and finally frustrate Japan from expanding at the expense of her neighbors. Since 1945, we have fallen heir to the task of redressing the imbalance in the Far East occasioned by the withdrawal of Japan and the European colonial powers from areas they formerly dominated.

Therefore, whereas our relations with Europe varied from disengagement, "hands off," and intervention to our present armed presence, our relations with the Far East remained basically the same. There we tended to react to what George Kennan has called "contingent necessity." That is to say, in the Far East we were inclined to maintain our equanimity until we noted a development. If we decided that it should not be allowed to go on as is, we proceeded to state our position, displeasure, or even make certain moves. Acquisition of the Philippines and the Open Door policy, as well as our current involvement in the war in Vietnam, seem to have been prompted by such considerations. On the other hand, had we kept in closer touch with the developments and taken appropriate measures at an earlier time, it probably would not have become necessary for us to resort to stopgap measures.

Basic to our understanding of relations with the Far East is the recognition that we are dealing with an area that historically and geopolitically bears no resemblance to Western Europe. Though our entry onto the Far East scene coincided with the period when China's influence was on the decline, the effects of that country's dominance in the area for over a millenium persisted. It was hardly an area in which a state system in the European sense could have developed, and it probably never will be.

Some key considerations in matters of security for the Far East are:

1. The fact is that the United States will remain a Pacific power. The overriding question is in what capacity? As much as our national goal to maintain the position of primacy in the world will require that we retain our leadership role in this area, there are signs, both domestic and in the Far East, which call for the United States to mute this role.

2. Strategic considerations will necessitate that our principal effort to contain Communist China and the Soviet Union be made from the selected ring of islands off Asia's mainland. This is not synonymous with the concept of the island *cordon sanitaire.* Military bases in South Korea, Thailand, and elsewhere on the mainland presently under our control are to be maintained so long as they can be held without undue cost and sacrifice. It is worth noting that of the number of wars we have fought since the War of 1812, none have been as inconclusive as the Korean War and the current engagement in Vietnam. Large-scale land action on the mainland of Asia should be eschewed in view of the vast land forces of Communist China and the ever-present danger that such action might escalate into a nuclear confrontation with the Soviet Union.

3. Though the nations on the fringes of Asia's mainland and the islands on the outer perimeter have shown an inclination to meet and form organizations such as the nine-nation Asian Pacific Council (ASPAC), the prevailing mood is against a regional collective security system.[1] In view of our strong anti-Communist biases, we have a problem here in coordinating the perspective of ASPAC nations with our efforts to further our own goals in the Far East.

If these considerations are to be reflected in our new approach to Communist China, punitive measures designed to frustrate her must give way to more patient, conciliatory, and manipulative tactics so as to elicit more moderate responses from her.[2] This does not necessarily mean that we should suddenly become charitable. Quite the contrary, if the remedial approach is to take effect, we must impress upon her all the more that we will remain ever constant and firm in our aims.

Adoption of this long-term approach will have a salutary effect on our own people by impressing upon them the gravity of the growing menace of Communist China. We shall have to accustom ourselves to the idea

[1] On this point, see Selig S. Harrison's articles in the *Washington Post,* June 10 and 13, 1969. It would stand to reason that Thailand, South Vietnam, the Republic of China, and South Korea would like to see a more security-oriented organization.

[2] For relevant remarks see E. O. Reischauer, "Trans-Pacific Relations," in Kermit Gordon, ed., *Agenda for the Nations* (Washington, D.C.: The Brookings Institution, 1968), pp. 421–24; John K. Fairbank, "On America and China," *Harvard Today* (Autumn, 1968), pp. 13–17; "Rethinking U.S. China Policy," *Time,* June 6, 1969, pp. 48–49.

that this is going to be a long struggle, a true contest in perseverance whereby we will be called upon to exercise prudence and circumspection such as this nation has never practiced before.

It will be well to recall the plight of Japan in the 1930s. Although it was the military might of this country that brought her to her knees, China was the anvil on which her back was broken. Our time-honored approach to the Far East of callously reacting to "contingent necessity" will sap this nation's strength and resources to the point that we may no longer be able to maintain our position of preeminence in the world.

In the final analysis, our security consideration in the Far East will not be so much a game of charades with the communist nations, but a question of how well we can maintain in our favor the orientation of the nations that surround them. We must remember, however, that every nation, regardless of its size or strength, has an orientation peculiar to itself. Therefore, to press another nation to strike an unnatural pose literally weakens the country from within and makes it an unreliable ally.[3] Not too long ago we were guided by a belief that the more firmly we committed friendly nations to our side, the more certain we could be of our own security.

Instead every effort should be made to invigorate the nations surrounding Communist China. In this way each will be able to develop its own brand of resistance to outside, that is, Chinese, pressure. We must be reconciled to the fact that a number of them may evolve a form of government not in consonance with ours. The essential thing is that each be endowed with a fierce spirit of self-reliance in managing its own internal security. These countries would then constitute a natural buffer for this country.

Let us take a closer look at the so-called "contingent necessity" as it confronts us today. Whether it be on the basis of its size, population, or the intensity of animosity displayed toward us, Communist China poses by far the most serious challenge at present and probably for many years to come. However, let us confine our prognosis for strategic considerations to the mid-1970s.

It seems particularly important to reexamine our relations with Communist China now, when some proponents of the highly controversial anti-ballistic missile program have referred to that country as the potential enemy against whose attack the missiles should be deployed.

At the root of the differences between Communist China and the United States lies the stern reality that the two nations are poles apart in their national goals and their means of achieving them. The fact that our prime competitor is still the Soviet Union and the fact that she is

---

[3] See my statement in *United States-Japanese Political Relations,* The Center for Strategic Studies, Special Report Series No. 7 (Washington, D.C.: Georgetown University, 1968), pp. 32–33.

presently more actively at odds with Communist China than we are tend to distract us from the more profound and intractable nature of the problems Communist China poses.

For the time being, at least, the United States and the Soviet Union accept the reality of nuclear stalemate and tend to deal with circumspection with the areas that lie in each other's sphere of influence, especially in the strategically sensitive zones. This is not to minimize the significance of the intense competition for achievements in space and for advantages in certain politically fluid areas of the world, such as the Middle East.

With Communist China, however, we manage to carry on only the barest minimum of dialogue with their representatives in Warsaw when necessity compels us to do so. We do not accord her the amenities normally proferred to a sovereign nation. In fact, we have indicated our hostility toward her by way of embargo, containment, support of rival regimes, and armed conflict short of declared war. On her part Communist China has not spared words nor deeds short of open war to display her intense enmity and hatred toward the United States.

At the bottom of this conflict lies the unwillingness of the United States to allow Communist China to round off her power base in the Far East in order that she may become the leading power in that part of the world. This country maintains a ring of military bases in Japan, South Korea, Okinawa, Taiwan, and the Philippines, thereby boxing Communist China in from the seas.

Experts on Chinese military matters agree that China's land force represents so formidable a defensive power that no invader would dare challenge it. However, she has only limited capacity to carry a war into foreign soil. Her naval force, which consists of PT boats and submarines, cannot support landing operations of any size. She has yet to recover the offshore island of Quemoy. It would be sheer fantasy to suggest that Communist China could invade Taiwan or Japan, let alone the mainland of the United States.

The United States has tactical nuclear devices in Taiwan and South Korea deliverable by Phantom jet planes (F4-E) and in Okinawa in the form of Maces. However, the fact that they have not been used even under extreme provocation as in the Pueblo incident or when our EC-121 was downed by a North Korean fighter plane has tended to detract from their value as weapons of deterrence at the substrategic level. The existence of these tactical nuclear weapons may also have impeded us from developing a style of warfare more suitable for the type of war we are currently engaged in.

Despite her present limitations, China may not be contained for long. She is proceeding at full steam with her nuclear program. By the mid-1970s, she may have as many as 100 medium-range ballistic missiles. An authority on Chinese nuclear strategy thinks that about then Peking's bargaining power will begin to outweigh that of the United States.[4] Although Communist China will not be in a position to launch a direct nuclear attack on cities in America, she could hold the cities of our allies in the Far East as hostages, knowing our reluctance to rattle our ICBMs lest such a gesture provoke the Soviet Union. The forecasts are that by sometime in the 1980s Communist China will have developed ICBMs of her own.

The prospect is indeed sobering, particularly if Communist China continues in her present state of mind. Though she may not take to terrorizing her nervous neighbors from the outset, she will have to make political capital of the ICBMs she has produced at such great cost. She will direct the momentum gained in her national prestige toward the nations surrounding her and will try to pry them loose from the orbit of the United States. The question is, how will each nation of the Far East react to Communist China's changing posture? The worst thing that can happen is that they panic and either capitulate to China or clutch at us even tighter. This will result in heightening the confrontation between this country and Communist China.

Japan may react to China's increasing nuclear strength by developing her own nuclear capability, an event neither ourselves nor Communist China nor the Soviet Union could view with equanimity. An era of extreme instability will have descended upon the Far East. Hence, it is necessary to reiterate the theme that the only way in which we can achieve a degree of stability in that region is to enable the nations surrounding Communist China to be as self-reliant as possible irrespective of their political style. We shall go bankrupt if in our insistence on ideological compatibility we try to maintain by military means regimes that have neither the whole-hearted support of their people nor the will to fight pressure from the outside.

In our relations with Japan, three issues hang fire for 1970. They pertain to the United States–Japan Security Treaty, the status of Okinawa, and our trade relations with her. These developments are being closely watched by the Japanese.[5] Seldom since World War II has there been an occasion for such sweeping adjustments.

The Japanese islands, no larger than California in total land area, extend in an arc nearly 2,000 miles off the mainland of Asia. Though the country is definitely overpopulated, its economy is so healthy (perhaps too much so) that its annual gross national product has grown at

---

[4] Morton E. Halperin, *Contemporary Military Strategy* (Boston: Little, Brown, 1967), p. 125.

[5] As of June, 1969, more than 200 pieces of writing on the pros and cons of the United States–Japan Security Treaty have been circulated by the government, opposition parties, labor unions, pacifists, and other groups.

an astonishing average rate of better than 11 per cent per annum over the last ten years. Her GNP for 1969 will be approaching $150 billion. Her economy has recently surged ahead of West Germany's, thereby placing her third among the industrial powers of the world.

Although Japan is now committed emotionally and through her constitution to a no-war policy, she possesses an air force and navy that are up to date and capable of holding their own against any belonging to other Far Eastern nations. She is deeply committed to a close tie with the United States by virtue of the fact that approximately 30 per cent of her import and export trades are with this country. Generally speaking, she has been cooperative with our aims and programs; but recently, spurred by growing nationalism, she has become more self-assertive.

Across the sea from Japan on the mainland are North Korea, Communist China, the Soviet Union, and North Vietnam. Their relations with us range from an unfriendly stance to open hostility. All this—the economic strength of Japan, her strategic position, her military capability —adds up to the fact that cooperation from Japan is essential if it is our objective to hold Communist China and the Soviet Union at bay by supporting friendly nations on the outer perimeter.

Japan serves as an anchor for our vast military system in the Far East. Currently, we have the use of 148 bases in Japan to give support to our forces in Thailand, Vietnam, the Philippines, Taiwan, Okinawa, and Korea.

The Seventh Fleet, the world's most powerful, makes Yokosuka and Sasebo its supply and repair bases. The Fifth Air Force, whose assignment is to defend Japan, Okinawa, and South Korea, makes Fuchu its headquarters. Bombers of the Strategic Air Command are stationed in Yokota and Misawa. Other important military bases are located at Zama, Atsugi, Tachikawa, Iwakuni, and other places. In all there are about 40,000 American military personnel stationed in Japan.

There exists a deep chasm in basic orientation between the United States and Japan, which goes deeper than a set of specific issues. In dealing with the United States, Japan stresses the point that she is today essentially the product of United States occupation policy, which directed and firmly committed her toward a nonmilitary approach to foreign relations. As embarrassing as this may be to the United States in view of what we would have Japan do now, Japan cannot be easily persuaded to change her tack, since in the meantime she has picked up momentum and is now awakened to her own version of a national mission.

At the moment the Japanese on the whole do not recognize any clear danger to their security from any direction. If anything they fear the possibility of becoming involved in a war through America's actions in Asia. China is seen as playing a cautious military role owing to unsettled domestic conditions. Japan does not believe that military buildup is the right answer to bringing about stability to this part of the world. Instead she pictures herself contributing to the lessening of tension as a mediator between America and Communist China, for the three divided nations, and between the Philippines and Indonesia, India and Pakistan. Thus strong feelings persist in Japan today that too close a tie with the United States has impeded her from assuming what she feels is her natural role.

Learned and respected writers in Japan express acute concern over the state of impasse in her national politics that has resulted from controversy over foreign policies. The political parties in Japan have been violently opposed to each other on critical issues affecting Japan's external relations. This conflict has paralyzed the proceedings in the Diet to the point that it is incapable of arriving at a workable national consensus. In general the writers who are examining the question of the true role or state (*arikata*) of Japan seem to conclude that a more autonomous foreign policy must be formulated.

At times, Japan's feelings have run high, particularly with respect to relations with Communist China. The fact that China is a neighboring nation with whom Japan has enjoyed a long history of past associations has made Japan take the position that she should be given more leeway in dealing with China and, incidentally, with Russia as well.

Secondly, Japan is sensitive to the fact that the heightening of the hostility between the United States and China adds to her nuclear insecurity.[6] As United States-Japan negotiations over Okinawa enter the crucial phase, the limitations of the "nuclear umbrella" thesis will inevitably be shown and brought to a sharper focus.

As previously stated, there are reasons to believe that by the mid-seventies Communist China may have as many as 100 medium-range ballistic missiles (MRBM), and this will mean she may choose to blackmail the United States by threatening our Asian allies like Japan. Seemingly, the United States could deter Peking by means of our own MRBMS or ICBMS. There the credibility factor may work in favor of the Chinese because of the uncertainties of Russia's reaction to our nuclear attack on Communist China.

Certain ruling elements of Japan's Liberal Democratic Party seem to infer that the continuation of the present security pact with America assures a nuclear umbrella that covers every contingency. This is in effect true with respect to Communist China given her present level of nuclear armament; but it is hardly so now with respect to Soviet ICBMS or to Communist China in the 1980s when she will have her own

---

[6] Japan is the only country against which Communist China has made threatening remarks about possible nuclear attack. Morton E. Halperin, *China and Nuclear Proliferation* (Chicago: The University of Chicago Press, 1966), p. 37.

ICBMS. It simply does not make sense to assume that this country would place its own cities in jeopardy in order that Tokyo or Osaka may be sheltered from nuclear attacks by either the Soviet Union or Communist China.[7]

Two things are bound to happen when these facts are driven home to the Japanese people. Japan will turn to a neutral position with resultant weakening of U.S. influence in the Far East or begin building her own nuclear weapons system.[8] Should the latter happen, the strategic picture of the Far East would be altered beyond recognition.

Bearing in mind the foregoing contingencies, let us see how the current demands and counterdemands between the United States and Japan square off:

The United States	*Japan*
1. Retention of Japan as a firm U.S. ally.	1. Reversion of Okinawa to Japan under the "homeland" formula.[9]
2. Remilitarization of Japan with conventional weapons to the point of backing up U.S. security policy in the Far East.	2. Ending of the war in Vietnam by the United States (non-negotiable).
3. Exercise of restraint by Japan in her demand for reversion of Okinawa; U.S. to retain the use of military bases with the presence of nuclear warheads.	3. Muting of U.S. military and political presence in the Far East (non-negotiable).
4. Trade and investment liberalization.	4. The Japanese majority, though not strongly opposed to continuation of Security Treaty, are split three ways between "for," "modify," and "noncommittal." Main concern is that there will not be a repetition of mass demonstrations on the scale of 1960.
5. Japan's exercise of further self-imposed limitation on the export of certain items to the U.S.	5. Stalling of trade liberalization until early in 1971.

[7] James H. McBride, "The United States–Japanese Security Treaty," *Sekai Shuho* (World Weekly News), Tokyo, April 29, 1969.

[8] The Japanese aversion to nuclear weapons is still exceedingly strong. But, as the post postwar generation comes of age, "nuclear allergy" will eventually give way to a more rational attitude toward the end of the 1970s. See Kei Wakaizumi, "Japan Beyond 1970," *Foreign Affairs* (April, 1969), pp. 510–12, 517. Also see a revealing story about changing attitudes toward nuclear weapons among Japanese teenagers in Henry Brandon, "Our Umbrella Over Asia," *Atlas* (February, 1969), p. 39.

[9] According to Article VI of the United States–Japan Security Treaty of 1960.

6. Further contributions by Japan in money and skill to Asian economic development.

6. No more self-imposed restraint on export of textiles to the U.S.

7. Feeling that she has assumed a fair share in promoting Asian economic development.

In the coming negotiations, America will be called upon to make a series of difficult decisions. There is no satisfactory substitute for Okinawa as a military base. Nevertheless, it is far more important to our over-all strategic posture in the Far East that we retain the good will and cooperation of Japan in order that the United States may retain the use of very extensive military bases in Japan proper. Thus, we shall have to give ground to Japan. Moreover, if our government persists in maintaining a rigid position, the result will in all probability be violent demonstrations, which the Japanese government may be hard put to quell. The new government that would emerge in the wake of such an upheaval could hardly be sympathetic to our aims and program in the Far East.

The Soviets' growing naval power in the western Pacific presents another problem in Far Eastern security. The presence of the Russian submarine flotilla in Vladivostok has virtually neutralized the Sea of Japan. Their ships allegedly have taken to traffic through the Strait of Tsugaru between Honshu and Hokkaido, which the Japanese claim as a part of their territorial waters. The question of how to keep the sea lanes along the coast of China from being overrun by Soviet submarines will tax the ingenuity of American and Japanese naval experts.

Even more formidable will be the task of patrolling the Indian Ocean after the British withdrawal from that area in 1971. The power that dominates the Indian Ocean will control the approach to the Strait of Malacca, which in turn is the key approach to the waters of the Far East from all points west.

Elsewhere, area after area remains fluid. It would be to our interest that neither North nor South Korea launch a military action against the other lest Communist China or the Soviet Union join the fighting on the side of North Korea. The internal situation in the Philippines has been deteriorating, making for political uncertainties in the future of that country. Indonesia continues to be plagued with economic and fiscal problems. Malaysia is currently in the throes of internal racial strife. Cessation of military action in Vietnam will enable Hanoi to tighten her hold on Laos through the Pathet Lao. For years to come, Communist China will continue to fish in the troubled waters of Southeast Asia. She is at present abetting dissident tribes in the mountainous regions in northern Thailand and Burma.

Unfortunately, there is no neat and tidy policy that can be applied to a nation like Communist China. Her policies are geared to a time span extended to the point of being meaningless to Western minds. The only pragmatic approach is to strengthen the nations that lie around her perimeter. Care must be exercised that we do not provoke her to the point that she may launch a nuclear war. The success or failure of our Far Eastern policy will be determined by the skill with which we maintain relations with the nations on the perimeter.

In the final analysis, our capacity to survive as a nation will depend on the quality of our thinking. That is to say, our ability to perceive the realities of the situations confronting us and then to make the necessary adjustments in our strategies is essential. In the Far East, we shall continue to be plagued with the difficult task of reconciling where we would *like* to hold the line with where we can *afford* to hold the line. This is the lesson, if any, which this country has learned from the war in Vietnam.

U.S. SECURITY THROUGH MULTILATERALISM

Urban Whitaker

"National security" is an inflatable goal. Affluence inflates it. Because we are so affluent we, who are nationals of the United States, have developed a concept of national security that is constantly expanding to include luxuries of prosperity and prestige well beyond the average world citizen's concept of his national security. We suffer from the same "revolution of rising expectations" that is usually said to be a condition (often considered a malfunctioning) peculiar to the developing societies. The more affluent American version of this upward explosion in expectations converts luxuries into "necessities" at an alarming rate. As a result, the American definition of "security" is becoming less and less distinguishable from nationalistic dreams of grandeur. To put it bluntly: it is common for Americans to assume that their national security requires the maintenance of a relative economic advantage that finds them consuming something close to half of all the goods and services produced in the world. Translated from economic into military expectations, such an assumption requires that American or pro-American power should predominate in such distant places as Asia, Africa, and Europe. In its most inflated form the concept of American security becomes an expectation of American domination.

It seems necessary to begin this essay with these definitional observations because they have a vital bearing on the outcome of the first question that must be asked about the title, "U.S. Security Through Multilateralism." The question is: Is "U.S. security" a justified end? That question ought to be answered, and the consequences of the answer ought to be accepted, before consideration is given to the further question of finding appropriate means (such as "multilateralism") to whatever end seems worthy of our extended concern. We cannot determine the value of the proposed end, however, without defining it.

Defined in its most inflated sense security means something like *empire*. It cannot be justified as a goal for any people. It is simply preposterous for the Americans—6 per cent of the world's total population —to believe that they have the right, or the duty, or the historical mission to be the dominant influence in the world.

Defined in its narrowest sense, security is simply *survival*. Survival hardly needs justification as a basic goal for *people*. But we should not assume that the survival of *states* is a prerequisite to the survival of those who inhabit them. The literature of international relations reflects a common error of scholars who have treated the nation-state as an actor rather than as a means to an end. There is little doubt, however, that on further reflection, most students of the subject would agree that the state was created by the people as a means to an end—primarily security —and that the ascription of ends to this abstraction is only a shorthand way of saying that a group of *people* seeks security.

Security defined as survival (survival of people rather than of states) can be justified as an end. In fact it can even be argued that the end is purely altruistic and that survival is a prerequisite for service to others. But if security is defined as "survival in the high style to which we would like to become accustomed" then it becomes "empire" and must be rejected as a gross distortion of the legitimate survival goal.

However, there is difficult ground in between. If empire is too much, survival alone is not enough. Usually it is little or no problem to achieve security, defined as simple survival of people. The United States, for example, probably could have achieved survival of its people by submitting to Japanese pressure rather than opposing it in the 1930s and 1940s. In fact, it could be argued that more Americans would have survived by submission than did by resistance. (Hitler's tendencies to genocide make this argument inapplicable in the case of the war with Germany.) Although people might have survived, however, their *power* probably would have diminished. Insofar as the American economy was dependent on rubber, tin, and other Asian imports, American living standards would have declined. And if American affluence had declined, certainly American ability to perform altruistic services for the rest of mankind would have declined. Where does one draw the line?

In practice, the line is most often drawn in favor of maintaining a relative power advantage greater than our relative numbers. Security is thus defined by most Americans as something greater than simple survival but short of world empire. We comprise only about 6 per cent of the world's total population but we have grown accustomed to controlling closer to 60 per cent of the world's goods and services.

This does not mean that there must be an exact correlation between population and consumption. Inequities in the distribution of resources, differences in values, and differences in effort may lead to legitimate differences in production—and therefore in consumption—of goods and services. But this writer objects to the idea that the security of *some* people is more important than the security of *most* people; he also rejects the commonly approved objective of "national" security, which provides that an American ought to devote his energies to seeking more prosperity and prestige for Americans rather than to seeking a better life for all of humankind. The emphasis instead must be placed upon the "greatest good of the greatest number" without regard to sex, creed, color, race, religion *or nationality*. Any narrower basic security goal cannot be morally justified.

It is often asserted that the goals of United States security and world security are coincident, that what is good for the United States is good for the world and vice versa. It may be true that the concept of an enlightened self-interest is consistent with the goal of universal security. But if the two really are identical no one should object to the larger goal. There is also ample evidence that true enlightenment suffers from a certain distortion when approached from the narrower vantage point.

United States security is a legitimate goal, but it is treated in this essay as a goal that does not remain in perspective except in the proper context of the greater goal from which it is not safely separable. Hence we should discuss "U.S. Security Through World Security Through Multilateralism," rather than merely "U.S. Security Through Multilateralism."

Given a broad goal like "world security" it is difficult to think of any human endeavor that does not belong in a discussion of means to that end. The concept of multilateralism, however, suggests that our concern is limited to the single question of selecting the proper participants in the process. Specifically, the question is: who are the relevant actors in seeking a goal such as world security?

"Multilateralism" as an answer to that question suggests only that more than two actors might be involved, but it leaves open a wide range of possibilities, from regionalism to universalism. Given that the goal is universal security, it is tempting to conclude forthwith that participation in the choice of means ought also to be universal. In the most basic sense that conclusion is valid. There is no other way that is both just and practicable to seek universal goals. However, a major qualification is necessary before this conclusion becomes meaningful: it must be assumed that a universal decision-making authority would choose to delegate a considerable portion of its powers to regional, national, and even more local levels. Moreover, one of the most significant roles of a world government would be to insure that individual freedoms were preserved —that is, to insure an absence of government, at any level, on certain subjects. If this role for a universal government is accepted, the question of determining appropriate levels regains relevance. It is not a matter of choosing regionalism (or some other multilateral arrangement) *in defiance of* a universal body, but of the universal body itself having to choose the appropriate levels of organization to which functions and powers should be delegated or reserved.

It is sometimes alleged that the choice of governmental levels is a simple philosophical matter. There is a popular, but fallacious, belief that conservatives favor the least government possible and that at the lowest, or most local, level whereas liberals prefer as much government as possible and that at the highest, or most all-inclusive, level. Even the most cursory review of major contemporary issues disproves this shallow conclusion. The same white, reactionary, "states rights" Mississippian who wants to eliminate the federal government's role in race relations is among the most vigorous supporters of such restrictive and expensive federal activities as conscription, "defense" expenditures, the FBI, the CIA, and subsidies for owners of very large (but not very small) farms.

There is a philosophical basis for two schools of thought about the proper functions and the proper levels of government. The two schools, however, are distinguished less by their preference for high or low levels of government than by their devotion to the interests of the many or of the few. If the goal is "freedom" and if the problem is to determine the best level of government to guarantee freedom, then the relevant question is: *"whose* freedom to do *what?* The Mississippi liberal, white or black, will choose federal intervention because he knows it is the way to achieve the freedom of black people to participate equally in the democratic process.

Similarly, if the goal is "security," the choice of an appropriate level of government depends upon the answers to two prior questions: "whose security?" and "against what threats?" In keeping with the humanistic biases accepted earlier in this essay, it is safe to assume that the answer to the first question is, "the greatest security of the greatest number of human beings." In recognition of the fact that the sources of insecurity are sometimes rooted in the actions of other human beings, and sometimes in the nonhuman environment, the range of relevant threats should be open to cover all of the major insecurities: poverty, disease, hunger, and weather; as well as discrimination, tyranny, and war.

This completes a rather vigorous assault on the title assigned. The writer does not apologize either for having questioned it at length or for having changed it to read "World Security Through World Co-operation." (Later a case will be made, in fact, for *"world government"* as the proper means for achieving the goal of world security.) Given these value assumptions, the relevant question becomes: At what level, or levels, of government can we achieve the greatest security for the greatest number of human beings?

The most basic rule that ought to guide us in choosing proper levels of government is that we should ask which level is the most efficient for getting a particular job done. Rule number one is efficiency.

If we are to have any realistic hopes for efficient government, we must recognize that efficiency is not a function of level alone but of the relationship between the level of government and the task to be performed. The level that is most efficient differs with the subject. It may be local for one, national for another, and universal for yet another. Rule number two is variety.

Some would propose a third rule (in fact, they would call it the first rule): that if government is instituted at all it should be at the lowest possible level. While agreeing that governments exist for men rather than vice versa, the writer rejects this argument as redundant and dangerous. It is redundant because the most efficient level of government (rule number one) *is* the lowest (or the highest) level possible. It is a dangerous argument because it is often used to give the appearance of less government in cases where, in fact, the absence of formal government merely makes it possible for the real governing to be done by private groups that represent the interests of privileged minorities rather than of the general public. Again, the preliminary judgment is vital: Whose interests do we wish to serve? After that judgment is made the question of levels is primarily a question of efficiency, and the answer varies depending on the subject to be governed.

One of the best examples for illustrating the full range of relevant government levels is the subject of waste disposal. Under certain conditions it is properly argued that there should be no government, no regulation whatsoever on this subject. Under other conditions it seems obvious that a measure of world government is absolutely necessary if mankind is to achieve security from pestilence, pollution, and disease.

At the lower end of the waste disposal spectrum there is no need, in many cases, for any government at all. An individual ought to be free to burn trash in his fireplace without anyone's permission. But, as local conditions vary, the need for government varies. In areas that suffer from temperature inversion, for example, the physical security of the populace may justify prohibition, by city or county government, of any fires in fireplaces or trash burners. Smog control may necessitate the creation of higher levels of government such as air pollution districts that cross county boundaries. In fact, national regulation of automobile manufacturing standards may be appropriate as an efficient means of protecting the right to breathe fresh air.

Waste disposal as a cause of water pollution also requires regulatory activity at a variety of governmental levels. A lake or other stationary body of water may be wholly within a city, county, or state. On the other hand, it may be an international waterway. Rivers, if they are to be controlled at all, often require interstate or international regulation. Detergent waste dumped into a river in one country may be a dangerous pollutant of drinking water in another, thus necessitating some regional governmental regulation.

Finally, if we are to keep both air and water free of pollution, the safe disposal of nuclear waste requires various levels of multilateral, and ultimately universal, government. No single nation-state can justly claim the freedom to contaminate the atmosphere, outer space, or the oceans with the radioactive residue of atomic-powered engines or weapons.

Transportation and waste disposal are only two common examples of the need to establish government at many different levels in the quest for human security. Even if there were not the danger of world war there would still be the need for world government. When we put into one big picture all of the threats to human security—from war, from weather, from disease, from hunger, from poisoned air and water—we should, all the nations as one, put the creation of world governmental institutions at the top of our priority list.

The case for world government is very clear. The cause of human security cannot be served without it. Yet, the opposition to world government is so strong that the case for world government is seldom made in public. Why?

There are two sets of reasons, the one held quietly by the timid supporters of world government and the other put forward by its more vocal opponents. The supporters are inclined to seek substitute language, such as "world community" or "world federalism," and to be satisfied with less than really governmental solutions such as the specialized agencies of the UN or even the UN itself. The opponents are of at least two widely different viewpoints, one on the far left and the other on the far right. If world security really depends on world government as it is argued above, it awaits persuasive answers to the arguments of both the federalists who work for world government so cautiously and the variety of anarchists who oppose it so effectively.

One of the things that many liberals need is a good lesson in how to plan for progress. What they too seldom understand is the true relationships between desirability and possibility on the one hand, and effective planning on the other. The common mistake is to ask the wrong question. Surprising as it may seem, it is actually very difficult for liberals to dream. They easily and regularly fool themselves into believing that they have thought seriously about the most desirable shape of society, that they have really developed a target model of a dream world. In fact, they almost always target in on the "best *possible*" world. That is their fatal mistake.

The author often asked graduate students (and most of them are generally liberal in their outlook) to begin a project by developing a dream model of some aspect of world organization. It is designed so that they should, first, have an idea of perfection; that they should, second, have an accurate picture of the barriers which exist between here and there; and, that they should, last, prepare a plan for achieving their dreams. But we always have trouble with the first part of the assignment. Dreams of the desirable, unmodified by worries about the possible (more accurately, about the impossible) are hard to come by. Yet, if we do not dream, we short-circuit the planning process. We try to perform in one step an operation that requires two distinct steps. We leap immediately into the final assessment of the relationship between desirability and possibility rather than first calculating the true dimensions of each, and considering whether they might be brought closer together by expanding the limits of the possible.

The reader has been led to this point for precisely this reason. The limits of the possible often *are* expandable. There are two kinds of impossibility. One is objective. Nothing we can do, at least within some reasonable time period, will bring the objectively impossible achievements within our reach. We can't build a network of highways across the Pacific. Not yet, that is. But, even objectively "impossible" dreams like this one have a way of coming to pass. A century ago, it was "objectively impossible" to fly across that same ocean. Transportation difficulties alone made world government an impossible dream a century ago. But the transportation and communications revolutions that have already brought us jet planes and orbiting tel-stars have expanded the possibilities for the development of universal political community. What, then, is holding us up? Why haven't we proceeded to convene a world constitutional convention and create the modern political institutions, which the new economic interdependence makes so necessary?

The usual answer still is that it is an impossible dream. However, the alleged impossibilities are now all subjective. Although it is sometimes suggested that an objective "human nature" makes world government impossible, the more accurate conclusion is that it is nationalistic habits and attitudes rather than some basic changeless human trait that keeps us behind the times. Attitudes can be changed. New and healthier habits can be developed. The relevant question is not whether world government is possible, but whether we are willing to engage in the extensive efforts that will make it possible. So long as the impossibilities in any situation are subjective they are also vulnerable. They can be eroded by a heightened commitment to the achievement of the most desirable. And, when the *desirable* is also the *necessary*, the entire myth of the subjectively "impossible" disappears.

What has all of this to do with the nature of the planning process?

It has everything to do with successful planning. A planner who limits himself to the "possible" admits in advance his failure to achieve the desirable. He plans only for what is possible *now* (in fact, because of normal information lags, he plans only for what *used to be* possible) and passes by the opportunity either to cash in on natural expansions in the realm of possibility, or to be a positive force in causing such expansions.

It ought to be a rule for liberals that their plans be aimed somewhat higher than their estimates of what is "possible." The essential first step in planning ought always to be: to develop a dream, to paint a picture of what is desirable. The appropriate second step ought to be: to make an estimate of what is possible. The creative third step is to plan somewhere between what our idealistic dreams tell us is desirable and what our realistic analyses tell us is possible.

Now, bolstered by this dedication to creative planning, let us return to those who favor world government (deep down inside) but make a case for caution. The argument that theirs is the "realistic" position and the writer's is somehow starry-eyed is untenable. In fact, the stars are the first target which the realistic planner's eyes should seek. These cautious "realists" argue that we should not use the term "world government" because too many people oppose it. It is probably true that a majority of Americans are opposed to whatever it is that this term conjures up in their minds. (In the next section we will try to learn what that negative image is.) Nevertheless, it is certainly true that we aren't going to change their minds about world government by talking to them about something else. It is both dishonest and impractical to try to fool people into supporting world government by camouflaging it.

Government is both an honorable and a necessary institution. It has developed, for many centuries, as a practical answer to the needs of people. It has not been at any other level, and it should not be considered at the world level, a kind of liberal-radical conspiracy plotted by a group of idealistic eggheads. It is simply a practical response to a need. The need is now clear at the world level. The adequate response depends upon a degree of commitment that is more courageous than cautious. If the friends of world government will not lead the campaign for it, then its opponents will be able to preserve the outmoded attitudes of the present into a future that deserves better.

As if its cautious friends were not problem enough, world government has to overcome a host of extremist enemies on both right and left, before it will see the light of day. Some of the opposition is against all government as an institution, and some of it is specifically against government at the world level.

Opposition to government as an institution comes from both ends of the political spectrum. From the radicals on the left there is a small but militantly effective minority that preaches, and practices, anarchy. The movement may still be growing. It has effectively used (its most vigorous detractors would say "subverted") some highly visible communication channels of which the most important is probably the folk-rock music that thoroughly saturates young radio and record audiences. The philosophy of anarchism is preached regularly, though not exclusively, through all the media of the drug culture. "Do your own thing" is widely accepted advice among a major segment of the most able and vital youth in America today. There is a rebellion against authority. ("Beauty is a defiance of authority" became a popular slogan for some elements of the radical movement.) There is a deep striving for absolute freedom without any external restraints.

Differences of opinion about the virtues of this total freedom are severe. Communication becomes rapidly polarized when "power to the people" movements defy established procedures. A significant segment of those who are resisting authority in numerous kinds of institutions are not hard-core anarchists. Philosophically they take the position of John Locke, as reflected in the Declaration of Independence, that after a "long train of abuses" a revolution may be justified. These idealistic, progressive liberals and radicals are willing to fight for freedom in exceptional circumstances where it has been curtailed by tyrannical authority. But there is a more doctrinaire core group that rejects not only all political authority, but in the most extreme cases, all authority external to the individual. They appear even to reject reality, sometimes claiming that it does not exist except in the infinitely flexible eye of the individual viewer.

It must be considered now an open question whether this spectrum of anarchy radiating out from a hard doctrinaire core will be a major negative influence on constructive political endeavors at every level in the next few decades. For the moment it is at least quite clear that some of the allies on which progressive liberal movements used to rely for support have become so disenchanted with "the system" that they oppose attempts to create or preserve, or even to improve, any kind of government. The young college student who wrote the following sentences illustrates the attitude of some who oppose world government from the left: "There has never been a government, and will never be a government that will not oppress its makers; therefore, I feel government must be eliminated. If the United Nations is merely a group of countries or governments, then it follows the UN must one day be abolished."

Opposition from the right is seldom so clear cut. It almost never admits to being anarchistic. It is, however, clearly aimed at removing governmental regulation from certain small groups of powerful persons who will, themselves, function as private governments. It is a type of selective anarchy. The conservatives (in fact, most of them are reactionaries, preferring earlier forms of socio-political organization in which the powerful few have a freer hand) vigorously contend that their distinctive characteristic is a unique dedication to individual rights and freedoms. It is not really so. Their dedication is to a selective freedom of a few privileged individuals to gain positions of great advantage without governmental restraint. What distinguishes them most clearly from the liberals and radicals is the narrow selfishness of their basic objectives. They want security—for the few. Their only interest in U.S. or world security is its sedative effects on the masses. Conservatives and their more extremist brothers, the reactionaries, are seldom really opposed to government per se. In fact, they are vigorously supportive of "law and order" as applied to the lower economic classes. In summary, they support government of most of the people, by some of the people, and for a few of the people.

Opposition to world government from the right-hand side of the political spectrum is much more often directed against the "world" than against the "government." The four most common arguments are that world government would be more expensive, less efficient, more restrictive, and less democratic (often stated "more communistic") than government at the nation state level. All of the arguments are false. Most of them are dishonest. Some of them are the exact opposite of the truth.

1. The argument that there is a correlation between the level of government and the cost of government is both fallacious and dishonest. In the first place, the cost of world government, or of any government, will depend on how much of it we decide to create. It is not the level, but the amount and the type of government that determines the cost. In the second place, if world government can replace world war (as it can and must) it will save more money than it costs. Government, like anything else we buy, can and should be a bargain or it shouldn't be purchased. Finally, the same people who claim that world government would be expensive are most vigorous in their support for a vastly more expensive substitute, which is euphemistically called "national defense." At the close of the 1960s the substitute was costing the United States more than $80 billion annually and about 12,000 annually in lives lost. In startling contrast, the U.S. share of the annual U.N. budget in 1969 was just over $30 *million* ($.03 billion). The total of all the UN budgets for all the members for all the quarter century of the organization's existence is not as much as the cost of the Vietnam war for one month. One cannot help but wonder what kind of world we would be living in if we had been willing, since 1945, to spend even half the amount on world government services that we have spent in national military services. Objectively speaking, it is possible. Subjectively speaking, we are split: Some of us want some world government because we

want security for all humankind; and some Americans oppose world government because they want selective security for some of mankind. The cost is pretty much irrelevant.

2. The argument that there is a correlation between the level of government and efficiency is nonsense. The efficiency of government depends on many things. The relationship between efficiency and level depends exclusively on the particular subject being governed. International air travel cannot be regulated efficiently by city governments, and the locations of parking meters in Kansas City cannot be determined efficiently by a world authority seated in Geneva. There is simply no necessary correlation between the level of government and its efficiency. We can have the grossest inefficiency at the most local levels, or the most remarkable efficiency at the highest level. The best way to insure efficiency in world government is first to make sure that functions and levels are properly matched, and then to hire the best people to administer the system and provide them with adequate resources and support.

3. It is nonsensical to argue that there is any necessary correlation between the level of government and the amount of government. The argument that world government would be more restrictive—in short, that it would regulate more of our activities—misses two essential points about government: that it can delegate its powers; and that it can, and does, often delegate powers to the people as individuals. A city government could be severely restrictive—regulating everything from the kind of grass which must or must not be planted in every "private" lawn, to the hours during which a citizen may be out in the street. And a world government could be extremely permissive, even to the point of insuring that no citizen need ever ask anyone for permission to go on a public street at any time. A world government could regulate many fewer, or many more, activities than are now regulated by national and local governments. It could, and most likely would, in fact delegate most regulatory powers to regional or more local levels of government. It could, and probably would, insure certain vital individual freedoms by prohibiting lower governments from enacting restrictive regulations.

One man's freedom is another's slavery. Our purpose, at all levels of government, ought to be to maximize the freedoms of the largest number of human beings. In virtually every case, this means governmental restrictions on the activities of individuals or groups who, left free to do so, would effectively curtail the freedoms of many in order to gain special privilege for a few. Freedom is not a value which can be supported in the abstract. It is essential to ask, "Whose freedom to do what?" Only when we are armed with answers to these questions can we properly argue the case for or against particular governmental regulations.

Those who complain the loudest about the restrictive nature of world government are not really so convinced that there is something inherent in the world level that would increase the amount of government. Their real concern is that world government would be government for the many rather than for the few. There is no necessary correlation between the level of government and the amount of government. The argument that world government would be more restrictive of freedom, conceived as an abstract value, is false. However, it is clear that a world government organized to serve the interests of a world majority would—and properly so in the author's opinion—be restrictive of the "freedoms" various privileged groups now use to acquire considerably more than their just share of the goods and services humankind produces.

4. Corruption, tyranny, dictatorship, and, inevitably, communism are commonly alleged to be necessary characteristics of government at the world level. At best, the argument is fallacious; at worst, it is scandalous. Corruption is possible at any level. One wonders whether it is even theoretically possible to find more corruption at some other level than has been regularly found in some big city government. Tyranny has always been more associated with peculiar social and economic conditions than it has with the level of government. Dictatorship, benevolent or otherwise, can exist, either by the choice of the many or the design of a few, at any level of government. Communism, if indeed it is possible at any level, seems much more likely in limited local conditions than at the world level. If the history of the past six or seven decades tells us anything about communism the message is probably that even in the most favorable conditions it cannot successfully be either imposed or voluntarily implemented even at the national level, let alone the universal. The deepening failure of the Russians and the Chinese even to coexist peacefully offers considerable evidence that the "inevitability" of international communism, which some have heralded and others have dreaded, is at best a myth.

Only two reasonable explanations exist for the persistence of the allegation that a world government would be communistic. One is ignorance; the other is malice. We can no longer afford such abysmal ignorance. We should no longer tolerate such dastardly malice. In fact, the Communists, in a *de facto* alliance with the extremists of the reactionary right, have regularly fought against the progressive development of United Nations authority and have stood vigorously for nationalist prerogatives.

There is no necessary correlation between the level of government and the type of government. To oppose world government on the grounds that it would be corrupt or communistic is like opposing big apples on the grounds that they will be bruised and brown. Big government is no more apt to be rotten than big apples. Any government could be bad. No government must be.

In summary, the arguments most commonly heard against *world* government—as distinct from government at any other level—are mostly nonsense and partly malicious. Government at the world level will be efficient or inefficient, expensive or a bargain, honest or corrupt, federal or unitary, Communist or not, in response to numerous factors, virtually none of which is a function of the level at which the government is instituted.

We may write "world government" in two ways: world government with a small "w" and a small "g" is already with us and it is growing fairly rapidly in response to the needs of an increasingly interdependent global constituency; World Government with a capital "W" and a capital "G" is still around the corner, and the need for it is rejected by some and not even seriously considered by most. It is sometimes argued that *de facto* world government is sufficient and that we only borrow trouble if we try to overcome all of the psychological nationalistic barriers between us and the institutions of a more formal World Government. It is even alleged that the most elusive element of world government, control of the use of physical force, is informally achieved by a nuclear stalemate, which has seen us through periods of intense challenge and danger without permitting a single world war since 1945. There is merit to the argument. The author does not believe that the world will fall apart next year unless we establish World Government next month. Yet, it seems clear to me that the desperate needs of human beings are outrunning the capacity of the casually cooperative "governing" institutions that emerge on a purely *ad hoc* basis. We are compelled by the reality of our circumstances to conclude that we will never achieve real security for all of humankind until we have created a World Government—of, by and for all the peoples of the world.

Can it be done? The answer is within us. The real question is, "Will we do it?" We can, and we will. We need only to rid ourselves of a very bad habit: the habit of thinking that all the great accomplishments were made in history by our grandparents, or will be made in the future by our grandchildren. We must come to realize that some of the great moments are ours to live and some of the great monuments are ours to build. We must summon from inside ourselves the courage and the commitment and the creative energy to build, now, a better world for all of humankind.

U.S. SECURITY AND THE COMMUNITY OF NATIONS

Lawrence W. Wadsworth

The review contained herein of some of the aspects of the present-day search for national security may appear banal to many readers. Indeed the writer claims no startling originality for it. On the other hand, the conclusions drawn are clearly not part of the intellectual furniture of many decision makers and scholars. They would seem therefore to bear repetition.

The most notable characteristic of the great powers' search for security in contemporary terms is the almost exclusive preoccupation with security through weaponry. We frantically concentrate on weapons of greater and greater power and longer and longer range, in the face of a technological revolution that renders each weapon obsolete as it is deployed. This phenomenon is not entirely new. One is reminded of the experience of World War I, when a new armor plate was developed for use in the then new-fangled armored weapons through which no existing projectile from a field weapon would pass. Within a matter of months, the same researcher who developed the armor plate produced the armor piercing projectile that would penetrate the plate.

The present situation of almost immediate obsolescence of new weaponry, however, is of a new order of magnitude. The overwhelming destructiveness of the new weapons, and the increasingly sophisticated means of delivery of such weapons, have created a situation in which even the superpowers lie virtually defenseless to their potential enemies. Traditional concepts of national security itself are thus rendered obsolete, or to use the current term of choice, irrelevant.

If anything is clear in the current international situation it is that national security can no longer be defined as the possession of enough coercive power to render the home country even relatively safe from external attack. This kind of national security is an unattainable goal. As this has become apparent the proponents of the search for security through weaponry have shifted the definition to something like the possession of enough coercive power to deter an attack for fear of a devastating retaliatory blow by the nation attacked. This thesis has both practical and logical flaws. Its major practical flaw is that "enough power" is a constantly escalating quantity, and the desideratum of a comfortably secure position is never reached. The logical flaw lies in the fact that power for deterrence contributes nothing to security. It merely puts the antagonists in the position of two scorpions in a bottle. They will inevitably kill each other; neither can injure the other and hope to survive.

As soon as parity or near parity between the superpowers was achieved the notion of overkill was hatched. Overkill is the development of enough coercive power not only to render an enemy state politically impotent in the event of nuclear exchange, but to assure that there will be an unacceptable loss of population and resources so that the attacking nation will be utterly desolated. Thus the overkill idea merely raises the deterrence theory to a new order of magnitude without correcting the flaws.

In spite of the unsatisfactory nature of the overkill theory, the buildup is still going on and intensifying. As a demonstration of this, one has only to take note of the development of multi-warhead and partial orbital weapons. To remedy the defects of the overkill idea, we are now offered the idea of defense through weapon-destroying weapons. According to this concept nations will not only have to accumulate enough power to achieve overkill, but also enough to destroy the overkill potential of any of her power. Even as we continue to debate the effectiveness of the anti-ballistic missile, the evidence accumulates that its effectiveness can be neutralized by raising overkill to still a new dimension, and developing a saturation force of missile weapons—which presumably could in turn be countered by stronger anti-missile missiles.

This aspect of the problem has been stated most trenchantly in a recent article by William O. Douglas, associate justice of the Supreme Court:

> The manufacture of the missile defense systems will make the military-industrial complex rich, will result in the production of high piles of junk, and will be meaningless in terms of survival. Indeed our preoccupation with problems of this kind reveals the growing political bankruptcy of this nation. The salvation of the world lies in the pursuit of a rule of law not in the anti-ballistic missile. . . . History demonstrates that preparedness is no deterrent to war. The failure of one nation to keep apace of the enemy may, of course, be disastrous . . . (but) the compulsion of nations to balance power only

accelerates the acquisition of more power by each side and invariably results in war.[1]

This writer would be less ambitious than Mr. Justice Douglas, and plead not for the "pursuit of a rule of law" in a specific sense, but merely for the maintenance of the orderly base of an international community within which there is a viable structure for interstate relationships and a degree of predictability in the behavior of states.

The problems attendant on the pursuit of weaponry are further complicated by the actual and potential development of mini-arsenals of weapons by nations that cannot hope, within the limits of their national resources, to achieve even the now *passé* status of ability to deter. Such mini-arsenals cannot confer security on their possessors in any defensive sense. What they do confer is the potential to trigger wholesale nuclear destruction of all nations. Apparently the possessors of such small nuclear forces can envisage situations in which such self-immolation would be necessary for the maintenance of *le gloire*, for they guarantee national destruction if used rather than national security.

The evidence is clear that security, however defined, is not to be found in the mere possession of coercive power. In the meantime this blind pursuit of an unattainable dream is serving to poison the whole structure of relationships among states. It is in fact the embodiment of that "lack of tolerance and self discipline" that Herbert Butterfield has assured us will promote "the modern Barbarism." This form of pursuit of national security is not only bringing about the abandonment of long cherished positions and policies, but is giving rise to reckless attacks upon the very structure of the international community.

For all its flaws in practice, the concept of international community has served the human race well for half a millennium. Much that is cherished by men everywhere is fostered and nourished by the maintenance of the state acting in community with other states. Stability within the international community is a better guarantor of national security than a fruitless accumulation of excessive power, if only because it results in greater predictability in the behavior of states. Security for all states can only be enhanced by the preservation and strengthening of orderly procedures in international life.

This is not a plea for the completion and codification of the rules of international law and the provision of enforcement and adjudicatory machinery to apply the rules, which is what is usually meant by "rule of law." Such a goal is supremely desirable, but is beyond the present apparent capacity of the nation-state system to devise and support.

This writer is not referring to such things as cooperative development

[1] William O. Douglas, "The Rule of Law," *Center Occasional Papers*, Center for the Study of Democratic Institutions (Santa Barbara, California: February, 1969).

of national economies, or of the extension of collective security, or of the definition and enforcement of basic human rights, however desirable such things may be. There is a need, however, to maintain and strengthen the basic norms of international intercourse, which are being eroded by the search for security through the accumulation of power.

Neither does this essay advocate security through moral regeneration, however desirable that might be. Despite Lord Acton, there is no intrinsic evil in power itself so long as it is not made an excuse for the erosion of the infrastructure of international life. Should the great powers engage in strengthening and extending the use of orderly procedures by the community of nations through their influence with each other, that would in itself constitute an application of power.

The following illustrative cases from recent events are intended to demonstrate the applicability of the foregoing assertions. Clearly no attempt has been made to be exhaustive in the selection of these cases. One may feel that more important and far-reaching issues might have been used. The controlling consideration in using these cases has been that they clearly indicate an attack upon and a weakening of the structure of the international community and not merely violations of the rules of conventional international law.

From the inception of the republic of the United States until the institution of the Volstead Act and the Eighteenth Amendment, the United States, without exception, defended the rule that a state's jurisdiction over territorial waters extended three miles to seaward. John Bassett Moore states:

> The littoral sea extends as far from shore as . . . three marine miles or a twentieth of a degree of latitude which was formerly the range of cannon shot.[2]

He supports this assertion by reference to authorities of the United States and other states, tracing it finally to van Bynkershork's *De Dominio Maris* of 1703, and noting that this has been the invariable position of the United States. He also makes it clear that this rule was almost universally observed by all the maritime nations.[3]

In 1922, for the special purpose of the enforcement of its prohibition laws, the United States asserted a claim of jurisdiction to a distance of twelve miles. After the repeal of these statutes in 1933 the United States returned to its traditional posture. Nevertheless, by making a claim to special jurisdictional limits for a special purpose, the United States had created a breach in what had formerly been a useful and well-settled

[2] John Bassett Moore, *Digest of International Law*, I (Washington, D.C.: Government Printing Office, 1906), 699.

[3] *Ibid.*, pp. 698–706.

rule of law. In the years since that time, and especially since 1945, many countries have made a variety of claims to special jurisdictional limits for special purposes. Some of these have gained international recognition through the Geneva Conventions on the Law of the Sea of 1958 and 1960. It can no longer be said, in fact, that there is any single limit to claims of jurisdiction over the marginal sea.[4]

The most extreme of these special jurisdictional claims, by some four hundred miles, is that of the United States, which established the Aircraft Defense Identification Zone (ADIZ). In this zone, the United States asserts a claim to jurisdiction over air space to a distance of one hour's flying time from the coast. At this time one hour's flying time is interpreted as a distance of 600 miles. Within this area the United States asserts the right to require any aircraft to identify itself and to announce an approved route and flight plan, upon pain of being shot down should it refuse. Perhaps it is too obvious to need mention, but the claim is made, of course, in the name of national security. Yet it is difficult to see what the zone's contribution to national security may be. The weapons that realistically threaten that security are expected to fly at orbital heights or to proceed from under the sea, and therefore are not subject to the ADIZ regulations. Intelligence that might be gathered from aircraft flying in the zone can be as well gathered by surface vessels or surveillance satellites, which are also not affected by ADIZ regulations.

In addition to its apparent uselessness in security terms, there is a more disturbing aspect to this extensive claim. It is that there is no admission of reciprocity on the part of the United States. No other state is admitted to have a right to defend its security in the same or equivalent manner. For many years a portion of the strategic bomber force of the United States was kept air-borne at all times. The planes flew attack courses approaching the Soviet Union, presumably to a distance of twelve miles over which the U.S.S.R. claims jurisdiction. To note a more recent event, American aircraft engaged on surveillance missions flying along the coast of North Korea are now protected by the fighter aircraft of an extensive naval task force. One can imagine the response should a similar right be claimed by the U.S.S.R. or perhaps by Cuba. This assertion of a right while simultaneously denying the assertion of the same or an equivalent right by another state is, at the very least, an attack upon the principle of the comity of nations.

Comity of nations has been defined by the Supreme Court in *Hilton* v. *Guyot* (January 18, 1895) as ". . . the recognition which one nation allows to the legislative, executive or judicial acts of another nation." In the same case the court stated, "it is neither a matter of absolute

[4] L. W. Wadsworth, "Changing Concepts of the Territorial Sea," *World Affairs* (The American Peace Society, Fall, 1960).

obligation on the one hand or of mere courtesy on the other but is the mutual observance of the rights of one nation by another." [5] It seems clear that, whatever the full and detailed meaning of comity may be, one of its essential elements is reciprocity. Moreover, comity is one of the essentials of the maintenance of international life. Without a basis in comity, nations simply cannot live in the world together, because none would have any respect for the acts of another and the behavior of each would be wholly unpredictable. For any state to behave in a manner that weakens the principle of comity, in a time when there is no assurance of security in coercive power, flies in the face of common sense. At such a time, on the contrary, the preservation and strengthening of this principle becomes doubly precious since it offers a possible alternative route to increased security.

The Soviet invasion and occupation of Czechoslovakia offers another illustration of the erosion of the basic principles of international life by an uncontrolled search for an unattainable kind of international security. At the time of its original incursion into Czechoslovakia the U.S.S.R. held that its action was justified under the terms of various treaties including the Warsaw Treaty and the bilateral mutual nonaggression treaty between the Russians and the Czechs. The justification arose from the fact, ran the Russian claim, that the territorial integrity of Czechoslovakia and even of the U.S.S.R. was threatened by the West Germans. Such a claim of a preemptive strike to forestall a threat is a frequent stratagem in the behavior of expansionist imperialist states, and is not to be taken with complete seriousness.

On this occasion, however, the time-honored tactic was a complete failure. The reaction of the Czechs and even of other Warsaw Treaty nations made it clear that the U.S.S.R. could no longer successfully lump together all those of whom it disapproves and maintain that they jointly constitute a plot against the security of the Soviet Union. To put the situation in the vernacular, nobody would buy it.

Whether for these or for more substantial reasons, the Russians shifted their ground in the Czechoslovak case. They solemnly announced that in the interest of their own national security they had to maintain a right to prevent members of the Socialist bloc from making dangerous changes in the constitutional structures of their own governments, because such changes would result in changing relationships with other Socialist countries. This so-called "Brezhnev doctrine" was first formally presented by Foreign Minister Andrei Gromyko to the General Assembly of the United Nations on October 3, 1968, but it is more succinctly stated in a *Pravda* dispatch of September 26.

---

[5] *Hilton v. Guyot*, 159 U.S. 113, January 18, 1895.

tional community offers a demonstrated alternative for the im-
ent of security as opposed to the chimera of seeking security
weaponry.

be freely admitted that the present state of international law
y itself is not a sufficient basis for security. The specific rules of
not always clearly agreed upon, and they are subject to change.
tem is incomplete and provides no guidance at all in many
nt areas. It has no firm procedure for adjudication and lacks
ently powerful enforcement system. Nevertheless, it fulfills a
nd especially in the area of basic organizing principles as op-
o specific detailed rules it is an ever-present guardian of the
security of all the member states of the international commu-
rthermore, the legal system is susceptible to improvement and
on without recourse to grandiose schemes of superstate institu-
he rule of law is not a cure-all for international ills, but it is an
nt tool, which should not be thrown aside when security through
ry seems clearly to be leading to less rather than greater security.
he diplomatic game not be played without damage to the very
e upon which the game rests? It can—for a time at any rate. But
tion of that period will be catastrophically shortened unless the
cognize that unlimited attacks upon the structure of the inter-
community in the name of national security are unacceptable
defeating. In the words of Confucius, "While pursuing a thief
man will not trample his own rice crop."

Any decision of theirs must damage neither socialism in their own
country, nor the fundamental interests of the other socialist countries,
nor the world wide workers' movement. . . . This means that every
communist party is responsible not only to all the socialist countries
but to the entire communist movement.

At a later point the same dispatch states:

The weakening of any link in the world socialist system has a direct
effect on all the socialist countries which cannot be indifferent. Thus,
the antisocialist forces in Czechoslovakia were in essence using talk
about the right to self determination to cover up demands for so
called neutrality and the CSSR's withdrawal from the socialist commonwealth.

Perhaps the most revealing statement of the true interest of the U.S.S.R.
occurs still later in the same article.

The Soviet Union and other socialist states, in fulfilling their internationalist duty to the fraternal peoples of Czechoslovakia and defending their own socialist gains, had to act and did act in resolute opposition to the anti-socialist forces in Czechoslovakia.[6]

These statements can only be taken to mean that in the view of the
U.S.S.R., Socialist countries have only limited sovereign control over
their own governments.

It is no doubt disturbing for an imperial power to witness a threat of
a diminution in its sphere of influence. Probably the United States also
wishes it could figuratively send some of its nominal allies to the wood-
shed. But what is the relationship of this instinctive reaction to national
security? Any real threat to the security of the Soviet Union or of Czechoslovakia comes from a distance and from weapons unaffected in their
danger and efficacy by the U.S.S.R.'s actions in the Czech case. Indeed,
if these actions serve to exacerbate relationships with the United States
(although this danger appears to be slight), they may have actually less-
ened the security of the Soviet Union.

In a more real sense this doctrine of limited sovereignty strikes at the
security of the U.S.S.R. and of all states. The basic principle under
which the state system exists at all is that of the sovereign equality of
all of its members. In circumstances in which weaponry of the U.S.S.R.
cannot confer security it appears to approach lunacy for that state to
attack the principle of sovereignty.

[6] Sergei Kovalev, *Pravda*, Sept. 26, 1968, in *Problems of Communism* (November–
December, 1968), p. 25.

Without doubt such examples could be multiplied into an extensive list. An outstanding one is the progressive erosion in the exactitude and propriety of diplomatic usage. In many instances diplomatic correspondence seems to have descended to a barrage of name calling, which serves no purpose of communication and seems designed primarily to be published in the national press to prove that that government is not being soft with its adversaries. This topic, however, is a study in itself, and is less directly related to the erosion of the basic principles of the community of nations than other ready examples.

Let us content ourselves with one more instance in which a basic principle of the community of nations has been attacked in the name of national security. The United States has always been in the forefront among the states in defending and enlarging the concept of the freedom of the seas. As a specific element in that effort it had been consistent in denying that pacific blockade can lawfully be applied to the vessels of third states not directly involved in a conflict. Charles Cheney Hyde has stated:

> The United States has never had recourse to pacific blockage. Its chief interest in the employment thereof by other states has been . . . to deny that such action could be designed to apply to the ships and commerce of a third power.[7]

As recently as 1938 the U.S. Naval War College held that:

> The United States has consistently denied the legality of interference with the vessels of third states by a squadron applying a pacific blockade.[8]

Nevertheless we imposed just such a blockade in the Cuban missile crisis of October, 1962. The blockade was publicly called a quarantine, although it is interesting to note that Robert Kennedy repeatedly referred to it as a blockade.[9] In any case calling a blockade a quarantine makes it no less a blockade.

As in our other two illustrations, it is difficult to see how the actions of the United States in this case added measurably to its security. The late Senator Kennedy, in the work previously cited, seemed simply to assume that a reaction to the U.S.S.R.'s initiative was demanded of the United States. To this writer, at least, the assumption that the Russian

[7] Charles Cheney Hyde, cited in Green Hafwood Hackworth, *Digest of International Law* (Washington, D.C.: U.S. Government Printing Office, 1947), Vol. VI, p. 157.

[8] *Ibid.*, p. 158.

[9] Robert Kennedy, *Thirteen Days* (New York: Norton, 1969), *passim.*

actions in Cuba substantially disturbed the ba vincing. The devastation that could have be missiles in Cuba could then, and can still, missiles in Russia.

Furthermore Kennedy noted that "In ad the Russians under the guise of a fishing large naval shipyard and a base for submarin fact was not mentioned again throughout raised since that time. Was the reaction of against the missile sites because missiles are than submarine bases? How do land-based of power in the Western Hemisphere m missiles?

Whatever the answers to these and oth been made. As a result of the U.S. actions i been little gain in security, but there has the United States to advance the concept o

It will be recognized of course that the c these illustrations were not wholly, or perh national security. Considerations of "savir role. The reactions to the actions taken, or action were not taken, were carefully calcu spheres of influence was an unacknowledg decisions made. In other words, the politic the usual fashion. The significance of thes which the states were willing and able to bases of international life, in the name of s

It will also be recognized that the pri equality of states, and freedom of the seas actions. At other times in other places the as loudly as ever by the same states that a hand, it seems clear that the principles c will be easier to attack them the next tim extent that these principles, and others, ha of international life itself has been weaken

The tragic irony is that in each case, wh compensated for by tangible gain. In thi useless and wasteful. Is it possible to cor without a framework of basic principles s sible, but not pleasant, for in such a worl would have to be undertaken by first work to be applied before substantive issues c other hand the maintenance and strength

[10] *Ibid.*, p. 25.

U.S. SECURITY AND REGIONALISM

James R. Jose

Military alliances and regional security organizations are unreliable vehicles for realizing superpower security interests. The assumptions upon which this theme is based relate to both the nature of international organization itself as well as the dynamic nature of alliance and international politics. International organization is viewed as a confining context for the realization of security objectives for all states, but particularly the superpowers. International organization affords small states the opportunity to mobilize a consensus, which more often than not is contrary or detrimental to superpower interests. This results in issues' being defined in terms of superpower-small state relationships. The implication is that the superpower loses the luxury of flexibility in terms of political initiatives and is cast in a defensive rather than an offensive mold. Furthermore, the nature of alliance and international politics has undergone such change in the years since the regional security and alliance organizations were estabished that the small states are less than resolute in their commitment to the collectivity. In addition, the relationship between the alliance leaders, the United States and the Soviet Union, is now increasingly being defined in collaborative rather than conflict terms. These factors of international and alliance politics combine to produce less cohesive alliances which are rapidly becoming irrelevant to contemporary international politics.

Critics would suggest that one who promotes such an idea is avoiding the reality of the past twenty-odd years, during which the growth of international organization has been dramatic, with most states attempting to establish the legitimacy of their policies through multilateral arrangements.[1] This reality is not denied here. Rather it is suggested that *because* multilateralism has become so accepted as a way of conducting

---

[1] See Inis L. Claude, Jr., *The Changing United Nations* (New York: Random House, 1967), Chap. 4, for an excellent discussion of this concept of collective legitimization.

the international business of state, the traditional *modus operandi* of great powers and small states alike has been modified, very often to the detriment of the former.

It is shortsighted to suggest that states *should* work through international organization because in collectivity there is a semblance of "international consensus" and hence "legitimacy." The assumption of such a notion is that whatever is sanctioned by the greatest number of states and "sanitized" by collective action through an international agency is inherently good. The assumption upon which this essay is based is that the *should* is best left to the moralists and those who have the unique ability to perceive the systemic value of something still to come but not yet fully understood. In short, this essay is an attempt to reflect what the writer has perceived *to be* and, on the basis of this, what *could be*, and does not attempt to develop the notion that what has been necessarily should be.

Regionalism as one manifestation of multilateralism provides a convenient analytical framework in that one can include both contemporary military alliances and the twentieth century innovation known as regional security organizations. The distinction between the two is clear.[2] The assumptions and implications of contemporary military alliances are not different from those of the traditional alliance notion in international politics. Military alliances are arrangements usually having an organizational structure, which would seemingly suggest an element of permanence and continuity, but which are based upon short-term political factors of moment in international politics. Such arrangements are responses to some perceived threat, the point of origin of which is external to the geographical area covered by the membership.

Military alliances do not exist primarily to deal with disputes among members, and hence their principal function is not to discipline an erring member that commits or threatens to commit aggression against another member of the arrangement. Their primary function is to provide military defense. Contemporary illustrations include the Central Treaty Organization (CENTO), the North Atlantic Treaty Organization (NATO), the Southeast Asia Treaty Organization (SEATO), the Warsaw Treaty Organization (WTO), and the security arrangement between Australia, New Zealand, and the United States known as ANZUS.

Regional security organizations, on the other hand, may possess the defensive function of traditional military alliances, but they also have

[2] James R. Jose, *An Inter-American Peace Force Within the Framework of the Organization of American States: Advantages, Impediments and Implications.* Doctoral dissertation, The American University (1968), pp. 2 and 240–41; Organization of American States, Inter-American Juridical Committee, *Differences Between Intervention and Collective Action* (Washington: OEA/Ser.I/VI.2 CIJ-81, January, 1966).

the capacity to discipline a member that commits or threatens to commit aggression against another member or some other state. These organizations normally possess nonmilitary functions and are based upon long-term considerations of a political, economic, social and/or military nature. Such organizations are probably the closest states have come to realizing what is popularly referred to as collective security. The Organization of American States (OAS) and the Organization of African Unity (OAU) are contemporary examples.

During the era of alliance and security organization-building in the late 1940s and early 1950s, the United States viewed these devices primarily as convenient tools through which to mobilize selected groups of states against the "Communist threat," capped by United States leadership. When the threat was sufficiently credible, the legitimization of an extended United States presence was assured. The peculiarities of recent history suggest, however, that as the threat has diminished so has the need, desirability, and legitimate base of an extended United States presence. The assumption seems to have been that so long as the threat could be sustained, the security organizations and alliances would remain cohesive, and selected groups of allies loyal to the United States would remain intact. The paradox is that while the United States attempts to maintain some semblance of threat-credibility, it also shows signs of wanting to establish more collaborative relations with the Soviet Union.

The evidence that leads one to suggest that regional security and alliance organizations are not reliable vehicles for realizing superpower—and particularly United States—security interests emerges partially from the nature of international organization itself. The concept of regional organization, being a facet of the more inclusive notion of international organization, by its very nature suggests a basic assumption of participation in and use of the organization by all members. We proceed on the assumption, in other words, that in any organization all members possess the basic right to participate in the general activities of the organization and to use that institution to their own ends.

A second assumption is that a special role is usually reserved for the dominant member(s), implicitly or explicitly, in certain organizations and alliance systems. Third, when states find their needs and interests to be similar, they will endeavor to act collectively. Such collective activity may be inclusive (engaged in by all members) or exclusive (engaged in by groups of members or factions). Inclusive collective activity is rare in contemporary regional security organizations and alliances. Factional or exclusive collective activity is the usual norm, with specific issues defining the personality and membership of the factions.

Increasingly, exclusive collective activity in regional security organizations and alliances is defined by issues revolving around the relationship between the dominant state(s) and the smaller members of the arrangement. When the latter perceive their needs and interests differently from the former, a clash develops, which tends to paralyze the organization, often resulting in collective pressure exerted by the smaller members on the dominant state. To be more precise, international organization provides a unique forum for developing consensus among states with similar needs and interests.

Increasingly this consensus is directed against the dominant state, which finds it difficult to identify with the needs and interests of the smaller members of the arrangement. When those smaller states choose to act outside the organizational context they are less influential, for it is the organization that provides their strength through the potential factor of *collective* influence. The dominant state, influential internationally, with world commitments, interests and needs, is weak by comparison when forced to play the game of international politics within the organizational context. This is particularly true when the small state consensus emerges from issues involving the dominant state-small state relationship. In short, the dominant state finds it difficult to reconcile its international interests and needs with the more exclusively national and regional interests and needs of the small-state majority.

Illustrative was the Soviet attempt to force a "supranational" regional military force on its Eastern European allies in the spring of 1969—an attempt rebuffed by the small-state majority under the leadership of Rumania. Shortly after the Dominican crisis in 1965, the United States similarly proposed unofficially a permanent inter-American peace-keeping force. It was rebuffed by a small-state majority because it failed to convince the Latin American states that such a force would produce national and regional advantages for them rather than advantages for the United States.

The theme that emerges from these isolated examples is that consensus mobilized against a dominant state forces that state into a particular mold of political activity that can be characterized as predominantly defensive; defensive of its policies, interests, and needs, and particularly, its dominant role in the organization or alliance. In addition, these illustrations reveal that dominant states are confined when this consensus is permitted to flourish in an organizational context. Dominant states are forced to play the game of international politics according to rules legitimized by the collectivity if they want to play the game at all within the organization. The alternatives are of course quite clear: (a) disregard the collective small-state pressures and be branded a dominating outlaw, bent on wrecking the very fabric of the organization, or (b) operate outside the organization.

It is too tempting to suggest that, on the basis of the above, international organizations give disproportionate influence to small states. It is possible to conclude, however, that the basic ground rule that is emerging is that superpowers, if they want to utilize regional security organizations and alliances to secure their interests and serve their needs, must take into account the interests and needs of the smaller members, which can be and most often are different. Often this rule is not fully appreciated or adhered to by either the United States or the Soviet Union.

The changing dynamics of international and alliance politics have been such as to question the continued utility of regional security and alliance organizations in serving the needs and interests of the superpowers. Particularly vulnerable are alliance organizations with a military focus (NATO, WTO, SEATO), rather than regional security organizations, which, in addition to military functions, have near-proportionate economic, social, and political functions (OAS).

Military alliance organizations can be viewed as little more than political contradictions today in that they deny the dynamic and fluid nature of international politics and the relativity of force, power, and influence. Such organizations that persist beyond their years of usefulness are irrational, because they pretend to institutionalize fluid variables such as the nature and perception of threats and a dynamic political process. It is difficult for such organizations to (a) desist once their purposes or original political assumptions have become obsolete, or (b) respond to changes in the political environment through structural-functional modification and a rerationalization of the purpose and validity of the organization.

The volume of evidence questioning the relevance of alliance organizations like NATO and WTO to contemporary political reality is ample. An examination of this evidence reveals such seminal factors as changes in the nature and perception of threats and preoccupation with domestic rather than alliance concerns. These factors are manifested in a reluctance to continue to accept the leadership of dominant members of the alliances—a reluctance to be confined to the structure of a system that is years out of date—and a desire to develop political and economic relations with members of competing alliances.[3]

One of the most obvious pieces of damaging evidence against the continued utility of NATO and WTO is the changed perception of threat on the part of the smaller members of these alliances. NATO allies, once obsessed with the threat of Soviet hordes sweeping across Western

[3] See Herbert S. Dinerstein, "The Transformation of Alliance Systems," *The American Political Science Review*, Vol. LIX (September, 1965), for a useful analysis of interalliance relations.

Europe, now view such a threat as a remote possibility rather than an eventual probability. When these nations relate to NATO today it is primarily—if not solely—in the context of regarding the alliance as an institution through which United States nuclear power can be used as a protective device for European security. Viewed in this context, these states feel free to operate behind the NATO protective shield unencumbered by alliance restraints. As the likelihood of nuclear war becomes less imminent, even this factor loses much of its credibility.

The evidence is all too familiar. Few, if any, of the smaller members of NATO have maintained troop and other commitment levels. The reduction of French participation in NATO would suggest a change in threat perception. (It is difficult to believe that the French action was solely motivated by the grand dreams of world leadership of an old man or a rebuff to United States influence in Western Europe, the usual explanation of this action.) The announcement in April, 1969, that Canada intended to reduce its commitment to NATO also confirms the fact that the original threat upon which the alliance was based is now conceived as only a remote possibility by that state.

Several important members of NATO are presently faced with domestic situations pressing enough to occupy the primary attention of their governments. The United Kingdom, faced with perhaps the severest economic crisis since World War II, has been forced to recognize that it can no longer afford the luxury of maintaining troops around the globe. The situation is so crucial that the country has had to accept a confining austerity program. West Germany, blessed with enviable economic growth, is straining to keep its economy in check. Simultaneously, the government is attempting to deal with domestic political controversies that have threatened political stability in recent years, particularly the neofascist movement. The resignation of Charles de Gaulle has complicated an already deteriorating French domestic scene, precipitated by the student and workers' revolt of May, 1968, and followed by steadily worsening economic conditions.

The short-lived reform government of Alexander Dubček in Czechoslovakia expressed a desire early in 1968 to seek financial underpinning and trade relations with Western nations (the "enemy" according to the strictures of the WTO). The question can be logically raised whether or not that government perceived the NATO threat to be what it was thought to be a decade ago. This desire for closer economic ties with members of a competing alliance is shared by Hungary and Rumania. Western economic "bridge-builders" include France, West Germany and Italy—countries interested in extending the hand of economic collaboration eastward.

These concerns and developments have resulted in a less-than-resolute commitment on the part of the smaller members of the Western and Eastern military alliances. The implication is that the fabric of unity is no longer as closely knit as it once was. Both NATO and WTO have been weakened to the point that neither the United States nor the Soviet Union can control their respective followings as they once could. Each has had to increasingly moderate the exercise of arbitrary influence. It is too easy to suggest that the Soviet influence over Czechoslovakia in August of 1968 belies this point. It is unsound to point to this example alone without at the same time suggesting that the exercise of such influence has its limits. One need only consider the inability of the Soviets to consolidate their hold by forcing a "supranational" Eastern European armed force on their brethren, alluded to earlier.

An important, though as yet undefined, factor in the changing dynamics of alliance politics has been the flirtatious affair between Moscow and Washington in recent years. This affair has had all the earmarks of improved collaborative relations and a tentative desire to formulate and execute joint policies in circumstances where superpower interests and needs coincide. The resolve of the smaller members of the Western and Eastern alliances has been weakened as a result of superpower collaborative policies. One need only consider the nuclear test ban treaty, outer space treaty, non-proliferation treaty, and closer commercial relations. Such collaborative activities may have weakened the confidence of the smaller members in the alliance leaders. Collaboration by leaders of competing groups indicates that the severity of the issues that separate the groups has been reduced considerably.

This improved collaborative relationship between Moscow and Washington may be explained in yet another way. The superpowers may have come to realize that because of thermonuclear weaponry they are only relevant to one another when considering the application of such power. Thermonuclear capability is not translatable into power vis-à-vis weaker states, which, recognizing this, have become restive, impatient, and reluctant to adhere to the alliance line regarding nuclear threats. The result is that the alliance leaders are faced with a situation wherein they share more interests between themselves than they do with their allies— hence increased collaboration.

Whatever the interpretation, the result has been a widening breach between the dominant and smaller states in each camp. There are those who would suggest that a Moscow-Washington rapprochement would tend to reconstitute the respective alliances because of potential small-state resentment at being neglected. It would seem more plausible to suggest that each alliance becomes weaker if its source of strength, that is, superpower inputs and competition, is compromised by increasingly harmonious relations among the superpowers. The ensuing breach between the small and the dominant states is the harbinger of weakness, eventual decay, and, perhaps, extinction. In short, it must be recognized that the cohesiveness and utility of both NATO and WTO are inversely proportional to the harmony of United States-Soviet relations. As relations between these two states become less competitive and more collaborative, each alliance system becomes regressive and weak and increasingly irrelevant to political reality.

Relevant to the central theme that regionalism is a highly unreliable context for realizing United States or superpower security interests, or both, is the Southeast Asia Treaty Organization (SEATO). Unlike NATO and WTO, this arrangement does not reflect the cleavage between the resident superpower and the smaller members of the alliance as the cause of the unreliability. Rather, the unreliability emerges from the fact that the smaller members do not evidence strong collaborative relationships among themselves; hence, the path to small-member consensus against the resident superpower is rocky at best. Even the regional threat of the Vietnam war has not served as a catalyst for closer collaborative relations among the smaller states. The reasons are many, but perhaps the central explanation is that the internal structure of each small member is too fragile to be able to serve as the foundation for a larger organization. These states cannot afford and do not have the capacity to support an organization such as SEATO.

The entire history of the Organization of American States (OAS) has been one of conflict and very little cooperation between the United States and the smaller members. At first, one might think of the 1962 Cuban missile crisis and the 1965 Dominican crisis and the joint actions taken in each as refutations of conflict, but upon closer examination, we see that such a conclusion is unwarranted. Superficially, the actions of the OAS in these cases suggested a "common cause" between the United States and the Latin American members.

Even though the OAS Organ of Consultation approved a resolution urging members to act to prevent Cuba from receiving additional missiles,[4] only twelve Latin American states responded with offers to participate in the quarantine and ultimately only two (Argentina and the Dominican Republic) aided the United States by providing naval vessels for a unified patrol force.[5] The *ad hoc* Inter-American Force, fielded

[4] Organization of American States, *Minutes of the Council Acting as Organ of Consultation* (Washington: OEA/SER.G/II/C-a-464, October 24, 1962).

[5] Note from the delegations of the United States of America, Argentina, and the Dominican Republic dated March 9, 1962 regarding the establishment of a combined quarantine force, in Pan American Union, *Inter-American Treaty of Reciprocal Assistance: Applications* (Washington: D.C.: Pan American Union, 1964), 11, p. 154.

by the oas during the Dominican crisis, was approved by a narrow margin and consisted of forces from only six Latin American countries in addition to the United States.[6] It would seem reasonable that had "common cause" genuinely existed in these cases, more Latin American states would have made at least token contributions.

Since the Dominican crisis the personality of the oas has reflected a continued desire on the part of the Latin American members to constrain the United States and prod it into relating its interests more closely with theirs. Successful pressures on the United States during the charter revision conference in Panama gained the Latin members more beneficial economic provisions.[7]

If it can be concluded that "regionalism" as it now exists in the context of regional security arrangements (military alliances and regional security organizations) is not suitable, what are the available options for the United States? The first and most readily apparent option is for the United States to reject regional security arrangements as devices for obtaining interests and make a determined effort to establish a United States-Soviet system of collaborative security. Such an alternative would seem reasonable to some in that these two states appear to have more mutual interests as great powers than they do with their smaller allies. The collaborative context would appear therefore to be less confining than the organizational context in that the superpowers would not be subjected to the collective pressures of smaller allies. However, such an arrangement would tend to assume that security continues to be defined today in physical and military terms. The validity of such an assumption is open to question.

A second alternative is that it may be desirable to modify the definition of "security interests" in such a way that they are no longer defined so exclusively in terms of military competence. The assumption here is that the real threats to the security of the United States are much more intangible and internally disruptive than the number of missiles paraded through Red Square.

Not unlike its smaller allies, the United States is facing a severe domestic crisis. Riots in the cities, demonstrations on the campuses, and increasing impersonalization of the body politic have done more to threaten security than the Soviet invasion of Czechoslovakia. A unified and only slightly dissatisfied society is the first prerequisite of security.

Internationally the most disruptive threat to stability lies in the de-

[6] "Establishment of the Inter-American Peace Force," *The OAS Chronicle*, I, No. 1 (August, 1965), 4.

[7] See Organization of American States, *Charter of the Organization of American States as Amended by the Protocol of Buenos Aires in 1967* (Washington, D.C.: OEA/SER. A/2, 1968).

veloping areas of the world. The emerging nations are engaged in the challenging process of human development and nation-building; it is to this task that the United States can productively commit its energies. It is to be hoped that the objective of identifying more closely with the regional and national needs and interests of these states would be achieved. International organizations, including regional agencies, are effective devices for accomplishing this objective. Particularly attractive are general regional organizations such as the Organization of African Unity (OAU) and the OAS. The former, of which the United States is not a member, could act as a multilateral funnel through which developmental resources could be channeled and human, national, and regional development encouraged. Although the latter could play a similar role for Latin America, the United States effort would be hindered initially owing to the abrasive quality of United States-Latin American relations that has developed over the years. However, such organizations can be effective only if they are permitted to serve the needs and interests of the members unhampered by any dominant state-small state conflict. Until such permissibility is evident, however, regional arrangements will continue to be inadequate and unreliable for securing United States interests.

It is tempting to suggest that a final alternative is available, namely, a combination of the preceding two, whereby the superpowers would establish a system of collaborative security and simultaneously and jointly relate their interests more closely with the tasks of human development and nation-building. However, it would seem that these two states would have to develop a more extensive collaborative base than is apparent at present before such could be considered a feasible alternative.

Military alliances and regional security organizations have not necessarily been failures. They may indeed have been highly successful in doing the job they were designed to do. It is argued, however, that the job has changed. If the Cold War has not yet reached a stage of advanced senility, at least it is no longer the controlling or compelling force of international relations that it once was. The compelling force today is human and national development—a challenge to which the current military alliances and regional security organizations are incapable of responding—a challenge to which the United States must respond if it is to provide responsibly for its security.

MILITARY TECHNOLOGY
IN THE 1970s

Walter C. Clemens, Jr.

Hiroshima has left its impact, not only on the lives of its inhabitants in 1945, but also on the minds of millions not directly affected, yet concerned lest atomic warfare occur again. As a result, great strides have been taken to control and regulate nuclear technology—by unilateral, bilateral, and multilateral action; by formal and tacit accords. True, nations have gone to the brink, but atomic weapons have not been used in combat; various safeguards have been installed; agreements have been signed to limit nuclear testing and to prohibit the deployment of weapons of mass destruction in outer space; understandings have pledged a reduction in the production of fissionable materials; hot-line networks have been established between major capitals to minimize inadvertent escalation. Nonetheless, such achievements do not inspire confidence in our collective future. Unless military technology comes under more effective control in the 1970s, civilization as we know it may not survive. Domestic as well as international issues are at stake—issues so vital that they return us to the basic purposes of government as discussed by such philosophers as Hobbes, Rousseau, Locke, and, for that matter, Marx and Engels. A common theme in their works is that governments are instituted to facilitate, not hinder, the realization of a modicum of physical security and economic well-being. These minimum objectives, however, in this country and globally, are threatened by the dynamism of the arms race and the dangers it portends.

Military technology has its own dynamic, but that is only part of the problem, for it interacts with international and domestic forces, which, when taken together, constitute a formidable challenge to human ingenuity, good will, and foresight. A futurologist might say that the forces making up this challenge develop synergistically, each gaining strength from the other.[1] An ancient Greek, on the other hand, might

---

[1] This paper derives in part from the author's study of the problems of arms control, strategy, and outer space, sponsored by the M.I.T. Center for Space Research,

view them as a hydra-headed monster; as soon as one head or one aspect of the challenge has been suppressed, another head strikes out with equal or greater power, so that the defender enjoys no respite. Let us consider briefly the three components of this hydra-headed or, in modern terms, synergistic challenge.

The first component is military technology itself. If a weapons system can be developed, there is an almost inexorable tendency for it to be developed. Further, if a group of military planners can conceive of a weapon that they might need or want, chances are—given the high state of the relevant arts—that a weapon of that kind can be developed and produced. Such weapons may be expensive, but the research and development (R and D) costs will probably appear low when considered as a marginal increment in the total human and capital resources already devoted to defense. This is certainly the case in the United States and probably in the U.S.S.R. Even in China, where very valuable, scarce resources have been channeled into the production of a small but growing atomic arsenal, the total cost has represented only a fraction of the gross national product.

Mention of these other countries brings us to the second major factor making it difficult to control military technology. This is the dynamics of interaction among nation-states. The nature of this interaction is not entirely understood, but several interesting models have been proposed, which at least approximate the real world. One has been termed a model of multiple symmetry; nations behave as though they had to respond to each challenge from their adversary by developing forces at least comparable to those he has mounted. Frequently, they overrespond, *inter alia*, because they perceive the adversary's moves unclearly and because they prefer to err on the side of strength in their own arms buildup. In addition to these human behavior patterns, the interaction of military deployment by partners in an arms race is often spurred by "out-of-phaseness." When country A feels it has reached an adequate level of preparedness, side B feels insecure and opposes any stabilization until it has reached some higher ceiling. By the time this ceiling has been approached, of course, A may well decide that its margin of security has been threatened in a way that warrants strong compensatory action.

The third major factor in the synergistic challenge before us derives from domestic political and economic forces within the United States and, by extension, in the Soviet Union and in other prime actors in the arms race. The term "military-industrial complex" used in President Eisenhower's farewell address, serves at least as a kind of shorthand definition of this factor. Earlier C. Wright Mills took note of the inter-

and the Boston University Graduate School, and from research on a modernist conception of arms control sponsored by the Stanley Foundation. Also see Walter C. Clemens, Jr., *The Arms Race and Sino-Soviet Relations* (Hoover Institution, 1968).

locking personnel connections between the ranks of military, corporate, and political power in this country. One need not subscribe to any devil theory of history to appreciate that—at a time when approximately 10 per cent of the national product goes to defense—persons who determine the direction and allocation of these resources will find themselves sought after and that favors traded among them will facilitate an upward climb for their own careers and bank accounts. Not only will it be in their interest to ensure the development and production of new weaponry; at some point it will also be in their interest that these weapons be used in actual combat. As retired Marine Commander David Shoup has written, the energies and egos of officers can be gratified and their own careers promoted most expeditiously only in time of war. The kernel of Shoup's thesis was articulated by the sociological theory of imperialism, developed by the economist Joseph Schumpeter, emphasizing the dynamism of the "warrior class."

It appears, then, that the theoretical insights of both C. Wright Mills and Joseph Schumpeter are needed to explain the domestic phenomena that Generals Eisenhower and Shoup observed in their own political and military experience.

In the U.S.S.R., no less than in the United States, the careers of industrialists, technological and scientific experts, and military leaders are intrinsically dependent upon government investment in military research, development, and procurement. The interests of these persons, in both countries, coincide also with the beliefs of political leaders fearful of detente and international agreements on arms control.

What are the consequences of the operation of these three factors in the United States, the Soviet Union, and in other great powers? The catalog of these consequences could fill many a shelf, but some of the most important can be summarized as follows:

1. Heavy concentration of human and capital resources in endeavors that have limited spillover benefits for urgent domestic needs;
2. Relative neglect of the cultural, social, and economic values that modern governments are expected to promote;
3. Engagement in an arms race that cannot assure even a relative increase in national security;
4. An increase in the destructiveness of war if it should occur;
5. Possibly a greater chance that war will occur, due to (a) anxieties about shifting balances of power, (b) the existence of large and growing arsenals, (c) accident, or (d) miscalculation;
6. A concentration of power in the hands of persons with special interests in the development and even in the use of modern weapons.

To control the dynamism of the arms race is an urgent task, but how can it be accomplished? A look at several recent cases may shed some light both on the severity of the problems being confronted and on the ways that they should (and should not) be approached.

The case of anti-ballistic missile defences (ABM) offers a classic example of how technology, international tension, and domestic factors can conspire to promote deployment as well as development of a new weapons system. For a while it appeared that the technology of defense could never compete with the resources of the offense. In that situation, there was little motive to go beyond the stage of research in ABM defenses. Improvements in computers, radars, and other components of the necessary systems, however, began to create at least some case for the cost-effectiveness of ballistic missile defenses. Whereas the cost of upgrading defensive capabilities to match improvements in offensive forces had once ranged from about 100:1 to 10:1, the ratio had been altered by 1967 to between 4:1 to 1:1—at least according to some scenarios.

The Soviet Union, for her part, did little to strengthen the hand of American leaders urging restraint in the deployment of ABM. Khrushchev himself had made extreme claims for the Soviet ABM as early as 1962. Soviet theoreticians and diplomats refused for a long time to consider the impact that a Soviet ABM deployment would have on U.S. planning and the resultant impact on offensive force levels of both countries. True, some Americans argued that if the Soviets wanted to waste their resources on an ineffective defense, Washington should cheer instead of emulating them in an unwise decision. But this approach was too rationalistic. As James Reston put it, the argument of Secretary of Defense McNamara and others against ABM deployment

> . . . would leave the U.S. vulnerable to intercontinental missiles, and the President would be left to face the charge that the Soviets were willing to provide an anti-missile system for the Soviet people while President Johnson was not willing to do the same to protect the American people.[2]

It was not surprising, therefore—although McNamara had successfully postponed any deployment decision for several years—that in September, 1967 the Johnson administration finally came down for the procurement of a "thin" ABM system.

The upcoming 1968 elections were one aspect of the domestic situation militating in favor of ABM deployment. Another aspect was the open disagreement between the Joint Chiefs of Staff and Secretary McNamara on the wisdom of proceeding with ABM defenses. Intelligence leaks from the Pentagon regarding the magnitude of the Soviet missile threat were another way that the professional military sought to override the judgment of the civilian leaders of the Defense Department. Thus, in censored hearing, a Defense Department official asserted that a major article

---

[2] *The New York Times,* December 9, 1966.

on the Soviet ABM program by Hanson W. Baldwin contained a "number of errors." Meanwhile, as signs mounted that pressures on the White House would compel it to proceed with ABM deployment, there was a corresponding rise in the stock prices of companies expected to take part in its building.

Once the Johnson administration stated that it would adopt a thin ABM deployment, the forces favoring an even thicker deployment were strengthened. A priority had been established and additional funds would be available to perfect ABM technology. In the Soviet Union, the voices favoring stabilization of the arms race would be confronted with the prospect that the United States was embarking on another round of arms competition and that only the naïve could hope for its restriction through negotiation. In the United States, as the Nixon administration came to power, military and industrial figures alike could take comfort from the apparent determination of the new Defense Secretary to promote ABM and to override whatever objections that scared landowners and dovish Congressmen and scientists might muster. Indeed, the very rationale of the thin system could be changes from city protection to missile protection without any apparent objections from the proponents of the system; its rationale seemed irrelevant. The important fact was the beginning of what promised to become, over time, a vast and expensive system in need of constant attention and upgrading.

Another case in the control of military technology concerns the effort to halt the spread of nuclear weapons. This effort goes back at least to the immediate postwar era when the United States proposed what has been called the Baruch Plan for the international control of atomic energy. The U.S. initiative represented what might be termed the first major instance of a "preventative arms control" measure in the postwar era. The Baruch Plan assumed that the control of atomic energy would be easier to accomplish before than after nuclear weapons had been perfected by additional states. The Soviet Union, of course, saw the plan as an American plot to retain for the United States an atomic monopoly while depriving the U.S.S.R. of equality in nuclear armaments. Indeed, Moscow's response to the Baruch Plan was very much like the reaction of Peking and the various non-nuclear weapons states to the nonproliferation treaty. The Kremlin, in the late 1940s could make a valid case, buttressed *inter alia* on the U.S. insistence on retaining nuclear weapons for enforcement purposes until, in Washington's judgment, the international control of atomic energy had been assured. Moscow then, like the nuclear have-nots today, demanded if it were to renounce nuclear weapons that existing nuclear arsenals be immediately destroyed so that no states were "more equal than others." Then, as now, the problem of security assurances for a non-nuclear state appeared almost insuperable. The result, as we know, is that no preventive arms controls were adopted and both Moscow and Washington went on to produce and deploy thermonuclear as well as nuclear weapons.

The next nations to become regular members of the nuclear club were Britain, France, and China. At some point it may have been feasible to provide alternative arrangements that would have satisfied their security, political, and scientific interests in some other way based on a special relationship with one or the other superpowers. In the end, as we know, each of these three states decided to develop its own nuclear arsenal, despite the great costs and—at least in the cases of France and China—over the objection of its more powerful ally.

Nevertheless, Moscow and Washington finally agreed that they should go to great lengths to prevent further spread of nuclear weapons. According to Chinese sources, this agreement came in August, 1962, but it was not for another five years that the superpowers concurred on most of the terms of a draft nonproliferation treaty. During that interval, China joined the nuclear club and moved ahead at a pace faster than any of the four atomic powers had done.

It remains to be seen how many of the potential nuclear-weapons states actually ratify the nonproliferation treaty. Among the key threshold powers should be listed India, Japan, West Germany, Israel, Sweden, and Switzerland. To a greater or lesser degree, we find in each country the same three factors that have impelled the United States to proceed with ABM deployment. Let us consider, for example, the case of India. To begin with, there is a technological capacity that can be exploited, although to do so will take men and materials from other projects desperately needed for economic development. Second, there is the stimulus of interaction with other states. There are external pressures resulting from the mounting Chinese nuclear capability, but also from the positions taken by the other nuclear powers, for neither Washington nor Moscow, it would seem, is likely to practice what they preach with regard to nuclear arms limitation; more important, the value of their security assurances made in a UN Security Council resolution in 1968 seems most dubious. The debates on the nonproliferation treaty in the U.S. Senate appeared to indicate that Washington was not taking on any additional commitments in the UN resolution, but it suggests how fickle and unreliable may be the security promises of another power with problems of its own. In short, if U.S. interests dictate support for India in the face of an external nuclear threat, she will have it; otherwise, she may have to capitulate.

Third, internal pressures in India and other threshold nuclear powers form a kind of analog to the military-industrial complex in the United States. The ruling party is faced with an opposition looking for a strong base from which to launch a critical assault. There are scientists, military men, and a variety of Young Turk intellectuals who, for a wide range of motives, believe that India should go nuclear whatever the absolute costs, the hardships for other sectors of the economy, or the relative benefits from an investment in a small nuclear arsenal and delivery system.

The effort to halt nuclear spread, to date, represents a partial defeat for the principle of arms control, but it may well yet afford at least a partial victory as well. Since the formulation of the Baruch Plan, four nations have joined the United States in the nuclear club. One may argue—from the standpoint of war prevention—that limited proliferation has been a good thing; that Moscow's acquisition of nuclear weapons has served to stabilize international relations. A bipolar balance of terror is symmetrical and somewhat manageable. With China's entry onto the scene, however, the principles and ground rules of the bipolar confrontation become much more complicated and difficult to apply.

Now that China has become a nuclear weapons nation it is at least conceivable that international stability would benefit from a further limited extension of the nuclear club, so that China might be balanced by India and Japan in the manner that the United States and Soviet Union have checked one another. It can be argued, however—citing an important essay by Stanley Hoffman—that it is important to confine the nuclear club to its present membership. With every addition to the club, the quantity and quality of the variables facing the decision makers of every nation begin to exceed calculation. Further, if we admit the utility of a regional atomic balance in Asia, then sooner or later we will have to concede the same principle in the Middle East and then in Latin America. And as each of these areas gets its quota of nuclear powers, the unpredictability and incalculability of international politics will soar. Hence, if we do succeed in closing the barn door—even though some prize cattle have passed through it—an important if qualified victory will have been won. Whether even this limited achievement can be consolidated remains to be seen.

Three other cases show that the superpowers have not always exploited military technology to its possible limits, at least in domains that did not seem likely to prove an effective means of enhancing over-all capabilities. First, in 1959, a treaty was signed declaring that Antarctica would be kept demilitarized and off limits for acquisition by any state. Second, in 1963, declarations by London, Moscow, and Washington stated their intention not to deploy weapons of mass destruction in outer space, a statement amplified in a multilateral treaty signed in 1967. Third, in 1969, both superpowers appeared to want an analogous treaty that would prohibit the deployment of mass destruction weapons on the seabeds.

The value of these agreements has been challenged by some who have argued that accord was possible only because neither superpower sought, in any case, to militarize the areas in question. Certainly there is some validity in this contention, but it overlooks several important aspects of these agreements. First, each accord served at least as a symbolic assurance that arms-control agreements were possible between adversaries. Second, each treaty helped to generate and perpetuate some momentum toward detente and further arms control. Third, and more important, these treaties helped to assure the major adversaries that neither needed to exploit a facet of military technology just because the other was likely to do so. In this way, these accords helped to interrupt the interaction process that has so often led to upward spirals in the arms race.

The relatively easy victories already achieved in Antarctica and outer space and those that may come in banning nuclear arms on the seabed are more important for the principle they establish—the utility of preventive arms control—than for their objective content. The essential task for the decades to come will lie in preserving and extending that principle to other domains of military technology. It will be difficult to maintain the principle of preventive arms control even in those areas where it has already been applied, but it will be still more difficult to secure its application in areas that seem militarily more promising or in which the adversary is believed to have a significant head start.

The hydra-headed challenge of technology, international interaction, and domestic factors remains potent and ever-growing. In the realm of technology we see that modern weapons of mass destruction are becoming more easily accessible—in terms of both the technical know-how and the financial resources required. Moreover, though some experts have predicted a kind of leveling off in the superpower arms race, it is clear that quantitative changes within the existing arsenal can create a qualitative change in the strategic balance: witness in particular the effect of deploying five or ten multiple warheads on the missile launchers already in place (MIRV). Looking ahead, it must be granted that changes in military technology or in other factors may make weapons systems more attractive which were earlier ruled out as being not cost-effective. Should this trend continue, it will be difficult even to hold the line on those arms control measures agreed to in the last several years.

Second, international interaction patterns are likely to become more complex and disturbing. Any increment in the number of nuclear weapons states will make it increasingly difficult to make policy decisions on a rational basis. But the problem of rational calculation will become more difficult merely by the rise of China to the status of a middle-rank nuclear power. Indeed, the U.S. and Soviet planners must already be reeling from the difficulties of computing deterrence requirements when the adversary has so many different kinds of lethal systems at his disposal. As difficulties of this kind mount, some planners will seek relief in simplistic solutions—numerical superiority across the board or, more ominous, the possible merits of a first strike.

The anxieties produced by international interaction patterns are not reduced by the general incapacity of the great powers to empathize with one another. Thus, American attempts to persuade Kremlin planners to consider the impact on the U.S. defense posture of a Soviet ABM deployment was spurned in 1965–1967, Moscow becoming more attuned to these dangers only in 1967–1968 when the White House announced its decision to deploy the Sentinel system. American confidence in the U.S.S.R. was not bolstered by the series of Soviet FOBS tests—carried out during and after the signing of the outer space treaty, contrary to its spirit though not its letter. On the other hand, the U.S. program of underground nuclear testing intensified immediately after the partial test ban treaty was signed in 1963, a program that the Kennedy administration exploited, *inter alia*, to obtain Senate approval of the test ban. The U.S.S.R., of course, has also carried on a vigorous program of underground tests, but with less publicity than the United States, and hence with somewhat less affront to the spirit of the 1963 Moscow treaty. The underground tests of both superpowers have vented a spirit of nuclear prowess, technically if unintentionally violating the letter of the treaty. Their behavior—coupled with the Chinese nuclear buildup—has done little to assure nations without nuclear weapons that they should sign the nonproliferation treaty because the arms race is coming to a standstill. As for China, her behavior has been circumspect, in part so as to minimize the danger of an external attack on Lob Nor.

Third, the growth of military technology under the influence of various military and economic interests seems likely to increase in years to come —not only in Western and Communist countries but in the Third World as well. Many of President Nixon's appointments have strengthened the voice of the military and industrial interests in 1969, although their position has been opposed by a growing and increasingly vocal cross-section of American citizens. In the Soviet Union, the prediction of Milovan Djilas—the ascendancy of a military ruling class—seems already to have been realized in a significant degree, though opposition from other quarters is difficult to measure. As for China, the Cultural Revolution seems to have spawned only one new institution of power, the armed forces, cultivated at the expense of the Communist party, with the Defense Minister groomed to succeed Chairman Mao himself. In the Third World, we have seen a growing tendency in the last decade for military juntas to replace civilian political leaderships. As the problems of national security and economic and social modernization intensify, the trend toward military government—linked with at least some economic interests—will probably continue.

Given the dimensions of this challenge, what can be done? To begin with, three technical approaches may be useful. One of these is to submit every weapons system decision to careful analysis. A second technical approach is to stress research and development instead of actual deployment of weapons systems in order that a nation can achieve some assurance that it knows how to proceed with a weapons system without doing so unless compelled by the actions of others. A third approach combines technical with psychological and other considerations.

These technical approaches, however, are at best palliatives. Perhaps the most important ingredient in gaining control over military technology (and technology in general) is the emergence of an informed, alert, and concerned citizenry, willing and able to organize and work for its beliefs.

The response of many U.S. citizens to the prospects of a "limited" ABM deployment in 1968–1969 contains effective guidelines for waging a constructive campaign against the mindless expansion of military technology and its products. First, this campaign enlisted the support of many segments of the population—not only liberal and leftist intellectuals and humanists, agitated scientists, and mothers, but also property holders, former members of the military and scientific establishment, and Congressmen—both Republican and Democratic—motivated by economic as well as arms control concerns. Second, it was an informed campaign with positive interaction, and feedback between defense intellectuals and the public at large, with sympathetic and fairly detailed treatment in the mass media. Third, it was persistent and high spirited, despite the heavy odds against victory. Whatever the long-term results of the campaign to prevent ABM deployment, the tactics and organizational ties used in the effort should be preserved and enlarged for other campaigns to come.

Even if the technical approaches such as those suggested are widely used, and if an alert and educated citizenry is ready to work for the common, not just the particular, good, the impact of the three synergistic forces driving the modern technology may still push the arms competition to even higher levels of expense and danger. To contain and reverse the thrust of military technology, a broader plan may be necessary, one that is accepted not only by a minority of concerned individuals but by the same kinds of sociological groupings that have joined in the struggle to prevent ABM deployment.

If we are to move toward a better, rather than a worse, world over the next decade, a new way of thinking about arms-control problems must be developed. The term "modernist" seems appropriate to characterize this new attitude, because the urgent task is to develop a way of looking at problems that accords with the imperatives of the present and—still more—of the future. If we look at the field of nation-building, a modernist approach denotes a syndrome of policies directed to enhancing economic growth and national unity. These objectives commonly lead to policies aimed at better planning of resource use, the cultivation of personal and community incentives, improved education, increased living standards, and so forth.

Similar objectives and means are appropriate to a modernist arms-control mentality, except that *world* rather than *national* community must be the criterion shaping the total constellation of policy. The arms race itself leads to feelings of insecurity, but the fact remains that the only way to throttle the roost of arms competition is to build a deeper sense of human community and global security. It would be unrealistic to assume that the underlying sources of international tension can be eliminated in the near or intermediate future, but we can specify minimum characteristics of a modernist arms-control approach that are within reach.

Though we cannot hope, in the foreseeable future, to fully eradicate the basic causes of competition in arms, we can still outline the kind of philosophy needed to contain and control it. This world view, it will be stressed, is probably a requisite but not necessarily a sufficient condition for world order. This outlook would build upon a basic insight, which was not widely accepted until the late 1950s: the principle that arms control, like defense policy, should be a means of enhancing national security. Though this principle suggested the need for cooperation among adversaries, and proved useful in providing the rationale for such agreements as the limited test ban, its stress on self-interest may be inadequate for the challenging problems of the late 1960s and the 1970s. The outlook necessary for dealing with these problems must contain a broader sense of the common dangers and opportunities facing all mankind—including of course one's own particular country. Some aspects of what we call a modernist approach propounded by arms controllers and other political analysts for some time is underscored by a focus on the contributions of the large and smaller powers.

A modernist philosophy of arms control will start from five axioms:

1. Preventative arms control is more feasible than corrective therapy;
2. Adversaries may share overlapping interests;
3. Power connotes responsibility;
4. *Noblesse oblige;*
5. Look to the future.

The first two notions have been discussed and need little elaboration here, except to note their place in the over-all strategy. The recognition that adversaries may have common interests, for example, has been accepted not only by U.S. game theorists (the notion of a non-zero-sum game) but by Soviet ideology (peaceful coexistence has elements of cooperation as well as conflict). But while Washington and Moscow may accept such notions theoretically, much more could be done in practice to implement them. The theory itself has been little recognized in tense relations between other sets of adversaries, for example, Israel and the U.A.R., China and the United States, and the black and white Africans.

The third and fourth axioms imply great responsibilities for large and small powers alike. They confront the crucial question of who will take the first step toward breaking a vicious circle or preventing one from evolving. No matter what area of arms competition we examine, we find a dynamism contributed to by many actors. The balance of power is rarely acceptable to all sides, so that agreement to freeze the situation requires a degree of sacrifice for one or more participants. On occasion, a few nations may take an initiative to stabilize a situation acceptable to them but not to others; for example, the U.S.-U.K.-Soviet accord on nuclear testing. Frequently, however, the major adversaries find themselves at odds regarding the opportune moment to stifle some aspect of their competition.

Mindful of the interaction patterns between states, Charles E. Osgood has suggested that the United States should announce and implement a series of first steps which, if the Soviet Union reciprocated, would be followed by still other initiatives to dampen and eventually to reverse the arms race. Many problems arise to complicate such a strategy; for example, whether Moscow will perceive a U.S. first step in the manner in which it is conceived in Washington; whether the Soviet reaction will be sufficiently prompt to convey a sense of reciprocity; whether—given the Sino-Soviet rift and the Vietnamese war—overt collusion of this sort is politically thinkable for either superpower.

Despite such problems, we are left with a need for someone to take the first steps to forestall a wide range of potential rounds of arms competition. Hence the axiom that power implies responsibility and thus magnanimity.

While the most powerful nations possess most abundantly the means, all governments with humanist aspirations should respond to the notion of *noblesse oblige*. What is needed is not mere lip service to such values as those spelled out in the Universal Declaration of Human Rights. What is needed is rather a restructuring of the priorities guiding the actions (as opposed to the words) of statesmen.

It might be argued that such an appeal is fruitless and even unnecessary; that enlightened self-interest is sufficient to guide governments to responsible steps to contain the arms race. Both allegations may be partially true. But we can not be sure what limits exist on the motivating force of internationalist, humanist sentiments—witness the popularity of the Peace Corps-type activities in many countries. In any event the resort to enlightened self-interest may well be insufficient to motivate the kind of first steps required to prevent the arms races likely in the next decades. An emphasis on self-interest has all too often led governments not to focus on the new forms needed for tomorrow, but has instead reinforced a myopic and conservative orientation aimed at safeguarding whatever advantages exist today.

The fifth axiom—look to the future—is implicit in other axioms. Looking to the future, statesmen will see common interests, not merely in survival but in the optimal use of resources, outweighing disagreements over ideology, boundaries, and spheres of influence. Looking to the future, they will act today to thwart the development and deployment of arms that will raise the cost and danger of weapons competition tomorrow. Looking to the future, the governments that are most powerful and those (large and small) that are the most noble will commit more of their energy and prestige to the initiatives necessary to build a safer and more prosperous world.

More generally, however, the call for a futurist orientation denotes the basic thrust appropriate for a modernist approach to arms control. This approach assumes that traditional ways of thinking and traditional institutions must be efficiently adapted if not profoundly revised just to keep pace with the dangers as well as the opportunities inherent in the ongoing revolutions in technology and society.

The notion *noblesse oblige* anticipates a world in which nations will be proud of themselves—not because they have exploded atomic bombs and wedded them to delivery systems—but because of their achievements in the humanities, sciences, in upgrading of their own and others' living standards. The idealistic appeal is reinforced by the realist argument that material objectives and national influence can be better achieved through economic growth than through stockpiling the tools of nuclear diplomacy.

Both conceptions—the realist no less than the idealist—require that statesmen look to the future, the last but not the least ingredient of a modernist approach.

The modernist approach, as we have seen, is far from a panacea. At best it is extremely difficult to implement, requiring greater degrees of altruism and foresight than governments or peoples have usually exhibited. Some optimism arises, nevertheless, from the premise that adoption of the five principles suggested might, in the long run, best serve the dictates of truly enlightened self-interest.

INDEX

DATE DUE

MY 2 '79			
JAN 26 '84.			